Psychodynamic Coaching and Supervision for Executives

Thomas Kretschmar and Andreas Hamburger provide an important overview of psychodynamic work in companies, presenting different viewpoints and explaining key psychoanalytic terms and techniques for coaching and supervision. Written in the form of a dialog between Kretschmar, an entrepreneur, and Hamburger, a psychoanalyst, the book provides unique insight into psychodynamic coaching and supervision.

Psychodynamic Coaching and Supervision for Executives begins with an overview of coaching, psychodynamic approaches, the unconscious and relevant psychoanalytic theory. Kretschmar and Hamburger then consider Operationalized Psychodynamic Diagnosis (OPD) in business, assess current research into coaching and supervision and present a selection of key case studies. At the end of each chapter, the authors compare their positions, giving important contextual information, exploring objections, complications and improvements, and providing a precise summary of the topic.

This book will be an illuminating guide for therapists and professionals who wish to learn how psychoanalytic theory and practice can be used for coaching, counseling and supervision in an organizational context.

Thomas Kretschmar is the managing director of Mind Institute SE and founder of Hypoport SE, Germany.

Andreas Hamburger is professor of clinical psychology and psychoanalysis at the International Psychoanalytic University Berlin, Germany.

Psychodynamic Coaching and Supervision for Executives

An Entrepreneur and a Psychoanalyst in Dialogue

Thomas Kretschmar and
Andreas Hamburger

Routledge
Taylor & Francis Group

LONDON AND NEW YORK

First published 2022
by Routledge
2 Park Square, Milton Park, Abingdon, Oxon OX14 4RN

and by Routledge
605 Third Avenue, New York, NY 10158

Routledge is an imprint of the Taylor & Francis Group, an informa business

© 2022 Taylor & Francis

The right of Thomas Kretschmar and Andreas Hamburger to be identified as authors of this work has been asserted by them in accordance with sections 77 and 78 of the Copyright, Designs and Patents Act 1988.

Translated by Diane Winkler

Published in German by W. Kohlhammer GmbH, Stuttgart, 2019

Library of Congress Cataloging-in-Publication Data
A catalog record for this title has been requested

ISBN: 978-0-367-77071-6 (hbk)
ISBN: 978-0-367-77070-9 (pbk)
ISBN: 978-1-003-16967-3 (ebk)

DOI: 10.4324/9781003169673

Typeset in Sabon
by Taylor & Francis Books

Contents

Illustrations

Preliminary remarks

For many years, supervision has been utilized in therapeutic, social, educational, medical and organizational fields of action. In consequence, over the course of the 20th century, various different trends emerged. The most important methodical concepts are psychodynamic, systemic, cognitive-behavioral and humanistic approaches, taking into account the many overlaps within the supervisory approach.

Since the first beginnings of psychoanalysis, and in the field of social work too, the fields of application of supervision have become further differentiated. Therapies and counseling for individuals, couples, families, groups and organizations are the main area of application of supervision. Alongside its occupational utilization, supervision is also an important component of many qualifications awarded to psychotherapists, medical specialists or social workers. There are also areas, such as educational and caring institutions or hospitals where the introduction or the intensive use of supervision on a regular basis is most desirable.

The special feature of this book is its dialog form. It is written by two authors with different backgrounds, who compare their positions at the end of every main chapter. In this way, readers not only get to know important topics, backgrounds and contestations, but also witness the lively communication of two dedicated advocates of their own subjects. This discussion in dialog form serves to examine the specific topic from different perspectives, addressing its essence one more time and discussing open questions, problems and suggested improvements.

Andreas Hamburger
Wolfgang Mertens

Preface

Although psychodynamic coaching is the most thorough and humanly satisfying form of consulting, it is not practiced often enough. This is because it not only requires psychoanalytic knowledge and skills, but also organizational know-how founded in experience in either an executive position or in some corresponding position in a business or social enterprise.

For coaching to be truly psychodynamic, the setting, of course, must also be psychodynamic. Furthermore, the process of understanding, right from the first few meetings, has to be such that it is accessible to consciousness, but also reaches a certain emotional depth. This is because the aim is not only to achieve cognitive problem solving, but also to arrive at emotionally relevant insights, which allow for new experiences to emerge without weakening the defense processes too much. This complex approach geared to the needs of one individual requires, on the one hand, a substantial knowledge of the organizational circumstances; and on the other hand, a great deal of intuition and experience on the coach's part in concentrating on relevant conflicts, corresponding anxiety and the defense against both. How then can this approach be adequately formalized, taught and evaluated?

It is one of the special features of this book that two authors with different social backgrounds and different professional experience, but in this case, with a mutual appreciation of psychoanalysis, engage in a fruitful and fascinating exchange of ideas.

Thomas Kretschmar is an academically trained entrepreneur who served as a full professor for bank organization at the Hochschule für Technik und Wirtschaft Berlin (University of Applied Sciences in Berlin), founded a technology-based financial services company and put it on the stock market (SDAX), worked as a coach for many years and finally studied psychoanalysis at the Sigmund Freud University in Vienna and at the International Psychoanalytic University Berlin.

Andreas Hamburger was a humanities scholar; he then studied psychology in Munich and after receiving his diploma and doctorate, trained as a psychoanalyst at the Akademie für Psychoanalyse und Psychotherapie München (Academy for Psychoanalysis and Psychotherapy Munich). He is a member of the German Psychoanalytic Society (DPG). After his habilitation (postdoctoral thesis), he was appointed as professor at the Internationale Psychoanalytische Universität Berlin (International Psychoanalytic University Berlin). In his private practice, he frequently counsels businesspeople and supervises coaches.

The dialog between the authors clarifies in many ways the frictions between two different areas of experience: To what extent is it possible to square the economic parameters of an entrepreneurial function with the need for self-reflection and honesty toward others and oneself? Is it even possible to put the purposelessness and anarchy of unconscious processes in touch with rational economic mechanisms? Does deeper self-awareness really lead to a better connection with colleagues, or does psychodynamic knowledge actually entice individuals into using it to control and manipulate? Or does the pleasing term "coaching" actually obscure the fact that many working conditions may entail psychological stress, which requires more than just coaching to be dealt with properly? How great is the danger that some psychodynamic coaches and supervisors time and again close their eyes to the truth and to unbearable knowledge, and sleepwalk into collusion with questionable social and economic processes?

Then again, why should all the valuable insights of psychoanalysis be reserved for patients in a therapeutic setting and not also benefit individuals and processes in a working environment? It is important for every human being to have a detailed knowledge of confrontational processes in work-related groups, of the difficulties of owning one's psychological processes emotionally and reflexively and the risks of being truthful to oneself. To secure the quality of these central values of human co-existence, psychodynamic coaching and the supervision of its processes is an essential method.

The courage to confront all these critical questions defines the framework in which this fascinating book about supervision and coaching covers its terrain.

Prof. Dr. Wolfgang Mertens
August 2018

Introduction

As the psychodynamic approach becomes increasingly important in management consulting, a need arises for training in psychodynamic coaching and psychodynamic supervision. On the one hand, business consulting calls for approaches to change psychological processes in a sustained manner. On the other hand, the management consulting industry requires new incentives beyond the scope of checklists and PowerPoint presentations. Clients expect methods that allow them a perspective on their issues beyond their usual horizon. The psychodynamic approach facilitates such a new perspective by making unconscious contents conscious and working them through.

So far, psychodynamic business consulting primarily reflects two trends: The first has its origins in group analysis and systemic psychology and today is mainly characterized by sociological thinking. This is a valuable starting point; however, in the case of a group of participants who all come from the same company, it may not reach deep enough. Time and again, this setting gives rise to conflicts of interest concerning privacy protection. No one likes to talk about his or her inner conflicts or private family history amongst colleagues. Thus, group analysis is more successful for the self-orientation of group members who are not acquainted and don't work together.

Based on our experience, it is more effective to work with 10 to 20 decision makers and multipliers (non-managers who influence colleagues) of a company in one-on-one coachings, as these offer the necessary frame for deeper work. Even if the results are kept confidential, those clients who undergo a one-on-one coaching show a good spillover for the company, based on their changed perception and behavior (Kretschmar & Tzschaschel, 2014, p. 213; Kretschmar & Senarclens de Grancy, 2016, p. 104).

Self-employed psychoanalysts who also guide executives in one-on-one coachings characterize the second trend. However, the majority of such psychoanalytic consultants have little experience as executives and therefore the analysis of their countertransference lacks a reference model. Furthermore, mere psychological expertise is less effective than a combination of psychological and organizational know-how (Möller, 2016, p. 7). Additionally, this psychoanalytic approach requires from the consultant a tremendously high training effort and from the client an enormous amount of time; this cost–benefit ratio prevents psychoanalytic coaching from being more widely accepted.

A further difficulty afflicting psychodynamic coaching is that the range of training programs offered for coaches is very wide. Training providers are applying many different methods in order to distinguish their own approach from that of their competitors. This makes it more or less impossible to identify clear structures, and the onlooker fails to understand which, if any, scientific findings underlie advanced vocational training. Hardly any recent research results or even scientific references to coaching can be found (Möller & Hellebrandt, 2016, p. 102).

All in all, we may conclude that the coaching and supervision market needs new approaches, and that psychodynamic counseling has the potential to serve this market if

- the basic approaches to implementing supervision and coaching can be operationalized efficiently;
- these approaches can be based on solid scientific ground; and
- they can be imparted to the practitioner through training of an acceptable length.

This is precisely why a new school of scientifically sound psychodynamic counseling within companies is needed. This book sets out to convey the authors' mindset on this topic.

The concept of this book aims to bring different approaches to a subject area under discussion and to enliven the debate by contrasts. Instead of presenting knowledge by only one author in a top-down way, the reader is able to reflect on his or her own opinion by following the pros and cons in the animated dialog of two distinctly different viewpoints. Even Freud used a similar trick of dramatization in his writings, by addressing himself to an imaginary counterpart whom he wanted to convince.

The two authors of this book represent the two trends discussed above: One is an MBA, psychologist and entrepreneur, who has opened up to psychoanalysis and has familiarized himself with psychodynamic thinking and acting. The other has his origins in the humanities and clinical psychology and is a dyed-in-the-wool psychoanalyst, who works partly therapeutically and partly in an occupational counseling setting with executives, businesspeople and consultants – as a result, he has acquired a deepened psychoanalytic understanding of commercial and organizational contexts. As the first few chapters deal with the basics, the positions of the two authors still lie close together. Further along in the book, their positions differ more and the dialog intensifies.

In counseling, processes can be either long-term or problem-orientated and brought to a close within a few sessions. The second author (Hamburger) prefers to call his work in the context of business and organizations, notwithstanding the questionable nature of the term, "supervision" instead of "coaching". He will explain why he does this in his comments in the book. He will also define his approach in contrast to coaching. And he will occasionally lodge a second objection, when the first author (Kretschmar) expresses his conviction about the usefulness of psychodynamic thinking in counseling; in other words, he strives to protect psychoanalysis against its followers. He sees psychoanalysis as a critical enterprise that cannot be turned into a mere social technique. This is also related to the question whether the issue of occupational functioning can actually be teamed with a psychoanalytic approach (see Chapter 4.9.1).

This book will take this question up consistently, and the authors will discuss how psychoanalytic theory and practice in all their facets can be used for counseling, coaching and supervision in an organizational context.

In fact, in their collaborative work on this book, both authors have experienced transformation. A certain guardedness in the beginning – to the business expert, the psychoanalyst seemed a little unrealistic; and the psychoanalyst judged the coach to be making slightly premature use of psychoanalytic concepts as tools – was overcome in the course of writing together, and the many face-to-face discussions brought about changes in the authors' attitudes. In dialog something new can emerge, that's what it is there for. With this in mind, the authors put the book in the reader's hands, hoping that they will still find enough of a difference between the authors' positions, but in the end also recognize the common objective.

Acknowledgments

We thank Ms. Leonie Derwahl, Ms. Sophie Grußendorf, Ms. Rebekka Haug, Ms. Julia Perlinger, Ms. Andrea Wurst and M. Hannes Gisch, all psychologists at the Mind Institute SE, for their critical review of the manuscript and their valuable suggestions.

1 Historical overview

Vocational counseling formats can be assigned to a field of interventional forms, which is characterized by numerous overlaps, but also by clearly visible differences. We start by analyzing and discussing similarities and distinctions between coaching, supervision and psychotherapy.

1.1 Similarities and differences in coaching and supervision

The term "coaching" has its origin in sports. The term has only been used in business and human resource (HR) development since the 1990s (Müller, 2012, p. 9). Before that, comparable services were usually described as "mentoring" (Western, 2012, p. 2).

Some authors apply "coaching" only to vocational and managerial topics. This is Müller's definition, with the recommendation of the Deutscher Coaching Verband: "Coaching is a form of distinct assistance, mainly for executives and experts and their personal development within a vocational context" (Müller, 2012, p. 10). The Deutscher Bundesverband Coaching takes a similar line: "Coaching is the professional counseling, accompanying, and support of persons with management and supervisory functions and of experts in organizations" (Dietz, Holetz & Schreyögg, 2012, p. 20).

The existence of further definitions by other federations shows, however, that coaching is not only understood in this narrow sense. The authors of this book have had the experience that even though executives call on a coach, initially, to meet a vocational need, in the end, topics from all areas of their lives are included in the process. The International Coaching Federation (ICF), for example, sees coaching as not limited only to vocational topics: Professional coaching is "partnering with clients in a thought-provoking and creative process that inspires them to maximize their personal and professional potential" (International Coaching Federation, 2016, p. 1). Health coaching – and its subforms, life coaching and stress management coaching – lies even further away from tangible vocational issues (Greif, 2013, pp. 230–231). We have previously indicated that there might be an overlap between reasons for psychotherapy and reasons for coaching. Stress management and health management are the most obvious examples.

DOI: 10.4324/9781003169673-1

Supervision, the second term to be discussed in this book, is much older – going back more than a century – and is based on various theories. Weigand (2000, p. 56) questions whether the term "one-on-one supervision" by now seems, perhaps, a little "tame, stuffy and bland", or whether it possibly constitutes "a concept within the technical language of supervision describing a specific approach, clearly marked-off against other dyadic settings", which deserves protection. This book aims to develop the concept of a task-based supervision in organizations and enterprises that is clearly marked off from coaching, and that refers to a specific – namely, a psychoanalytic – methodology of counseling.

The term "supervision" was originally used for the counseling of volunteers in social work, or was understood as an accompaniment for the therapies that aspiring psychotherapists undertook as part of their training. This means that the term was focused on health and social services (see Chapter 1.4). Even its extension to teams and – after the *systemic turn* of the humanities in the 1970s – its incorporation into the institutional context, together with a growing influence from organizational sociology on supervision ("Soziologisierung der Supervision"; Belardi, 1992; Hermann-Stietz, 2009, pp. 15–16), focused mainly on the social, healthcare and educational sectors. Supervision in profit-orientated corporate contexts was used mainly in respect of teams and staff, and only tentatively became a part of the discourse on supervision (Böhnisch, 2002). By contrast, coaching positioned itself firmly within the framework of executive counseling; the profit motivation of enterprises, which was challenged by those within the discourse on supervision who were leaning toward sociology, was taken for granted by the up-and-coming coaching discourse. This decided orientation of coaching toward executives is the reason for the common division of the field of application within the literature. Supervision is usually discussed with reference to the operational level of organizations, whereas coaching is allocated to the management level. The result is that changes brought about by supervision begin from "below", whereas changes set off by coaching begin from "above" (Kühl, 2008). However, this object-related distinction makes the third, but decisive, difference fade into the background: While supervision traditionally includes the whole person, in coaching, the stress is on the functional improvement of an organization's staff (Kühl, 2008). This created differentiating definitions, both within the development of conceptual distinctions and within field expertise: In the field of coaching, for example, "psychodynamic coaching" generally includes the personality as a whole and particularly its unconscious functions; while the field of executive supervision ties psychodynamic counseling in with the traditional concept of supervision, but specifies its field of application. For conceptual clarification, Pannewitz (2012) suggests using the terms "executive supervision" and "executive coaching" synonymously, and defining them as the "advancement of the technical, conceptual and social competence needed for the solution of managerial tasks or as support of self-management" (Buer, 1999, p. 186, cited by Pannewitz, 2012, p. 23).

Compared with coaching, supervision has a different target group and a different tradition. Supervision doesn't primarily target HR development. Indeed, supervision often aims also to promote vocational functions, whereas coaching also supports the client's personality. Supervision developed in parallel to social work and psychoanalysis (Hamburger, 2016a), whereas coaching has developed within HR management in companies. Accordingly, as Schreyögg argues (2012, pp. 26–27), supervision doesn't necessarily need managerial and organizational concepts, but therapeutic approaches instead. However, the opposite argument can be made, that supervision actually does need organizational concepts, but they must come from a different perspective.

Meanwhile, in Germany, the DGSv's equation of the terms "supervision" and "coaching" has not met with universal applause from the coaching federations (Schreyögg, 2013, pp. 232–237). However, viewed from the psychodynamic perspective, we do not always see the need for a strict differentiation. As we shall show later, the development of the personality plays a major role in the psychodynamic approach. The counselor's demeanor is closer to that of a psychodynamic psychotherapist and the theoretical concepts arise from the psychodynamic paradigm.

The comparable requirements of business coaching and supervision are often considered to be equal, since the client expects the coachee or supervisee to become better equipped to do a given job. However, if we use this interpretation, we lose sight of the fact that both approaches rely on different procedures and reference systems, which we shall keep coming back to throughout the book. The process of psychoanalytic supervision (Mertens & Hamburger, 2016) is characterized for the most part by abstinence (see Chapter 4.9.1) and mainly refers to developmental and personality-based concepts, while coaching predominantly pursues an approach of change.

1.2 The history of psychodynamic work in business

1.2.1 The history of psychoanalytic supervision

Supervision had its origins in supervising and training the volunteers of the American Charity Organization Societies. This arose in the late 19th century as a result of a long-lasting economic depression and the consequent impoverishment of large parts of the population. To optimize the effort of these volunteers and to shape it to meet the needs of those concerned, the volunteers were instructed by "paid agents" in the main offices. Important changes were made in 1920 when the psychoanalyst Otto Rank came to the United States and applied himself to social welfare. Due to Rank and the other psychoanalysts immigrating to the United States in the 1940s, supervision soon developed a psychoanalytic component: It became clear that work in social welfare could be complicated by defense processes and entanglements, and that for good results, it would be helpful to reflect on these (Lohl, 2016). In Vienna as early as the 1920s, August Aichhorn, Willy Hoffer, Anna Freud and Siegfried Bernfeld had offered case reviews and workshops for youth welfare workers and teachers (Aichhorn, 2011; Steinhardt, 2005, p. 32). In 1927 Michael Balint established "training-cum-research" workshops for medical doctors and visiting nurses in London. They were pioneers in their use of a psychoanalytic technique: The manner of case presentation and the resonance of the groups were used as a key to the understanding of the unconscious working relationship (Balint, 2002 [1954]).

Social casework developed on the basis of this psychoanalytic tradition, in which supervision played an important role in promoting self-reflection as part of understanding one's own professional role (Hechler, 2005; Steinhardt, 2005). From this, an independent line of supervision developed in social work and healthcare. Alongside the psychoanalytic paradigm, other concepts were added and gained importance. Systemic and sociological approaches drew attention to institutional contexts and team dynamics. From the 1960s, a transition from a psychologizing to a "sociologizing phase" of supervision is noticeable (Hermann-Stietz, 2009, pp. 15–16). Through the dialogue on this and other paradigms, supervision has developed into a distinct format of counseling (Rappe-Giesecke, 2013; Gröning, 2016).

Psychoanalytic supervision advanced predominantly within the framework of psychoanalytic training and was also further utilized in healthcare (Bergmann, 2016) as well as in business (Weigand, 2016). Since the mid-20th century, the relationship dimension of psychoanalysis increasingly took center stage. The term "the unconscious", which had at first primarily been understood as an internal psychological memory system, was now seen increasingly as an interpersonal field. In the 1960s and 1970s, the classic one-person psychology was revised in the context of numerous new models such as object relations theory and self-psychology as well as in the context of interpersonal approaches. Infant research revolutionized assumptions about child development, which in turn affected the treatment practice. From the perspective of field theory and relationship, the unconscious is not an intra-psychological, but an interpersonal-systemic process (on the origins, see Conci, 2005; also Baranger & Baranger, 2008 [1961]; Bauriedl, 1980, 1994; Stern, 1996). "Thus in supervision or when presenting cases, you not only speak about clients but also to a certain extent about yourself. The supervisorial situation in psychoanalytic training thus becomes a very special field of force" (Mertens & Hamburger, 2016, p. 19).

This "very special field of force", however, can only partly be transferred to psychoanalytic supervision beyond training. Supervision within the framework of psychoanalytic training is a case apart, as the skills taught are precisely those that enable the trainee to establish an open, alive, analytic situation and to maintain it. Thus, there is a strong parallel between the learning content and the learning situation. With supervisees with a background in organ medicine, economy, social work or pedagogy, this does not apply. They are supposed to heal patients, manufacture cars, guide youths or teach students.

The question we ask in the following chapters is this: Which elements of the psychoanalytic attitude can be transferred to supervision in fields of application beyond training? The analytic attitude, according to Alfred Lorenzer's method (1970), is based on "scenic understanding". It is neither the conceiving of the analysand's message content (logic understanding) nor the comprehension of his[11] message intention (psychological understanding) that allows access to the dynamic unconscious processes. Rather, it is the reflection on the interaction unfolding in the analytical space, the "scene", in which the analyst is complementarily involved. The transmission of this psychoanalytic attitude to supervisorial processes also has to mirror the quite different assignment. Nevertheless, in supervision, a psycho-analytic attitude seems possible and useful – even in cases not aimed at the training of psychoanalysts – because "evenly suspended attention" and "scenic under-standing" (Lorenzer, 1970) are adopted and facilitated in oscillation with the focal work on the supervisorial assignment.

Supervision in a work context requires an adaptation of the psychoanalytic attitude. The supervisor is not himself in the field; his participation comes about via the supervisee, who is the field expert. The supervisor's participation in the supervisee's field expertise usually happens *analogously*. Occasionally, however, the supervisor, too, may experience a complementary participation in the field, especially in situations where the unconscious reflection of the scene repeats itself strongly within the supervision (Baranger & Baranger, 2008 [1961]; Vollmer & Pires, 2010). The subject of supervision is, of course, always the (therapeutic, eco-nomic, organizational) process run by the supervisee and not – as in psychoanalysis or therapy – the client. In the diverse forms of supervision common in organiza-tions, systematic institutional references are being established; these have to be considered accurately, named and constantly managed. The specificity of the supervisorial field has consequences for dealing with abstinence. Interpretations in an institutional framework are always given with respect to work assignment and to the supervisor's position. This constraint has practical consequences: One of the most common traps of the supervisorial process, which has often brought it to a halt, is the non-reflective assumption of the supervisor that he knows better what the supervisee is supposed to do. Just as psychoanalysts should not thoughtlessly give in to the temptation to consider themselves to be "better parents", so should the supervisor not see himself as the better therapist, the better CEO or the better department manager. While the supervisor needs to listen empathetically to the supervisee's complaints about institutional dysfunctionalities, reflection on the scene as well as the work assignment require the supervisor also to keep in mind the perspective of the institution and others involved in the supervised process. The technical neutrality of the psychoanalyst also has to be re-defined in the super-visory application. Assessment (as in therapeutic settings) compromises the further development of the scene; all the same, in certain work assignments, it may be inevitable if it serves to accomplish given objectives. The supervisees themselves will wonder (and will perhaps be asked) if the supervision achieved its goals, and if it was useful. Since the supervised activity itself serves a purpose and is evaluated, it would be inappropriate and self-defeating to eliminate assessment from the supervision. However, an abstinent assessment is advisable – where the supervisee and supervisor regularly check together whether the supervision has brought the participants any closer to reaching their objectives. This is abstinent in so far as it is not the supervisor who appraises and not the supervisee who is being appraised; instead, both word their perspectives according to the agreed objectives and their implementation. Moreover, it is always the supervisee who has the field compe-tence, whereas the supervisor is responsible for the present process. Supervision is about clarifying the conscious and the unconscious incorporation of the supervisee in his field of work. Therefore, supervision does not aim at the development of transference in the relationship. Nevertheless, sometimes the unconscious dynamics of the field are reflected in the cooperative process of the supervision (for example, a very tense or a casual atmosphere may arise); the appearance of these mirror-processes may be used to clarify a dynamic process active in the field that is not yet clearly understood.

1.2.2 From couch to company: Use of psychoanalytic supervision in social contexts

The Tavistock approach

The Tavistock Institute of Human Relations (TIHR) was established in 1947 to look into current problems and societal phenomena with the help of academically orientated, psychodynamic approaches. Such topics would have had no hope for funding within the newly established National Health System (NHS) of Great Britain (Trist, Murray & Trist, 1990).

Miller and Rice (1967) see in an organization a task-fulfilling, sentient system. In organizations, several tasks are consciously and unconsciously being handled at the same time. The work objectives of the enterprise are understood as being the "primary task" (Rice, 1958, p. 32). Organizations also satisfy the social and psychological needs of their members. If members of the organization develop anxiety while accomplishing their tasks, defense arises.

According to Rice (1958), assessment of organizations rests on clarifying what their primary tasks are and how well these are being accomplished. If the defense against anxiety stays in the unconscious, the company will be unproductive (Jaques, 1951). According to the Tavistock model, the psychodynamic approach of organizational counseling is characterized by an integrated view of the business tasks on the one hand, and the people who act according to their tasks on the other hand (Miller & Rice, 1967, p. xii).

Group analysis according to Bion

Wilfred Bion was a leading founding member of the TIHR and worked in group research. His book, *Experiences in Groups* (1961), makes the key assumption that group members have unconscious fantasies about their function. The contact between the group members is made via projective identification. This is a defense mechanism whereby individual members dissociate their own feelings and project them onto other group members, who then feel them in their place. The projective identification serves as a defense against overwhelming emotional conditions as well as helping to establish empathy. When such identification occurs, the object has lost its independence from the subject on the unconscious level, and may henceforth be controlled and manipulated by the subject. This means that, on the level of emotional exchange, the group member regresses to become a part of the whole group (Bion, 1961). The unconscious wishes of the group can differ from the consciously reflected tasks.

In an organizational context, the maintenance of identity and integrity can be threatened from within and without. Uncertainty and threats cause anxiety to which employees might react with defense (von Ameln, Kramer & Stark, 2009, p. 49). Structural order serves as a defense mechanism to protect the group against affective tensions at the unconscious level, and to enable cooperative conduct when confronting reality in terms of the working task. In this sense, Bion assigns the group, by analogy with the psychoanalytic concept of the mind, an instinctual primary process and a rational secondary process (Bion, 1952). The weaker the group ego, the more rigid the defense will be and the greater the constraint on the group's working capacity.

Bion differentiates between two modes for groups. In the first mode, the "work group" is defined by a rational working atmosphere and productivity. Every group member tries to understand the nature of the task and the other group members and to contribute his expertise to accomplish the group's task. However, when they confront the primary risk in choosing a task that proves unmanageable, the group regresses into the second mode – the "basic assumption group". Now the primary energy of the members is no longer used for the primary task, but for the primary defense mechanism. All "basic assumptions" may be deduced from three emotional states:

- Dependency: In a dependent or immature way, the group follows a leader or a vision. As inflated expectations cannot be fulfilled, the group vacillates between a good and a bad appraisal of the leader, or the vision, or splits up.
- Pairing: The group is supported by a fantasy of salvation through a pair within the group, which will maintain the group and lead it to a better future. Because of the defense character of this fantasy, it may never be realized.
- Fight–flight: The group concentrates its energy on fighting against an opponent outside the group or takes flight to fend off negative emotions.

It is possible that a group moves back and forth between these three basic assumptions. A combination of the basic assumptions and a shift in their respective dominance is characteristic for the group (von Ameln et al., 2009, pp. 53–54). Up to the present day, Bion's findings are still being communicated in Group Relations Conferences (GRCs) at the Tavistock Institute. Primarily, it is all about experiential learning on the functioning of groups. In laboratory-like settings, the participants concentrate on how group members relate to one another, how they use each other to accomplish important purposes, and how individuals and groups assign authority (Lohmer, 2004). Group Relations Conferences have been held yearly in cooperation with the University of Leicester since 1957. Bion's original model was further developed in the 1960s to study authority, with a focus on the processes of transference and countertransference between members of the conference and the leadership team (Tavistock Institute, 2016).

Developments of the ISPSO

The International Society for the Psychoanalytic Study of Organizations (ISPSO) had its predecessor in the First Cornell Symposium on the Psycho-dynamics of Organizational Behavior and Experience, held in 1983 in New York by a group of like-minded individuals, and continued for several years thereafter (Sievers, 2009, p. xv). The ISPSO was established in 1989 and holds yearly international meetings in North America, Australia, Europe or Asia. The Society aims to bring together scientists and practitioners who are interested in a psychoanalytical perspective on businesses. Its former presidents have included Larry Hirschhorn, Susan Long, Burkard Sievers and Jim Krantz, all of whom have long-standing experience in utilizing the Tavistock model, head their own institutes or consultancies and publish regularly (International Society for the Psychoanalytic Study of Organizations, 2016).

As at 2017, the ISPSO had nearly 400 members from approximately 40 countries (oral report of the board on occasion of the annual conference). The members are scientists, organizational consultants, psychoanalysts, psychiatrists, psychologists and HR experts. Further developments of ISPSO members will be discussed in greater detail in later chapters:

- The splitting between top and line management as a defense mechanism: If organizations do not succeed in tolerating their risks, as the Tavistock approach suggests, defense is activated (see Chapter 2.1.2);
- Primary risk and primary tasks (see Chapter 2.1.1);
- The enterprise as a psychologically safe haven (see Chapter 2.1.3);
- The perverted organization (see Chapter 2.1.4);
- The emotional experience of being part of an organization (see Chapter 2.2.1).

The Kets de Vries Institute (KDVI)

Apart from the Tavistock Institute itself and the ISPSO, there is a third approach to developing the Tavistock principles, which we want to mention for the sake of completeness. It is based mainly on the work of Manfred Kets de Vries, who today is considered to be the most prominent proponent of psychoanalytic work in organizations. He received his Doctor of Business Administration in 1970 from Harvard Business School, became a visiting professor at INSEAD, and then a full professor at McGill University in Montreal in 1975, where he obtained his own academic chair in 1979. At the same time, he was training to become a psycho-analyst in the Canadian Psychoanalytic Society. Subsequently, he opened his own psychoanalytic practice, but continued to work in commercial enterprises at the same time. Among his many new approaches, Kets de Vries can take credit for framing the psychoanalytic view on organizations and their individuals in an understandable language and for writing for businesspeople rather than psychoanalysts. Although he was one of the founders of the ISPSO in 1986, as time went on, it became clear that he did not want to integrate himself and his school of thinking into official organizations. The result was the Kets de Vries Institute (Kets de Vries Institute, 2016), which offers training and coaching. One of the major models developed in the Institute is the concept of the neurotic organization (see Chapter 2.3.1), which Kets de Vries published in his basic work *The Neurotic Organization* (Kets de Vries & Miller, 1984).

Continuation in universities of economics and business

As a visiting professor, Kets de Vries established a psychoanalytically orientated economic theory in several international universities of Economics and Business (including the global business school INSEAD with its European office in Fontainebleau and the Higher School of Economics [HSE] in Moscow). Konstantin Korotov, one of Kets de Vries's successors and a professor of coaching at the European School of Management and Technology (ESMT) in Berlin, brought the approaches of the Tavistock Institute and Kets de Vries to Germany in 2005.

This development is important, as psychoanalytic approaches are not supposed to be carried into business enterprises by consultants only. For the concept to be permanently established, the managers themselves have to practice and convey it. "Peer coaching" is Korotov's name for coaching that is conducted by managers, who themselves have business responsibility. He sees this as a mutual learning process of coach and client in one-on-one and group settings (Korotov, 2013).

Our economic life has radically changed since the time when the Tavistock approach was developed. Nowadays, we are dealing more and more with challenges and fears caused by loneliness in leadership, jealousy, a lack of perspective after the achievement of great goals, the feeling of being under surveillance, addiction to power, feelings of guilt, and a constantly steepening learning curve (Kets de Vries, Korotov, Florent-Treacy & Rook, 2016, pp. 3–4). Psychoanalytic consulting is therapeutic, but it is not psychotherapy. Nevertheless, it needs a comparable setting of confidentiality, as the work to be done is very intimate. From the viewpoint of Kets de Vries and Korotov, the important elements are: the staging of the inner theater within the enterprise, transference, defense, and as a particular focus, the coherence of narcissism and leadership development. On the last point, in particular, Kets de Vries et al. (2016) see a connection between early childhood conflicts, containing by the parents and compensation by the child, all important elements in shaping the personality. Constructive narcissism exists if there was enough early childhood frustration to promote compensation, but not so much as to overpower it. Reactive narcissism, on the other hand, develops when there is either too much or too little frustration. As a defense against the fear of not sufficing, a mental image of greatness can be developed. Whether narcissism takes the constructive or the reactive form, it later greatly influences the fantasies and reality perception of executives (Kets de Vries et al., 2016, pp. 19–21).

Another aspect of early childhood imprinting is the helper syndrome, which, in a clinical setting, is termed the active care mode. Active carers believe that they always have to help, they are not allowed to show any negative feelings and they feel dependent on the approval of others. Such drivers force executives into a self-maintaining stress cycle (Korotov, Florent-Treacy, Kets de Vries & Bernhardt, 2012, pp. 33–34).

These examples show that all psychodynamic methods in business counseling based on the Tavistock approach have a lot in common with clinical therapy, from where the Tavistock approach had its origin in 1947.

1.3 Usage in psychodynamic coaching

Basically, the Tavistock approach and its "offshoots" cover general concepts, theories and case examples, which are hardly comparable because individual enterprises differ so much (by size, industry, country, etc.). Nevertheless, these approaches constitute a good theoretical basis for psychodynamic counseling and should be part of the training for psychodynamic work with individual clients. Since psychodynamic coaching and supervision of executives, as already stated, should include psychological as well as economic aspects, it is important to recognize unconscious processes and to keep them in mind during coaching. Apart from this, the approaches of Bion, the Tavistock Institute, Kets de Vries and other ISPSO members are a good basis on which to sensitize executives within the context of psychoeducation for the handling of unconscious processes.

1.4 Usage in psychoanalytic supervision of organizations

Typically, psychoanalysts as supervisors work with individuals or with teams; less frequently they offer coaching or training. Other than the occupational field of coaching, their work is not organizationally constituted. This is easily explicable based on the fact that psychoanalysts receive their occupational training at psychoanalytic institutes, and usually negotiate their further professional identity in the framework of their professional associations and in the numerous specialized periodicals of their trade. Despite the long history of institutional distortions and divisions during the century-long history of psychoanalysis and the resulting different schools and identities, it can be easily specified what a psychoanalyst is and what he or she does. But for the use of this method within other contexts, existing outside therapy or education, this specification is much more difficult. To be sure, there are institutions and periodicals for the use of psychoanalysis within cultural and educational fields – for example, the long-standing journal *Imago* (since 1912) – but in the area of organizational and business supervision, no such institutions or periodicals exist.

This can hardly result from psychoanalysts feeling that they are only responsible for therapeutics. Freud's culture-theoretical and socio-psychological works, namely "Massenpsychologie und Ich-Analyse" ("Group Psychology and the Analysis of the Ego"; Freud, 1921) and "Das Unbehagen in der Kultur"

("Civilization and its Discontents"; Freud, 1930) cover the interlocking of psychological and social development, sometimes postulating radical assumptions; his writings on religious and cultural history also have to be mentioned in this context (Freud, 1913, 1914, 1927, 1939). The reluctance of psychoanalysis to develop and maintain its own approach to working with organizations could be connected with the fact that Freud's culture theory was mainly taken up by the socio-critical debate; from this point of view, any cooperation with business smelled like conformity with the system. Nevertheless, even these positions of criticizing the political and social system that have arisen since the 1980s have produced approaches to the supervision of enterprises and organizations; these, however, stayed aware of their societal obligation and would not devote themselves to a target of profit maximization only.

After World War II, a program of "executive workshops" was developed at the Menninger Foundation, Topeka, Kansas. It was based on the experiences that William C. Menninger (brother of the famous psychoanalyst Karl Menninger) had had as a leading psychiatrist in the US army during World War II. Mental illnesses amongst the quickly mobilized soldiers had caused a huge number of exemptions from military service (North, 1986). Menninger observed that dysfunctional and arbitrary leadership behavior, caused by the poor training of officers, increased the likelihood of soldiers falling ill (Mertens & Lang, 1991, p. 235). The workshops held at the Will Menninger Center for Applied Behavioral Sciences (CABS) were aimed at participants who had risen to leadership due to their high technical qualification, but had not received an appropriate training for this type of task (Craig, 1986a; Mertens & Lang, 1991, pp. 238–240). Leading lights were psychoanalysts like K. Menninger, H. Levinson, and from 1970 to 1982, the German psychoanalyst T. Brocher. Alongside such training schemes, specific counseling formats were also offered. A team composed of various experts, including a psychoanalyst, arranged individual counseling for executives, regularly involving their spouses (Craig, 1986b; Mertens & Lang, 1991, p. 244). The work of the Menninger Foundation ended in 2002 with the business failure of the Menninger Clinic and its fusion with the Baylor College of Medicine.

In 1975, Sir Charles Goodeve, with the support of the Tavistock Institute and the Industrial Society, founded the Organisation for Promoting Understanding of Society (OPUS) in London. The society's goal is to achieve a more rational and efficient form of social co-existence by deepening the understanding of confrontational dynamics in economy and society. "Reflective citizenship" – using this understanding to act authoritatively and responsibly as members of society and organizations within society – is encouraged there. For that purpose, training programs, research projects and publications as well as organizational consulting and coaching are also offered (see www.opus.org.uk/history, accessed 1 April 2017). The yearly OPUS conferences usually discuss topics at the interface between economy and society. Since 1975, OPUS has organized yearly so-called "listening posts" in 38 countries: In the framework of a small group event, a snapshot is taken of the current unconscious social topics in the respective country. This method assumes that a small group addressing itself to current social issues actually depicts the unconsciously pivotal topics of their society. Since 2000, the journal *Organisational and Social Dynamics*, which is affiliated with OPUS, has published theoretical discussions, case studies and controversies on economical and political topics.

Organizational analysis as a research area has been established at the Sigmund-Freud-Institute in Frankfurt am Main, Germany, under the direction of Professor Rolf Haubl. Research projects cover topics like "Arbeit und Leben in Organisationen" ("Work and Life in Organizations"; see Haubl & Voß, 2011; Haubl & Alsdorf, 2012; Haubl, Voß, Alsdorf & Handrich, 2013), the social history of supervision in Germany (Lohl, 2014, 2016) and burnout. The Institute also offers Balint groups, supervision for groups and teams, psychodynamic executive coaching as well as methods for the analysis and development of institutions.

Some training institutes, and even the journal Freie Assoziation (Free Association) for organizational psychoanalysis in Germany grew out of psychoanalytic institutes. One of the editors, Ullrich Beumer, founded the international coaching and training organization Inscape. Also, the Institut für Analytische Supervision Düsseldorf (ASv; Institute for Analytic Supervision Düsseldorf) and the Institut für Psychodynamische Organisationsentwicklung + Personalmanagement Düsseldorf e.V. (POP; Institute for Psychodynamic Organizational Development and Human Resource Management Düsseldorf) are led by experienced clinical psychoanalysts, group analysts and supervisors.

In 2012, the Mind Institute SE, financed by the Kretschmar Familienstiftung (Kretschmar Family Trust), was established in Berlin; it does research mainly in the area of psychodynamic coaching of individuals and started its own coaching school on the basis of its research results. The Mind Institute specializes in individual coaching based on the classical psychoanalytic concept. In the case of enterprises or groups, the approach is to give clients one-on-one coaching, and to work through systemic topics as introjection from an individual perspective using the approach of object relations psychology.

Other examples for institutes that focus on psychodynamic supervision and coaching in Germany are the Munich Institute for Psychodynamic Organizational Consulting (IPOM) or the Institute for Psychoanalysis and Psychotherapy Düsseldorf (IPD).

Apart from these company setups, which for the most part are very successful in the market, most psychoanalytic supervisors work in organizational or business contexts, but typically as individuals and usually not on a full-time basis, doing this in addition to their therapeutic practice or their job at an institution of higher education or other institution.

1.5 Present state of coaching and organizational supervision

As this discussion has shown, the work of supervisors and coaches in organizations and enterprises has become professionalized and organized due to individual initiatives or a transfer of expertise from other areas. The individually chosen paths have led either to the establishment of institutes that compete with one another in the market, or the foundation of organizations that pool various interests.

The supervisor's position in psychotherapeutic training is defined in different ways, according to national rules and regulations, generally by legal and conduct rules and additionally specified by professional associations and the institutes. It is all about assigning the correct status under varying conditions. It is a specific feature of psychotherapeutic training that a qualification as supervisor is nearly always combined with a qualification as training analyst or self-reflection trainer.

The qualification of future supervisors within the framework of international psychoanalytic training generally requires a demonstration of advanced ability of conducting a psychoanalytic process practice, as well as teaching experience and sometimes knowledge of, but no experience in academic research – a sophisticated selection procedure, where a specific supervisorial qualification, however, is not demanded. Moreover, the qualification as a supervision trainer is usually bestowed in conjunction with the qualification as a training analyst – even though both occupations actually do demand disparate skills. By contrast, behavioral therapy developed a specific training for supervisors (Sulz, 2016; Freyberger, 2016), while in social work, at the example of Germany, it is usually expected that supervisors not only have work experience, but that they have also completed a supervisorial training certified by the DGSv.

There are few programs worldwide that aim at qualifying psychoanalysts for their future task as training supervisors, notably the Swedish model (Szecsödy, 1994) and the Munich Model, a peer-to-peer system for psychoanalytic training supervision qualification (Hamburger, Rauch-Strasburger, Bakhit & Schneider-Heine, 2016), where experienced practicing psychoanalysts can familiarize themselves with institutional, didactic, legal and research questions in order to learn how they may usefully contribute their clinical skills and knowledge to the supervisorial process.

1.6 Coaching reasons and methods

Currently, there are few research studies about the coaching market. According to the coaching market analysis of the University of Marburg, commissioned by the Deutscher Bundesverband Coaching e.V. (DBVC: German Federal Association of Coaching) in 2011, coaching is utilized to remedy shortcomings in the standard of knowledge as well as in the performance and flexibility of human resources, to embrace preventative measures in protecting the standard of knowledge and performance level, or to develop and promote potentialities in the standard of knowledge and the performance level of human resources (Deutscher Bundesverband Coaching, 2011, p. 37). Amongst the reasons for needing coaching, based on the coachee's own perceived shortcomings, which were assessed by coaches and clients with replies of "often" or "very often" to more than 30 per cent of questions, were the need to reflect on one's own leadership behavior (such as shortcomings, receiving external feedback) and improving one's own presence and analyzing strong and weak points (Deutscher Bundesverband Coaching, 2011, pp. 38–39).

The only reason for needing coaching as a preventative/preparative measure, which was assessed by coaches and clients with replies of "often" or "very often" to more than 30 per cent of questions, was change of paradigm/position within the company or reorientation (looking for a new company) (Deutscher Bundesverband Coaching, 2011, p. 40).

Amongst the coachee's reasons for needing coaching based on potential, which were assessed by coaches and clients with replies of "often" or "very often" to more than 30 per cent of questions, were the unleashing of untapped resources, analysis of problem-solving competence, and career-coaching (Deutscher Bundesverband Coaching, 2011, p. 42).

Even though this research study, based on the DBVC's focus on HR development, is neither representative of the German nor the international coaching market, it is evident that aspects of relationship, resources and personality permeate all topics of coaching. It becomes clear that coaching mainly offers a framework for the further development of the coachee himself. Concrete changes of perception and behavior in organizations come about only in a secondary manner from this individual development.

There is currently no market survey regarding the methods and qualifications of coaches. In their field study on conceptions of the human being and ethics in coaching in a random sampling of 87 German coaches, Richter and Marchioro (2013) found that 35.6 per cent of their sample failed to mention any methods on their web sites and 9.2 per cent merely revealed a methodology that ranged from vague to incomprehensible. From 48 indications of a theoretical approach, systemic therapy with 45 indications (93.8 per cent) was the number one method (Richter & Marchioro, 2013, p. 154).

To obtain a specific overview of the importance of psychodynamic coaching, Kretschmar (2016) analyzed the web site of the DBVC as a good representative of the German coaching market. For this purpose, all information on the 353 coaches of the DBVC (as at 2016) was transferred into a database and their self-presentations (Deutscher Bundesverband Coaching, 2016) were systemized. These were the results.

From N = 353 coaches, 319 (90 per cent) stated that they had a university degree. Ninety-three (26 per cent) of them were economists and thus the largest professional group, followed by 83 (24 per cent) psychologists and physicians. Twenty-one (6 per cent) of the coaches were also psychological psychotherapists. Further frequently mentioned professional groups were 38 (11 per cent) graduates of social-scientific studies and 23 (7 per cent) engineers. Less frequent were natural scientists, theologists, pedagogues and lawyers. Most coaches offer coaching only in German; 105 (30 per cent) offer coaching also in English. Further languages are rarely provided.

Regarding the applied methods in coaching, 68 (19 per cent) coaches didn't specify any methods, either in their self-presentation on the DBVC web site, or on their linked-up web sites. The sample is therefore reduced to N = 285. The methods mentioned most frequently by these coaches were (multiple answers possible):

- 213 (75 per cent)systemic coaching or therapy training
- 42 (15 per cent)transactional analysis, following Eric Berne
- 40 (14 per cent)mental images and imagery techniques
- 36 (13 per cent)hypno-systemic training, in particular following the Milton-Erickson-Institut, Heidelberg
- 32 (11 per cent)resource-orientated, in particular following the Zurich Resources Model
- 26 (9 per cent)gestalt psychological coaching or therapy training
- 21 (7 per cent)psychodynamic coaching or therapy training
- 18 (6 per cent)neuro-linguistic programming (NLP)
- 17 (6 per cent)group dynamic methods
- 13 (5 per cent)360-degree feedback
- 13 (5 per cent)psychodrama, following Moreno.

As field study of Richter and Marchioro (2013) has already shown, systemic approaches dominate. This stands to reason, as the systemic approach lends itself to relationship issues between client and employer. The core topic of this book, psychodynamic methods, is offered by at least 21 (7 per cent) of the coaches. For the most part, they stated they had been trained in a depth psychology therapy.

1.7 Discussion: How and whom do coaching and supervision serve? Organizational and individual perspective – train or reveal?

In the chapters comparing psychotherapy and coaching or supervision, we could show similarities and differences and determine some primary elements that are features of the two discussed procedures. At this point, a cross-comparison between coaching and supervision, without the detour via therapy, will once again name parallels and differences.

The roots of coaching and supervision in personnel psychology, social psychology and psychoanalysis are indicative of differing objectives and methods, which may not be hastily reconciled. Supervision has its origins in the training and supervision of volunteers. Thus, supervision works purposefully on the object of cognition (the case, the client, the patient, the employee, the student, etc.). This means that psychodynamic supervision in its analytical attitude has to be collegial/analog (both looking at the same subject) and in its transference interpretation, rather more illustrative. The reflection is concentrated on the institutional role. Coaching, on the other hand, has its origin in sports. The development of the coachee's individual attributes has priority. Psychodynamic coaching is all about self-awareness of one's own personality and finding out whether the solutions that the coachee develops for his objective are right for him. The coachee develops his self-awareness in the relationship that he experiences with the coach. The analytic attitude can definitely be complementary and the work can be done within and through the process of transference. Reflections on the coach's limitations as well as his individual resources may for some time play a central role. In many psychodynamic coachings, the work to be done on the coachee himself actually takes up most of the time. Often the solution of those problems, which originally were the reason for the coaching, arises from the self-awareness all by itself. In distinguishing psychotherapy, coaching and supervision from each other, one must consider that clients often do not want to admit to themselves that they have an issue that needs therapy. From time to time, the boundaries between coaching and therapy seem fluid.

Implicitly, this brings up the question of how deep the need for change is set in the coachee. What psychodynamic coaching and psychodynamic supervision have in common is that they reach deeper than their equivalents in other paradigms. This is what the psychodynamic approach per se entails, as it seeks with its techniques to make the client conscious of the unconscious – whether it be predominantly in the client's working relationships as the object of cognition (then we are talking about supervision) or mainly within the client himself (then we call it coaching). The following chapters are concerned to a considerable extent with the unconscious and with these techniques. In the process, we shall describe in detail how a profound elaboration can be achieved even if time is limited, which, of course, means that, compared with the seemingly limitless work of psychoanalysis, the breadth must be reduced.

Depending on the client's objective, he may either want to start out from an organizational or an individual perspective, choosing his starting point on the basis of where he thinks solutions lie. If he thinks that his objective has more to do with his organization, then he might first choose supervision to refine his role in this organization as his object of cognition. Depending on the knowledge of the supervisor, some reflection about the unconscious within the enterprise might be incorporated into the supervision. Supervisor and supervisee look together as colleagues from different angles at the working relationship of the client within the enterprise. As part of the supervision, the individual perspective will also be addressed; for example, when the supervisee begins to analyze the countertransferences that are triggered in him by occurrences within the enterprise with regard to his individual matrix.

If the client thinks that his objective mainly has something to do with himself because he keeps encountering the same problems or roles in differing organizations, then he will possibly choose coaching as a means of self-improvement. With progressive work from this individual perspective, he will be led to relate his increased self-awareness to his organization and thus include also the organizational perspective.

Within the psychodynamic approach, coaching and supervision have this in common – that they reveal *and* train. Working on the object of cognition or on the client discloses wishes, conflicts, role behavior, unconscious enactments, relationship patterns, resources and limitations. At the same time, self-perception and the analytic interpretation of this perception are being trained to a considerable degree. In this way, psychodynamic work imparts to the client essential skills that are very useful in many areas of life. In the end, in a constantly changing world, these basic skills will be more useful, particularly for executives, than the ability to work on a specific objective, which might no longer be in place tomorrow. In this respect, the authors are convinced that psychodynamic coaching and psychodynamic supervision are capable of conveying important skills to every executive.

Note

1 Gender usage: For better readability, we have used the male form throughout, but this must be taken as encompassing also the female form.

2 The unconscious at work

2.1 Unconscious structures on the systemic level

The transfer of psychoanalytic concepts for principles of endopsychic functioning onto the level of social interaction is, on the one hand, connected with the ego-psychology tradition, which explores the individual's adaptation to a social environment; and on the other hand, and much more efficaciously, with the object relations theoretical modeling of Wilfred Bion and the Tavistock approach deduced from it (see Chapter 1.2.2). According to Bion, a group is more than the sum of its members; within it is displayed an unconscious function matrix or an autonomous defense (see Chapter 4.3) to prevent the emergence of unpleasant requirements within the interaction, based on the "basic assumptions" fight–flight, dependency and pairing (see Chapter 1.2.2; cf. also von Ameln et al., 2009, Chapter 4). The kind of impact that the predominance of these basic assumptions can have at the organizational level is described by Heintel and Krainz (1994) from a systemic perspective as forms of "defense against the system: the search for culprits, the yielding up to one's fate or actionism". With the last of these three defenses against the system, we must remember that Bion describes pairing as the anticipation of the Messiah; in this context, Heintel and Krainz (1994) speak of the managerial principle "shoot first, aim later", which in situations of crisis feigns activity instead of targeting the task (according to Bion, the work-group mentality) more precisely. This kind of pseudo-activity is common in business; it absorbs energy and gives an "impetus" comparable to the pairing in therapy groups, but without actually precipitating a real solution.

2.1.1 The primary task

The concept of the primary task plays an important role in the Tavistock approach. Initially, this approach ignores the environment conditions (markets, suppliers, customers, competition) and focuses on the work, which has to be done primarily in the organization.

Focusing on the primary task helps us to understand the *operations* of an organization, though not the process that leads up to finding a strategy. An architecture firm, for example, has the primary task to plan houses. The strategy of individual

DOI: 10.4324/9781003169673-2

partners, however, might be either to develop a firm with equal partners or a firm named after one expert within it. These two strategies, of course, are conflicting and mutually exclusive. From the viewpoint of its agent, every alternative strategy carries risks. Amongst equal partners, the expert might want to avoid the risk of investing in marketing for a new brand. If the expert leaves the firm, the investments made in his name might have been in vain. This example shows that anxieties do not arise from the primary task, but from an ambiguous choice of strategy. At this point, Hirschhorn (2009 [1997]) introduces the concept of "primary risk" – the risk of choosing the wrong primary task, which then might not be accomplished. This origin of this risk does not lie within the environmental conditions of the firm, but in the alternatives for action and the anxieties that result from them. A solution in the case example described could be the highlighting of these anxieties and the negotiation of a compromise (Hirschhorn, 2009 [1997]).

When human beings run a risk, ambivalence figures prominently. If managers cannot decide on a clear direction, if there is an obvious gap between the primary task and the employees' activity, if the employees feel that the enterprise is drifting – then there is the assumption that the enterprise will not be able to withstand the primary risk (Hirschhorn, 2009 [1997]). In addition, employees might get sick and symptoms will then shape the organizational routine (Kretschmar & Senarclens de Grancy 2017a, p. 30). The inconsistency of different strategies and the anxieties that are linked with the strategy alternatives must therefore be kept in mind. Moreover, the interference in performance that ensues from such ambivalence should be explained. The processing of the executives' anxiety and hostility regarding the unpopular strategy alternative helps the client to find a compromise that allows the primary task to be accomplished and the anxieties to be endured (Hirschhorn, 2009 [1997]).

In 1997, Hirschhorn highlighted the limits of the Tavistock approach and suggested important additions. He explained that the analyst runs the risk of focusing on those fantasies that employees use to construct their worldview and to then ignore the pressures that beset organizations. Employees react to the primary task using their psychological resources. But the task may be influenced by realities over which the organization has only very limited control. Furthermore, the primary task represents the practices of the employees rather than their convictions. A differentiation between the task as the employees see it and the real task is needed. In this sense, the primary task could be defined as a combination of primary actions that serve the business goal (Hirschhorn, 2009 [1997]).

2.1.2 The splitting of leadership and management

In 1986, Krantz and Gilmore carried out research on the splitting that occurs between the top management and line management, due to fear of change. Just as with a splitting in the psychoanalytic sense, one part of the organization is idealized and the other is depreciated. This social defense makes its appearance in the scenario of a cult about the operationally applied management tools and techniques, as well as in the scenario of idealization of a charismatic leader. However, the idealized application of management techniques cannot succeed with a depreciated leadership. Nor can a leadership succeed if the management techniques are being depreciated (Krantz & Gilmore, 2009 [1986]).

In the first scenario, the management techniques come to be seen as magical. Starting out from a strong belief in methods and techniques that have stood the test in other projects, they are now applied to all sorts of settings. Based on many case examples, management techniques have indeed proved capable of uniting employees who believe in them. In the process, however, objective and mission can be lost from view. If a charismatic leader is being rejected, the involvement of the employees becomes unsuccessful and the implementation of change in respect to the original goal fails. Outwardly, such projects are often passed off as successful implementation of management techniques. If, however, the employees are asked for their view, it can be quite surprising to discover what things have been changed and how. In the second scenario, although there is good leadership through a "rescuer", this leadership ignores formal processes and trusts its intuition rather than an exact analysis. The celebration of a new hero is accompanied by the depreciation of the administration (Krantz & Gilmore, 2009 [1986]).

Fears generated by the two splitting scenarios are typical: the fear of greater complexity, more competition, more customer responsibility, higher requirements and loss of security or autonomy. It is a paradox that sometimes cooperation generates more fears than competition. To avoid such fears and the resulting defenses against them, managers should substantially contribute to the enterprise's primary task through the changes that they make. Vision is not enough; they also need a good grip on administrative processes (Krantz & Gilmore, 2009 [1986]).

2.1.3 The enterprise as psychological refuge

Another aspect of the Tavistock approach is that enterprises must endure the primary and other risks if they are to avoid defense mechanisms arising. In this sense, entrepreneurs and enterprises have to offer a certain containing.

Bion (1962) framed the concept of containing by analogy with the mother–child relationship. He developed this model from the earliest interactions between mother and child. The baby is not yet able to understand its sensations, much less its impulses surging from within or to pin them down. It (inherently) expects satisfaction via the "good breast" and if this doesn't happen promptly, it enters a state of becoming overwhelmed. This state gets transferred to the mother who, with the highest sensitivity (Bion calls it "reverie", a sort of dreamlike empathy), suffers vicariously with the child and internalizes the baby's panic. Because she is an adult and capable of explaining and naming her feelings (for example, she is able to understand that the baby's life is not in danger, but it is merely hungry), she can help the child out of its distress. The relief she transmits to the child enables it to gradually evolve its feelings of vague panic to those of a specific need, which will be realistically and perceptively fulfilled. Thus, she has functioned as a "container", first internalizing the child's emotional distress and then returning it to the child in a moderated form. Analogously, this procedure, which is typical for many benevolent parent–child relationships, also happens later in life – intuitively and without conscious thought.

When it is transferred to the situation and function of the helper in the case of stress, containing is the helper's ability to internalize identifiably their colleague's overwhelming feelings, to help her/him endure them and to name them in a form that is acceptable for their colleague. This exceeds the usual empathetic listening and constitutes a mentally and emotionally strenuous task, which requires experience. According to Bion, the ability for reverie plays an important role. In a therapeutic or counseling setting, reverie is a sort of daydreaming whereby helpers can personally relate in an emotionally involved way to what is being told or has been experienced, and mull it over. The consultant allows himself to be "impressed" (in the sense of being moved, but at the same time still maintaining a certain distance). In this way, the situation and the colleague's experience can be subjectively perceived by the helper and "reintroduced" to the colleague in a palatable form. For example, from a reverie, an image or metaphor can emerge which serves the colleague as a new way to access his problem (for example, the image of a rollercoaster to convey constantly changing feelings). In this context, it is important to know that it takes time to develop containing, as well as the willingness to initially allow one's own emotional involvement, in order to then reflect upon it and not to dismiss it as annoying. Both aspects – acceptance of anxiety as well as reflective interpretation – belong to the containing function.

The containing function is also used to visualize dynamic relationships within an enterprise. In 1998, David Armstrong became engaged with the concept of the psychic retreat within an enterprise, when this retreat develops to pathological levels. According to Armstrong, every organization incorporates a pathological version of itself, its so-called downside. This pathological version of the enterprise is constructed collectively and unconsciously. It functions as a psychic retreat when anxiety becomes unendurable (due to a lack of containing). Under such circumstances, hierarchies may be viewed as illusionary containers. The activation of or retreat to this pathological version can be temporary, long-term, or in the extreme, chronic. The retreat is not necessarily destructive. However, there is the risk that employees get used to this state or even get addicted to it. In the therapeutic framework, an analogous addiction would be the retreat into the therapy room (Armstrong, 1998). The pathological version of the enterprise offers at least some retreat, and thus repose. However, there is no interaction between individuals aimed at making feelings conscious and reflecting on them.

Therefore, a containing provided by leadership, as Armstrong suggests, may be neither illusionary nor lead to addictions. Containing is all about executives enduring unavoidable risks, together with employees, in the "here and now" and providing them, if needed, with a mature emotional reaction. This approach gives rise to important questions but, as yet, research has not found the answers to them. How is the containing capacity of leadership to be measured so as to distinguish real from illusionary containing? Is it even possible to develop this ability to contain, or does leadership have to bring it along as environmental conditioning? And then there is the question of how to handle containing ethically, so as not to allow abusive dependencies to develop.

2.1.4 The perverted organization

From the experience of the first author (Kretschmar), which he gained as a business consultant and member of the ISPSO, it can be noted that the Tavistock model is not always practicable in enterprises with high margins. If an enterprise is a market leader or monopolist, the primary task has obviously been chosen well. Also, there seems to be no primary risk, as the selected strategy seems to be successful. In terms of the customers, suppliers and competitors, no danger threatens. Nevertheless, there seems to be a risk in such enterprises, arising from the aspiration to make no economic mistakes. At first, this seems like a paradox. It is, however, certain that enterprises operating in difficult markets are always forced to act in a disciplined and targeted manner, in order to overcome the tough competition. This kind of pressure toward discipline and goal-directedness does not necessarily affect enterprises with high margins. In several cases, the first author has noticed forms of moral decline in such enterprises, including molestation of employees, cheating on expenses, visits to brothels paid for by the enterprise or initiation rites for new employees. All of these behaviors constitute criminal offenses. The interesting part, however, is the origin of these wrongdoings, which are often of a sexual nature. This is not essentially a new phenomenon. In Susan Long's view,

> This behavior ... resonates with ideas of hubris, exhibitionism, pride and arrogance, with the underside being shame – a public emotion. ... most [of this behavior is not even undercover but] is open within the organization. ... an organization that develops a culture based on pride and arrogance, so that their primary risk is the dark side of pride: a blindness. Pride is also a defense against shame. This also echoes Adler's work on the superiority complex as a defense against an inferiority complex. This makes me think about the nature of their work. What may be found shameful in their tasks? In their histories? In how they recruit their people? I think it is important to explore how this culture developed historically. Yes, current leadership probably has a lot to do with the culture, but it may have been established earlier. Finance is often unconsciously linked to shame. [This can also be found in] Freud's ideas around the anal meaning of money.
>
> (Long, personal communication, 8 January 2016)

Susan Long has looked in depth into such perverted organizations. She describes the origin and consequences of pride, greed, jealousy, idleness, negligence, anger and rage in enterprises from the psychoanalytic viewpoint (Long, 2008). Christopher Scanlon and David Cooper (personal communication, January 2017) also share the experience that moral aspects do not generate the necessary pressure and that clients are skeptical when it comes to non-quantifiable dimensions, whether they derive from business or culture. Cooper sees in them "narcissistic drivers, which provide some release from the anxiety which comes from an awareness that their success is derived as much from luck as from business nous and leadership finesse" (Cooper, personal communication, January 2017). This discussion makes it clear, once again, that the primary risk, just as Hirschhorn originally defined it, primarily emerges from within. The only difference in the cases discussed in this chapter, is that here the primary risk does not derive from the fear of making the wrong strategic decisions, but from underlying conflicts within leadership and among employees.

2.1.5 The succession problem on the systemic level

One of the most pressing problems for the sustainability of structures is the transition from the pioneer phase to succession. In the context of this chapter, it will be treated as a systemic risk; personnel aspects and systemic–personnel interactions will be dealt with later (see Chapter 2.2.2, Chapter 2.3.4). Using the example of science organizations, Dieter Ohlmeier, one of the leading lights of psychoanalytic organizational research, has described the appointment of a successor as a "risky situation":

> A successor cannot avoid being measured against the founder, not even avoid measuring himself against the founder and thus replacing his own internal ego-ideal with an external one. However, such a process must cause a severe identity destabilization, even if at first, he is unaware of it. Also, the members of the institution experience a destabilization in the confrontation with the successor. If possible, they try to see the successor as a continuation or even as a copy of the founder. Or they soon assess the successor as falling short of the achievements of the founder (who is more and more glorified and haloed in their memory).
>
> (Ohlmeier, 2009 [2004], pp. 105–106)

Scientific and economic history is full of sometimes tragic examples of successfully established and perfectly balanced organizations producing a valuable output and nevertheless developing severe dysfunctions or even collapsing in this transition phase; this is not because they could no longer survive in the market, but for internal, mainly unconscious, reasons. Gilmore (2009 [2004]) mentions an alarming example of how dangerous a badly managed transition can be: "In the end the explosion of the Challenger rocket was the result of a group of executives leaving the NASA, who had not imparted their knowledge about the vulnerable construction of the toric joints to their successors" (Gilmore, 2009 [2004], p. 223).

The succession problem has three dimensions, which at the same time may be defined as goals of change:

1   Release: The founder must have the ability to hand over his work.
2   Accede: The successor must have the ability to accept his place and to develop it.
3   Accept: The institution must have the ability to honor the successor.

Release

Gilmore (2009 [2004]) describes the dynamic of denial about final situations as a fear of becoming a "lame duck", and its compensation with the fantasy of having control over the organization even after leaving. In psychodynamic terms, this fear is often linked to fear of death. The question as to when it is time to change from the operational side of the business to a counseling senior role is fore-shortened to the term "quitting" and then quickly denied; the question is then supplanted by the conviction of being irreplaceable. This denial, however, has not only an intra-psychological, but also a systemic aspect. In psychoanalysis, which is mainly concerned with child development, the complementary role of parents was often underestimated. The emphasis was mainly on the son's dilemma between his love for and his rivalry with the father, which was described by reference to the Greek myth of Oedipus. For a long time, the fact that Oedipus had already been abandoned as an infant, by command of his father Laius, was overlooked – the feared patricide committed by Oedipus on his father Laius was preceded by the father's assault on the life of his son (Devereux, 1953; Teising, 2009). This tragic decision, however, was already an involuntary, unconscious re-enactment, which points even more clearly to an inter-genera-tional, systemic dimension: In Greek myth, both Laius and his father Labdacus were under-age kings, for whom, after the premature death of their fathers, an older relative assumed the reins of government. Laius himself had to leave Thebes when he was only a year old, and he re-enacted this fate with his own son. When his uncle prophesied to Laius that his son would kill him, he had the child's feet pierced (thus his name Oedipus, meaning swollen foot) and ordered him to be abandoned. Oedipus survived, was brought up by a childless royal couple and later, without realizing it, murdered his biological father and then married his biological mother, Jocasta.

When executives, particularly in family businesses, don't accept or wish for a successor or fight him as soon as he becomes autonomous, this pattern is referred to as the so-called "Laius complex" (see the case example of Hirsch [2000] and its discussion in Chapter 2.2.2).

Accede

The difficulty of releasing corresponds with the difficulty of acceding. Goethe's Faust's adage, "What we are born with, we must make our own / Or it remains a mere appurtenance" is widely quoted to illustrate the role of the active successor who assures himself of his own authority. However, this is easier said than done. The demanded active succession can be confronted with mighty resistance. As we have used the Laius complex to illustrate the founder's fear of handing over to his successor, the even more well-known Oedipus complex is the paradigmatic myth of the successor. He seeks to step in for his father, but this implicitly means that he has to get rid of him; it actually requires the father's "death". This is neither an individual nor a pathological character or role; it results simply from the logic of a leadership-centered enterprise. To the same extent that the leader is idealized and worshiped, his replacement is tabooed. Anyone who succeeds is consequently a taboo-breaker. As Burkard Sievers states,

> even if an individual successor may be convinced that his situation is unique, and because of it thinks that no-one else can really understand him, so also the takeover of an inheritance is characterized by patterns, dynamics, and myths of succession, which are a part of the respective culture and its history.
>
> (Sievers, 2002, p. 489)

Accept

During the succession phase, typical reactions arise, not only affecting the leaving and entering executives, but also the entire institution in the form of uncertainty, a search for orientation and resistance. Uncertainty will already be rampant during the phase in which it becomes known or expected that an executive position is to be staffed. Usually, employees then adopt a waiting attitude. "Such behavior may cause the organization to drift along without a direction, at a moment, of all times, when the remaining executives are crucially in demand" (Gilmore, 2009 [2004], p. 224). A change within the leadership always necessitates a re-orientation of the social field within and outside the organization. It cannot be foreseen what sort of impact or reciprocal effect any succession planning might produce, if it isn't known how all the people involved interrelate. Moreover, it is not the formal allocation of tasks and competences, but the finely tuned system of implicit expectations which is influential. In this situation, the boss, even if he is not concerned with individual processes in his role, plays an important part as a projection figure. A concrete task in the enterprise can be tackled with determination and other participants involved if it is expected (and successfully conveyed to them) that the result will be social approval, valid for all. This is, of course, dependent on the successful fulfillment of the task; however, often the success is not immediately obvious and cannot be noticeably measured. What counts is the perceived success, the social recognition within the enterprise itself. If, for example, a professor at some university establishes a new degree course, he must involve a large group of colleagues and staff as well as committees. He needs to receive financial support from the university administration to set up the degree course and, often, it can only be determined years later whether or not the effort was worthwhile – for instance, if enough students registered for the course – and it takes many more years to ascertain if this degree was accepted by the job market as well as esteemed by the academic field. Only then can it become clear whether this extraordinary effort has generated a sustainable success. It is difficult to implement such a project if the university's administration is going to be changed in the next year, because such a developing process needs the support and approval of the administration during all stages and at all levels. It is easier to secure the support of colleagues if it is known that the university president backs the project. Committees will negotiate more favorably if this president can be expected to be on board for many more years – long-range investments are often not granted during the last year of tenure. In the departure of an executive, Gilmore (2009 [2004], p. 226) also notes that the containing of potential tensions within the enterprise is discontinued. Employees react to such a situation either with manic denial (for example, by working particularly hard on one single task), with retreat (for example, from cooperation with colleagues) or with nostalgia (for example, by relishing past successes).

This search for orientation within the group, which starts with the announcement of a change of leadership, intensifies as soon as the change is happening. Due to the aforementioned systemic signs of paralysis during the incubation period, considerable tension has accumulated and tasks have been neglected. As soon as the "novice" is on board, he is confronted with a significant need for speedy directional decisions – just at a moment when he is still adjusting to his new position and is not yet able to get an overview of the complexity of the decisions to be made or their associated social processes. From the viewpoint of those involved, this systemic process often assumes the form of resentments or frustrated reactions. In sum, these can accumulate to create unconscious group dynamics. Ohlmeier (2009 [2004]) describes the reaction of rejection toward the successor from the employees' perspective: They quite commonly take out

> their ambivalence towards the founder – in particular, their aggressive potential (usually suppressed until now) and their rebellion against him, which they, considering his real presence and power, have deferred until later – on his successor, whom they identify as being weaker and "younger". Finally, they also feel insecure in their group identity as members of the institution … they lose their contact with reality or with what realistically can be expected of an individual as they assess the noticeable weaknesses of the successor as "bad, insufficient, and detrimental" to the work of the institution. This is tantamount to a splitting tendency and they anxiously and worriedly experience the institution as threatened. They see the successor, for example, as misjudging the external enemies, not having the savvy and overview or even the connections, nor the legendary boosters and allies of the founder.
>
> (Ohlmeier, 2009 [2004], p. 106)

The succession problem is one of the main application fields for psychodynamic supervision. Lutzi (2003) sheds light on the situation of leadership change from a different perspective. She notices a principal paradox emerging at the breakpoints of the developing enterprise and describes it using Winnicott's terminology of the "transitional space". In such phases of strong change, there is always talk of "innovation, creativity and flexibility" (Lutzi, 2003, p. 452), but the concrete steps of change are planned with the increased "meticulousness of an accounting clerk" (p. 452). According to Lutzi, this kind of structural defense can only be understood and overcome if one drops the assumption that processes of change must be thought through before they can be implemented, and that a "hierarchical-linear relationship between thinking and acting" (p. 452) exists.

> The world within and the reality without are subject to different conditions and are not unambiguously relatable to one another. If an idea is to be realized, there needs to be room for the "bulkiness" of the objects – that is to say – for the difference between an imagined and an actually experienced encounter with the object. An intermediate room is needed in which both ways of interacting with the object can be correlated in the knowledge that they are different processes.
>
> (Lutzi, 2003, p. 452)

2.2 Unconscious structures on the individual level

People in organizations are part of the unconscious matrix of that organization and internalize this matrix. From the psychoanalytic viewpoint, various terms have been suggested to name this internalization: Hutton, Bazalgette and Reed (1997) call it "organization-in-the-mind"; Armstrong (1997) refers to it as "institution-in-the-mind"; and Long (1999) labels it "institution in experience".

> If we take on a role in an organization, then we introject parts of that which happens, and according to Melanie Klein's concept, develop inner objects and sub-objects. These objects form an inner matrix, which is partly conscious but because of its threatening character, must remain partially unconscious.
>
> (Beumer & Sievers, 2000, p. 12)

This introjection is based on the fact that the human psyche relates to social interactions right from the beginning. Intra-psychic structural formation happens in the context of the primary family, in particular through the establishment of a "controlling object" (König, 1986) – and this is the position for organizational contexts to be inserted later in life.

> This "internalized organizational matrix" decisively determines our perception of organizations and the transferred conflicts, defenses etc., as well. Combined with that, and with what the individual takes in consciously and unconsciously as a part of the organizational reality, a complex inner landscape is formed of the organizational perception: the so-called "organization-in-the-mind".
>
> (Beumer & Sievers, 2000, p. 16)

In the following sub-section, we will describe the incorporation of the individual unconscious into the matrix of the organization and some of the ensuing problems.

2.2.1 The emotional experience of being part of an organization

Richard Morgan-Jones (2010) does research on the health of employees and the organization from the psychoanalytic perspective. He focuses on the experience of being in one's own body as well as in the body of an organization. The starting point of his reflections is the individual health of body and mind, the desire for objects, and the concomitant disappointment of wish fulfillment. Organizations likewise have bodies and minds, with aims and wishes which are formed by their employees. Healthy organizations keep mind *and* body together. For his interventions, Morgan-Jones combines his experience from his psychoanalytic practice, his observations on group relations, his practical experience in coaching and consulting based on the Tavistock approach, as well as the findings of socio-analytic and psychoanalytic research (Morgan-Jones, 2010).

Psychoanalytic techniques can be employed for the processing of feelings. They help us to understand how relational experiences manifest themselves on a bodily and mental level. Important concepts are destructive defense mechanisms, the self-destroying aspects of the super-ego, progression and regression, the ability to dream and to wish, as well as the identification with various individuals. The findings of the psychodynamics of psychosomatic illnesses can be transferred to socio-somatic phenomena. Using findings from group analysis, it is important to see how the connections between different groups and sub-groups influence the perception of their representative group members regarding their conscious aims and unconscious psychodynamics, which lead to the subjective perception of their tasks. These connections also influence significantly the ethics and motivation in organizations. The Tavistock approaches to the psychodynamics of open systems help us to understand how the organization correlates to its members and to its environment. Its primary task, which secures the viability of the organization, is the exchange of goods, services and money (Morgan-Jones, 2010). With his approach, Morgan-Jones augments the management of operational health by bringing in the aspect of psychic health.

2.2.2 Family business and the succession problem: The inner-psychic level

Hirsch (2000) describes in detail the case of a father–son conflict about the succession in a major family-owned business. The enterprise founder's grandson had come to see him for psychotherapy. Ten years previously, he had succeeded his father in corporate management and had since developed an eating disorder and an alcohol problem. Even as the therapy was still ongoing, wild outbreaks occurred: The father threatened the son with legal measures and public exposure. The containing in the therapy prevented an imminent scandal and allowed an appropriate differentiation. As the background to this family quarrel, Hirsch depicts a transgenerational traumatization. The father of the client had been scorned by his father, the founder of the enterprise, but nevertheless had had to take on the business, because the brother actually chosen as successor, who shared the grandfather's name, had died in World War II. The client grew up as the father's "crown prince", whereas his mother rather turned her back on him. The father named his firstborn son after the grandfather and, as was expected, the son assumed the management of the enterprise. Thereafter, the father's trauma seemed repaired. As long as Hirsch's client managed the firm according to the senior partner's expectations, there was no conflict. This changed once he became more independent: Escalating disputes became more frequent, his old father demanded ostentatious privileges (such as company planes, expensive consultants, etc.); he began to damage the business reputation of his son, and thus of the enterprise, by deliberate indiscretions and, in the end, he sued him for damages. The father knew about his son's therapy and even tried to influence the therapist (Hirsch, 2000, p. 41). The client was incapable of disassociating himself from all of this effectively; his sense of duty toward his father, he maintained, was too deep. Hirsch interpreted the interlocked psychodynamic of father and son as follows: The client's father, who himself had been the unloved child, had projectively generated in his son a reparation figure by treating him like the crown prince – a model which could only go well while he could identify himself with this crown prince. However, as soon as the son began to think for himself and to fill his role as the boss, this unconscious construction crumbled and the elder leader relived in his son (the client) the experience of his own father announcing to him "that he was no longer the 'right' one". This, however, reopened his old wounds and he was forced to prove once again, just as when he had taken over the business, that in all respects "he was, nevertheless, the right one" (Hirsch, 2000, p. 41). From the client's standpoint, this corresponded with his identification with the powerful and significant father (once he had labeled him as "godlike"), which was also reflected in the therapeutic relationship. Behind the interlocked dynamic, Hirsch sees an Oedipal constellation: For the competing men, the firm had taken on the role of the mother they had to fight for.

> Both rivals had respectively an extremely [high] filicide and patricide potential, whereas the father being less inhibited, [was] even willing to risk the existence of the enterprise, obviously thinking that it was his achievement and that he could do with it what he wanted. On the other hand, the son was ... Oedipally inhibited: he was incapable of "killing" the father because he could not remove him from the firm, in his perception: from the mother. ... The client is unable to overcome the Oedipus complex and to separate from his father, because he is tied to him in a dyadic, alliance-like and identity-establishing relationship.
>
> (Hirsch, 2000, p. 42)

This interpretation, however, remained speculative, as the client was not prepared to work through it and was only willing to use the therapy as coaching (see also Chapter 4.4, where this case example is taken up again to illustrate the resistance concept).

2.3 Interaction of personnel and systemic level

2.3.1 The concept of the neurotic organization

The concept of the neurotic organization ascribes the unconscious as being an "invisible hand" in enterprises. Decisions grow out of invisible long-standing psychological forces. These covert forces often lead to irrational and dysfunctional behaviors. Management consultants with psychoanalytic training are capable of identifying symptoms in organizations which imply a destructive change (Kets de Vries & Miller, 1984, pp. 1–2). Based on Bion's concepts, Kets de Vries and Miller initially developed a theory as to how anxiety may cause varying forms of shared fantasies. Anger, hate or suspicions necessitate fight or flight. Depression, envy, guilt or reverence lead to dependency and the desire to be protected by a leader. Hope, faith, enthusiasm, despair and disillusionment give rise to utopian ideals about a future salvation (Kets de Vries & Miller, 1984, p. 53). By transferring the findings of clinical psychoanalysis onto businesses, they developed a concept that covers the following aspects: the neurotic personalities of executives in stressed enterprises; the influencing of feelings in interpersonal relationships through the transference of patterns from superiors and employees; the dysfunctional handling of personnel; life-cycle crises during a management career; psychodynamic defense strategies; mourning and resistance in the event of a loss of status (Kets de Vries & Miller, 1984).

2.3.2 Occupational burnout

At the interface between the enterprise and the individual, "fatigue breaks" often occur in the form of depressive reactions, which today are mainly termed "burnout".

Weigand (2000) notes that numerous supervisees from a business context, and in particular, achievement-orientated personalities, report the formation of symptoms based on their systematic disregard for the limits of their own resilience:

> Psychosomatic complaints, sleep disorder, tinnitus, burnout syndromes. Occasionally a supervision came about because an alert boss suggested to the supervisee: "You desperately need to do something for yourself, in order for you to remain with us for many more years".
>
> (Weigand, 2000, p. 56)

Such clear psychopathological symptoms would rather suggest the need for psychotherapy instead of supervision or coaching. Why there is a failure to perceive one's own limits against one's better judgment, and why the organization's requirements are nevertheless uncritically accepted, needs to be clarified in a personal context. Clients, however, rarely accept this; even with all the symptoms of burnout, they typically wish only to go in for further self-optimization – to become even fitter and even more efficient. This is why they opt for vocational consultation instead of therapeutic counseling. Often enough, the outcome of such consultation is the insight that the problem actually has further personal dimensions, at which point clients manage to overcome their prejudice against therapy. On the other hand, it needs to be recognized that burnout is an organizational symptom. The job requirements and communications structures of some enterprises generate a high rate of burnout problems and a heightened absence rate due to sickness among their employees. In such situations, it is the business that needs therapy and organizational consulting or organizational development in order to provide relief. At the interface between individual and organizational pathology, work-related symptoms can always be located and it is these which motivate the client to go into supervision or coaching. Then it becomes essential to concentrate on exactly those fields of consulting; even then, however, neither the institutional failure nor the possible personal pathology need to be excluded. The focus of consulting must be directed to what can be changed in the "here and now"; the necessity for other changes may need other forms of intervention. This constraint is psychodynamically justifiable, as the illusionary expectation that coaching or supervision is capable of changing the enterprise, or can heal neurotically related over-commitment in itself, is an idealized transference. This can possibly trigger countertransference in the supervisor and make him feel like an almighty healer, which should itself be reflected on and utilized for the analysis of the idealized transference.

Burnout is such a frequent reason for consultancy and appropriate support being urgently sought (and offered) that the advice, to stay exactly within the limits of the process, is all the more important. This was confirmed by the DGSv's research project, "Arbeit und Leben in Organisationen" ("Work and Life in Organizations"; Haubl & Voß, 2011), which was based on a systematic questioning of supervisors and utilized their privileged access to the everyday reality of their employees and their vocational activity in organizations in Germany. Since the 2000s, excessive demands on employees and the substantial stress that follows has led to an increase in mental illnesses that are clearly work-related. In particular, the DGSv's second report, *Belastungsstörungen mit System: Die zweite Studie zur psychosozialen Situation in deutschen Organisationen* (*Systemic Stress Disorders: The Second Study on the Psychosocial Situation in German Organizations*; Haubl et al., 2013) shows that according to 88 per cent of the supervisors interviewed, the work intensity has remained at a steady high and jobholders are still under pressure in terms of time and performance (Beumer, 2013). Researchers warn against pathologizing the subjective manifestation of these social issues as they appear in the form of exhaustion and overextension, by assigning jobholders to therapeutic categories (Haubl, 2013).

The question as to whether or not working can make people ill is passionately debated in this context. Gabriel (2009) speaks about "the miasma of the toxic organisation" and Stein (2009) of the "totalitarian organisation". Of course, it is imperative to substantiate such claims by research – for one, to check if it is actually true; and for another, to find out where and exactly how this happens in order to provide adequate relief. The controversy about the (generalized) assertion that capitalism makes us ill shows us that this is not always easy. With the diagnosis in his book, *The Weariness of the Self*, the French sociologist Alain Ehrenberg (2010 [1998]) recognized the increase of autonomy and accountability in democracies with neo-liberal economies as a cause for the epidemic increase of depression. The philosopher Byung-Chul Han, in *The Burnout Society* (2015 [2010]), partially denies Ehrenberg's assumption of increasing autonomy by accusing him of having overlooked the growing pressure to achieve. Martin Dornes, a much-read author in the German psychoanalytic community, who advocated, above all, the opening of developmental psychology for empirical results, disagreed with both authors, and in his paper, "Macht der Kapitalismus depressiv?" ("Does Capitalism Cause Depression?", 2015) points out that since the 1980s, mental illnesses have not increased substantially in Germany. This triggered a fierce controversy. Brede (2015), Egloff (2015) and Engelmann (2015) accused Dornes of wanting to shut down a socio-critical debate by presenting only epidemiological data. This controversy, which will not be elaborated on further here, shows that the perception of stress in modern economic life, which is articulated in various theories, demands an open discourse to establish a sufficiently differentiated picture. The distinction between "ill" and "not ill" is not enough to describe the individual dimensions of exhaustion, fatigue and depression in working life. And to refer these individual dimensions to society as a whole is certainly to generalize unduly. In order to have a proper discourse on this subject, research is needed, not only through an epidemiological survey, but also through a qualitative analysis of intimate counseling dyads under the auspices of a culture of deliberation.

2.3.3 Female leadership: A personal question of organizational development

One topic often brought up in coaching and organizational supervision, but rarely in public, is the importance of gender, gender-specific roles and respective role expectations. Both authors' conversational experiences show that men, in particular, do not dare to publicly speak their minds, when it comes to gender equality for executive positions in the economy: They fear being considered anti-progressive and anti-women, or being accused of not wanting to vacate a position of power and of being fundamentally paternalistic. In private conversations, it is often pointed out that nowadays women have excellent prospects in executive positions and that appellate bodies and HR managers are highly committed to finding suitable female applicants. The reverse side of the coin is, as we often hear in such conversations, that the man was refused the appointment to an executive position even though the preferred female candidate was less well-qualified. Bitter remarks on "Quota-Hilde" are no rare occurrence in such talks. Of course, the topic is not only raised in conversations with men. Female executives occasionally comment that these days, it could even be called an advantage to be a woman when applying for a job; but they also confidently add that in earlier days, when it was easier for men and careers were more accessible for them, men had no problem with seizing the advantage – "such is life". However, in public discourse and in research, the prevailing view seems to be that women are systemically disadvantaged. Beyond a judgmental/normative comparison, it is worthwhile, in our view, to determine impartially to what extent and in which ways gender characteristics affect vocational progress in organizations and businesses, as well as the subjective experiences of the parties involved.

In her sociological dissertation, *Das Geschlecht der Führung* (*The Gender of Leadership*), Pannewitz (2012) looks into those discussions in executive supervision and coaching where the lack of gender equality in leadership becomes apparent. She argues that it is not so much the hard personnel figures that matter – for example, the only slowly increasing numbers of female executives despite the subject being addressed in politics and the media for a long time – but rather the stories about leadership being dominated by "male success-and-strategy-stereotypes, or by an eloquent silence when it comes to leadership and gender and to dominating masculinized metaphorical concepts" (Pannewitz, 2012, p. 25). "Leadership is subject to an andocentric norm … which is shrouded in secrecy but which against its backdrop guarantees that 'female' lifeworld experiences and expectations of behavior are overwhelmingly excluded from the interactive interpretation of leadership" (Pannewitz, 2012, p. 25). Pannewitz reckons that this reproduction of stereotypes cannot be eliminated by supervision and coaching. Such stereotypes "are a part of the interactive negotiation process about the personnel criteria, which are compatible or incompatible with leadership" (Pannewitz, 2012, p. 353). If these really alarming sociological research results lead us to conclude that specific "gender coaches" should be brought in, or raise the question as to whether gender should be incorporated into the extended critical self-examination of supervisors and coaches, this is the subject of a controversial debate (Knoppers, 1987; Ludeman, 2009).

2.3.4 Family business and the succession problem: Individual–system interaction

The role of executives in family businesses represents a particularly virulent example of the intersection of individual and systemic levels. No matter whether an enterprise has grown to the size where the founding family only holds a fraction of the equity, which has meanwhile mainly passed over to shareholders, or if it is a medium-sized business, still owned by the family, "the firm" always plays a central role in the fabric of the family and vice versa.

Even if executives in family businesses are not relatives of the owner family, but employed "external" managers, they will certainly feel the mighty dynamic of this invisible force field.

When the subject of succession comes up in the family business, the meshing of system and individual plays a particularly important role. This interactive level differs from the system level described above (see Chapter 2.1.5). Here we are talking about individual unconscious processes (as described in Chapter

2.2.2) making themselves felt in the "social unconscious" of the enterprise; and conversely, about the role the business plays in the socialization of entrepreneurs' children. Admittedly, we should not overstrain the term "social unconscious" (Busch, 2001). "What society does with the individual and how this individual reacts psychologically and subjectively, social psychology must patiently collect, instead of patronizing and covering it over with speculative, analogizing, supra-individual concepts" (Busch, 2001, p. 418). But, of course, this "patient collecting" can actually lead to specific findings, which allow a better understanding of the complex mélange in family businesses, especially at the moment of handing over to the executive successor.

One of the most striking dramas about legitimacy and the earning of the fatherly or God-fatherly blessing, which allows the succession in the first place, is the legend of Jacob in the Old Testament. "The assertion of one's own origin and one's place in the succession is far beyond the scope of the narrow space of one's individual life and enables overcoming [of] the frame set by one's birth and death" (Sievers, 2002, p. 489). From his work with successors, Sievers reports on "succession transferences … in which many of them were entangled since their childhood" (Sievers, 2002, p. 507).

The succession problem in family businesses is particularly aggravated if the takeover of leadership happens along the direct descendant line. The tabooed patricide, which makes it difficult for any successor to assume his position, is even more powerful if the predecessor is not only a symbolic, but also a true father. The takeover of a family business by a daughter and its very specific difficulties has only recently been studied in detail. The German psychoanalyst Almuth Sellschopp in cooperation with Helga Breuningner (Breuninger & Sellschopp, 2013) dealt with this problem extensively. In a chapter in their book, *Von der Kunst der guten Führung* (*About the Art of Good Leadership*), Sellschopp (2013) describes a project in which a group of 12 women, who one day will have to decide for or against the takeover of a business, hold regular workshops on female leadership. All the participants hold a post at the board level and possess an excellent education, usually in two different fields. They are well prepared for their future role. The process was backed by two research projects, and out of these emerged a structured training for executives (female and male) in perception and utilization of emotions for leadership action. The findings revealed two sub-groups of female successors, depending on whether the father or the mother was handing down the business. On the one hand,

> in businesses led by mothers, our female successors showed an open succession climate. Conflicts in terms of rivalry and differentiation were definitely daily fare and were staged quite affectively and intensely – who had the say where and when. Otherwise inherent conflicts as, for example, the lack of appreciation, the feelings of not being sufficiently perceived, or basic helplessness in handling the structures predetermined by leadership, were lacking.
>
> (Sellschopp, 2013, p. 78)

With mother–daughter handovers, the authors noticed an early adaptive preparation and an active participation by the mothers, including supporting their daughters in overcoming the role splitting between executive and spouse. On the other hand, in businesses led by fathers, a division was revealed between the status of the "chosen" daughter and a simultaneous visible, subliminal devaluation of the gender role (Sellschopp, 2013, p. 79) on the father's part; correspondingly, on the part of the female successor, there was extreme performance orientation alongside a high valuing of modesty and restraint. As a contrast to the often described general pattern where executive daughters strive to attain their position by employing a coaxing and caring stance toward the father (a strategy often doomed to failure), Breuninger & Sellschopp (2013) describe a "kind of double-bind" manifesting "a need for authentic independence coupled with affectionate attachment to the father and therewith adoption of his working and business structures – a sort of permanent balancing act" (Sellschopp, 2013, p. 80). In a qualitative-empirical study from the project, Mörtl, Kirnoha & Pos (2013), using the grounded theory method, found various types of female successors – (1) "the controlling", (2) "the independent", (3) "the social", and (4) "the modest" (pp. 116–118) – which they, falling back on Operationalisierte Psychodynamische Diagnostik (OPD; Operationalized Psychodynamic Diagnosis; see Chapter 4.10), grouped in two overlapping, pure types: "the lone fighter" and "the team player" (pp. 122–123).

2.4 Discussion: Organizational perspective, individual perspective, and the big picture. Where do the central issues of coaching and organizational supervision lie?

In this chapter we have gathered, from our viewpoint, the important and prevailing issues concerning unconscious structures in enterprises. On the system level, these are issues of division, anxieties and risks resulting from the primary task, withdrawal and operational deterioration. On the individual level, the issues are those of emotional experience in organizations or the influence of feelings on decisions. At the level of interaction between the individual and the system, the issues are the invisible hand, burnout and gender in leadership. The issue of "business succession" extends across all these levels.

Initially, pivotal issues are to be perceived rather fundamentally and theoretically. From studying psychodynamic literature, and from our casework with clients, we know that groups have certain reaction patterns; that the unconscious within businesses can be operatively dysfunctional, too – in the form of anxieties, defense or regression; and that a business presents a great stage for many role players. However, in the end, these insights are useful only as background knowledge. In coaching and in organizational supervision with individual clients, every case is different and a pivotal issue can be hard to determine (see also the case examples in Chapter 6). Thus, on the abstract level, it can only be noted that the bringing to mind of unconscious puzzle pieces, which have to be assembled to create the big picture, is the pivot of psychodynamic work. This, however, is a very fulfilling assignment for coach, supervisor and client.

Of course, this knowledge finds expression in practical coaching and supervision work. In particular, if, according to the psychoanalytic attitude (see Chapter 3.1.2), you do not allow yourself to be tied down to an assignment for change, but first open your view in "evenly suspended attention" to what is seemingly irrelevant, the connection between the client's individual subjective perception and the institutional defense processes operating in the business's "unconscious" can be noticed. Psychoanalytic supervision that reflects this institutional dynamic can help one to deal with it successfully. In addition, the search for the interlocking of the institutional dynamic with the psychodynamic does not happen in a distanced, object-related examination setting, but in a transference space. Thus, it can be examined using the model of the ongoing consultation which reflects how clients behave in their institutional world. For instance, in his own countertransference, the supervisor can often sense his defense impulses being set off against the client's impulses for reform, which evoke anxiety in the subconscious of the enterprise. For example, he can feel "annoyed" by the client's aggressive and forceful proposing of reforms, and his reflecting on this countertransference can become the bedrock for a joint discussion about how the client and his institutional environment have internalized the unconscious fear of change. The "annoying" aspect of the client and the "annoyed" reaction of his team could then be reconstructed as complementary role splitting, an unconscious interaction between "annoyer" and "annoyed". Once this is understood, the client is capable of searching for creative ways of stepping out of his role.

The discussion of coaching and supervision in this book clarifies the following: Classical coaching can benefit from the psychoanalytic attitude and put its orientation toward the conscious assignment into perspective. The coach has to disentangle himself from the pressure of the assignment in order to identify the unconscious interaction between system and individual. And classical supervision can extend its familial paradigm of interpretation by concretely including knowledge about organizations; this comprises acceptance of the client's assignment pressure (without yielding to it) and recognition of it as being part of the institutional dynamic.

3   State of the art

3.1 Attitude, setting and ethical principles

3.1.1 The attitude of the coach

A coach's attitude is based on the assumption that he sees the client as expert. The coach restricts himself solely to facilitating the process without pre-determining its content or giving advice (Müller, 2012, p. 10).

As an important ethical bedrock of coaching, Müller (2012) mentions:

- The independence of the coach
- The secrecy of the coach
- The voluntary nature of the coaching for the clients
- The imperative to avoid private contact between coach and client
- The imperative to avoid role conflicts
- The transparency of the coaching processes
- The consideration of the client's self-reliance by the coach
- The coach's transparency with regard to the general limits of coaching and to the limits of his personal competence.

(Müller, 2012, p. 71)

Alongside ethical principles, there is, similar to psychotherapy, a duty of care. This includes a thorough clarification of the coach's objective and its concomitant circumstances, the management of his coaching as a legally regulated business, as well as his vocational education and further training (Deutscher Bundesverband Coaching, 2012, pp. 55–57).

As a rule, coaching takes place with individual clients in a setting which is comparable to a psychotherapy session where the client and therapist sit facing one another. Coach and client work together on a confidential basis in a closed room. According to the experience of the first author (Kretschmar), this is the most common coaching variant in Germany; In a one-on-one coaching session, the client is being coached on her/his own; there is no interconnectedness with other individuals in her/his business (Deutscher Bundesverband Coaching, 2012, p. 30).

DOI: 10.4324/9781003169673-3

There are also multi-person coachings of different types. In team coachings, the members of a team work together toward a goal. The team members also work together vocationally outside the coaching. In group coachings, members work together on mutually chosen topics, which are not vocationally dependent on one another. In organizational coachings, several individuals within an organization will be coached at the same time or in parallel. Such coachings are tailored to suit a common goal. Last, but not least, there are special formats which integrate other forms of developmental support such as training (Deutscher Bundesverband Coaching, 2012, p. 30).

3.1.2 The psychoanalytic attitude in organizational supervision

If clients from enterprises and organizations approach a psychoanalyst with a request for supervision, then their choice is already a statement. They are targeting a platform outside the familiar business world with its coaching and consulting facilities, and assume that a psychoanalyst can accordingly offer an external perspective – this is usually justified. Often, the client decides on this course when he perceives that the problem to be dealt with is very private; the fact that psychoanalysts are always therapists too may be another deciding factor. Generally, when someone chooses a supervisor or a coach, their background qualification is a relevant issue. If, for example, one calls upon a consultant whose background is theological, existential doubts may play a role, and the client hopes to speak with someone who is familiar with such questions. If one requests a coach who is a former CEO in an enterprise, then the client values managerial competence and looks for a meeting on an equal footing. With a psychoanalytic supervisor, the client is looking for someone who is open and well-equipped to advise on an individual motivation for change (Bauriedl, 2001).

But will this psychoanalyst be adequately equipped to deal with this objective appropriately? The question as to whether or not psychoanalysis (particularly modern psychoanalysis) and psychoanalytic treatment techniques, based on scenic re-actualization of earlier object experiences, are transferable to other contexts of application is a controversial subject for discussion in the psychoanalytical community. Wellendorf (1996), who supports such an application of psychoanalysis, frames the challenge clearly:

> Without the secure frame of the setting, unconscious elements seep away into everyday communication and it becomes impossible to analyze them. It is known that attempts and temptations of both the analysand and the analyst to break the mold and to overstep the limits of the analytic situation, are a central part of the analytic process and that the most hidden impulses, emotions and fantasies are brought to light by analyzing those attempts and temptations. What is meant by "unconscious" manifests itself in breach and violation of the limits.
>
> (Wellendorf, 1996, pp. 80–81)

If the frame itself is defined as such a vital element of the psychoanalytic method, then there seems no space left for its usage outside the classical analytic situation:

> As supervisors and consultants, we don't move in our own well-defined territory but in that of the clients. It is unavoidable that the psychoanalyst shares everyday activities, contacts and locations with the client. At times it can be difficult to clearly separate social and vocational contacts (Menzies Lyth 1989 [i.e. 1988], p. 38 f.). Even the principles of free association and evenly suspended attention in that form, which we utilize in the protected space of the psychoanalytic setting, prove to be largely illusory when working in the "social field". … To be talking about transference, countertransference and resistance in the "social field" seems a mere manner of speaking, relaying what actually happens between client and analyst or consultant only in a diffusely and subjectivistically distorted way.
>
> (Wellendorf, 1996, p. 85)

With respect to this gap between the genuine field of psychoanalytic exploration and its utilization in the social field, Wellendorf (1996) stresses the importance of not falling prey to the illusion that, armed with trusted analytic-therapeutic tools, it is possible to likewise analyze social matters. To be equipped with extensive training alone does not prepare psychoanalysts to work in the social field. "In their work with complex and permanently changing social networks", says Wellendorf, "psychoanalysts are, generally speaking, self-educated" (Wellendorf, 1996, p. 86). This, of course, is also their opportunity. What could actually help psychoanalysts in the social field is their competence in enduring uncertainties and their ability to take on the role of the uninformed, already tested in the analytic space (Becker, 1995a).

This means that the psychoanalytic attitude is not so much a "toolbox", but rather more like the research stance taken by an ethnologist exploring an unknown culture; he is open to experiencing the foreign, ready to expose himself to it and to reflect on it. Of course, it would be unrealistic to expect a psychoanalytic supervisor or an ethnologist to go out into the field without any prior knowledge whatsoever. Both of them have technical and process-linked expertise. Georges Devereux (1967) was the first to describe meticulously the process-driven application in the field of social science. At the intersection of object and process competence, there are those psychoanalytic *concepts* (for example, the assumed dynamic unconscious, basic defense processes such as denial, splitting and projection) to be found which facilitate the analysis of the object as well as the handling of the supervision process.

The supervisor's understanding of the process and his psychoanalytic attitude can also be conceptualized in various different ways. In contrast to a coach, a psychoanalytic supervisor will not aim for direct specific changes, but, depending on the working concept he adheres to, will always first allow a working space to develop, which can be modified according to the assignment, and thus achieve room for the unexpected and the unwanted. He will glean his understanding of the psychoanalytic attitude from classic psychoanalysis – from concepts like abstinence or evenly suspended attention, for example; then he will have to decide how this attitude can best (i.e. appropriately in relation to the assignment) be realized in the context of an organizational consulting supervision. He can, complying with the Klein–Bion school, volunteer to act for the client as a container, thus assisting the process with reverie and ultimately raising the client's reflective faculties and, consequently, his freedom of action. Of course, this concept of action must also be developed in accordance with the work assignment. The concept of supervision as containing has its origin in the psychoanalytic training supervision (Ungar & Busch de Ahumada, 2001; Vollmer & Pires, 2010). In that context, supervision can be understood as a space where those anxieties, evoked by the mobilization of unconscious dynamics in the field between patient and supervisee, as well as between supervisee and supervisor, can be contained. A containing triangle between patient, supervisee and supervisor emerges. In order to adapt this model for organizational supervision, it must be kept in mind that the task itself is different. In psychoanalytic training, the triangle is formed around the collective task to make the unconscious conscious. All three people work together on this task. Outside the context of psychoanalysis and psychoanalytic training, there is no such common task: The supervisor is supposed to (partially) make conscious that which is unconscious, whereas the supervisee works only on a task within his own enterprise (see Figure 3.1).

The difference of task also requires a difference of method: Because there is one agreed task during the supervision of psychoanalytic therapies, a homogeneous field is formed, in which all involved can fantasize themselves in the comparable scene; however, in the social field, tasks and fantasized functions are heterogeneous. A supervisor can fantasize himself into the position of a supervisee, but then in his fantasy, he is no longer the analyst, but a manager. The tasks as a manager differ distinctly from his own tasks as an analyst. Thus, the supervision of psychoanalytic processes (as well as the psychoanalytic training supervision

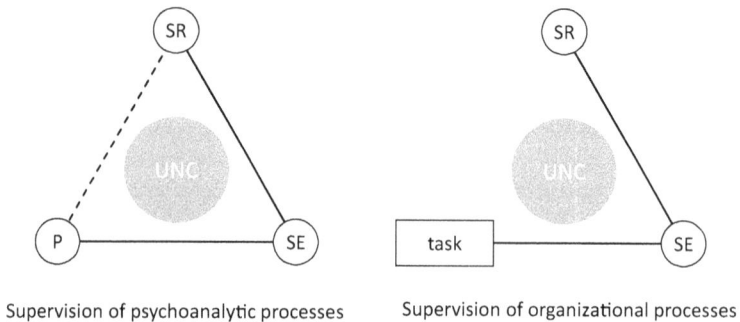

Supervision of psychoanalytic processes   Supervision of organizational processes

Figure 3.1 Supervision of psychoanalytic and organizational processes (P = patient; SR = supervisor; SE = supervisee; UNC = unconscious)

generally; cf. Freitag-Becker, Grohs-Schulz & Neumann-Wirsig, 2016) can be seen as an exceptional case, exhibiting homogeneous tasks of supervisee and supervisor. What is also true for the psychoanalytic field becomes clearer in the social field: The supervisee's work field is not directly accessible to the supervisor. This divide is just as constitutive (analytic work is only possible when this is accepted) as in psychoanalysis itself. Only when it is accepted that there will be no "looking into" the patient, let alone a remediation of his biographical wounds, but rather that we, as analysts, stand always at the frontier to the realm of the other, can we reflect the patient's experience by observing from the outside and forming hypotheses about the "here and now" in which the unconscious re-enacts itself. Fritz Morgenthaler describes this almost ethnographical role of the analyst thus: "I am always the delayed guest of my analysand and sit with him in front of half empty glasses and plates. No one ever sat like this before. It is a new experience for both" (Morgenthaler, 1986, p. 90). Only the role of the "non-knower" (Becker, 1995a) provides the opening up for theatrics (Lorenzer, 1985). This is why in any form of application of psychoanalysis, the probe into the realm of the "other" is crucial. Wellendorf (1996) puts it in a nutshell:

> Psychoanalytic work in the "social field" in its substantial sense is always work on the surroundings, or in other words, a complex border management: at the level of the working relationship between psychoanalyst and client, at the level of the internal and external borders of the client system, at the level of the inner borders of the involved individuals, and at the level of the psychoanalytic institutions.
>
> (Wellendorf, 1996, pp. 86–87)

3.2 Working with the unconscious: Practical basics

3.2.1 Providing an analytical space

Claudia Sies and Marga Löwer-Hirsch (2000) describe an amusing example of a first contact in coaching:

> [The] manager of the sales department of a large enterprise enters the office of a psychodynamic consultant because a coaching process had been "recommended" to him. Due to customer complaints, he was advised by his human resource department to allow himself to be helped by a coaching-specialist, male or female. Thus, this strongly built, exquisitely dressed manager with his shaven head and standing 6 foot 5 inches tall, at entering, knocks the consultant backwards into the room. She thinks: "This kind of behavior will definitely be of use once we get started." The indignant man plants himself in the middle of the room and complains with a loud voice about his HR department's recommendation to look into his way of dealing with clients: "For me there is no choice, I have to sell and sell and sell

again. Sometimes you precisely have to be a dirty swine!" "Yes, indeed," the consultant remarks with a friendly voice, "and you probably think this isn't immediately noticeable!" Thereupon the coachee drops onto a chair and remarks: "And what is going to happen right here now?" The problem of our leading sales expert was soon solved. He had entangled himself too thoroughly in the clichés of male self-assertiveness without considering the effect he was having on others.

(Sies & Löwer-Hirsch, 2000, p. 31)

Urban (2011) has listed numerous questions and aspects influencing the first contact for all those involved. Both parties are under close scrutiny. Urban recommends that the supervisor or coach first "endure the necessary initial confusion" (Möller, 2001, p. 32), and then, after the first interview, reflect on questions like one's own curiosity about the process; the fit of one's own field competence, consulting expertise and crisis know-how; the theoretical orientation with respect to the client's targets; whether or not his targets are realistic; and whether change is actually desired. These recommendations are definitely helpful, especially since, in comparison to therapy, in coaching and supervision settings, business relations take priority: A therapist "is looked for", a supervisor or coach "is taken". First contacts with coaches and supervisors, who have to hold their ground in a competitive market, occur in the context of acquisition; first contacts with a psychoanalyst made by patients with a desire for healing occur in the context of need. When psychoanalysts are requested as supervisors in a business situation, both contexts are often relevant. Normally psychoanalysts are working to capacity and have long waiting lists – but there are psychoanalysts who are very eager to carry out supervisions in an organizational context, particularly if they are better paid than for therapeutic interventions. On the other hand, there are renowned organizational supervisors and coaches who can choose their clients and have leeway in terms of what they can charge.

On the unconscious relationship level, it is not a question of real market position but of felt difference. Idealization, projection and transference are effective from the beginning and it is the task of the coach or supervisor to give them sufficient space. Even clients who are used to being in a position of power need to have a chance to idealize the analyst and to perceive him in transference as the superior father (or, projectively, as a fortune teller or similar); on the other hand, the supervisor has to be able to work with the fact that clients often occupy superior positions in society, which may trigger envious feelings or a corresponding transference attribution in the supervisor. The specificity of the analytic space, which is also established in supervisorial work, means that all these phenomena are admitted, appreciated and explained, and thus are interpreted as indicators of an (as yet) unconscious dynamic.

Löwer-Hirsch and West-Leuer (2017) describe the consulting space as a *transitional space* in the sense of Winnicott. In this intermediate space, the unconscious level of an enterprise is free to enact itself. Against the backdrop of an interactional psychoanalytic approach, Löwer-Hirsch and West-Leuer utilize this opportunity for a re-enactment to work together with the client on the unconscious of the enterprise. This occasionally necessitates addressing very personal issues. This kind of work is always correlated to the unconscious dynamic of the organization and has to be clearly set apart from psychologizing group coachings, which have become established for the high-potential executives of international businesses. The self-disclosures expected in this frame are seen as dysfunctional by the authors; according to their observations, these are also regularly undermined. Speaking about personal feelings is not an end in itself; it only makes sense to bring these feelings up if they can be used for working interpretatively; in other words, if emotional self-perception helps to access the unconscious aspect of the working relationship and brings about its alteration.

3.2.2 Interpretation

Interpretation is the crucial and distinctive type of intervention in psychoanalysis. Based on the sequence of the analysand's associations, his manifested behavior (acting out, re-enactment) and the reaction which both evoke in the analyst, the goal of interpretation is to make unconscious contents conscious. According to the classical perception of psychoanalysis, the unconscious, to which the interpretation refers, is that which defense mechanisms prevent from becoming conscious. According to newer conceptualizations of structural disorders, the unconscious is often seen as the not yet symbolized, as there are, for example, benevolent manifestations as well as the pursuing "other" and these remain unconnected. In this context, it would be deemed as unconscious (and could be addressed here in the sense of a split), that both of these manifestations belong to one and the same relational figure which is ambivalently experienced. In psychoanalysis, interpretations always require preparation; until an interpretation can be hypothesized, a longer process of confrontation and clarification, or of developing an interactive scene, is often needed. In scholarly literature on treatment techniques, interpretations are actually distinguished according to their focus; for example, resistance interpretation, genetic transference interpretation, and transference interpretation in the "here and now".

Even though interpretation is considered to be the pivotal psychoanalytic intervention, it is rarely or never referred to in the literature on psychodynamic supervision. This may be because the term refers mainly to the psychoanalytic situation. Psychoanalysts reflect on their encounter with the patient and combine these introspections with the available information on this person's background and symptoms. This procedure is clearly explained for clinical interpretation in terms of the triangle of insight (cf. Menninger & Holzman, 1973): Conjectures about a symptom deduced from the biography are validated by the analyst's self-perception in the field of the transference. The completion of the triangle (symptom – geneses – transference) yields the foundation of a psychoanalytic interpretation.

In a supervisory space, however, this triangle is not easily established; supervisors have good reasons to be particularly careful in their interpretative work. In coaching, this triangle could principally be established out of the constellation of coach and coachee; however, its scope and depth would be limited. But alongside interpretation, coach and coachee frequently also agree on other means, such as clarification or confrontation (Migge, 2005, p. 315). In his paper about psychoanalytic control-supervision, West-Leuer (2000, p. 20) terms interpretation as a key element. Its utilization, however, differs from the therapeutic setting: Interpretations in (control-)supervision are (1) focused on secondary processual thinking; (2) more explicit and thus more confrontational, as there is no necessity to take into account psychological instability; (3) inter-subjective and helpful: "Control-supervisors are confronted directly with their own defense mechanisms and unconscious conflicts. They may question, criti-cize, accept or reject interpretations, without it being interpreted as a resistance phenomenon" (West-Leuer, 2000, p. 20). Accordingly, interpretations in super-vision are characterized by authentic answers, clarification of affects and how to deal with them as well as with reality, as well as by functions of the auxiliary ego and super-ego. Busse (2010) likewise emphasizes the specific demands con-cerning timing and relationship clarification in the context of attempted inter-pretations in the supervisorial space: He notices that

> consultants ask their clients for permission to be critical and at the same time are attentive toward them. The fact that this permission or reassurance is even needed at all indicates a communicative catch 22 situation, as authenticity as well as protection against exposure are norms of correct and appropriate communication. Respect and caution are advisable also, because it is all about the maieutic recovery and freeing of the subjective world by the advice seeker himself (cf. Schmidt-Lellek, 2007 [2001], p. 195). So this is less about "cri-tique" of what the advice seeker says or does not say, and more about a "substitute interpretation" (Oevermann, 1996) to address the unsaid and the self hidden within the dialogical attempt and make it discussable, actually to raise it to consciousness in the first place and thus into the discourse.
>
> (Busse, 2010, p. 88)

Becker (2003 [1998]) sets psychoanalytical interpretation apart from super-visorial interpretation by deriving it less from work practice, but more from the subject itself. He differentiates between the "clinical-familialistic" and the "organizational perspective of interpretation".

> In the context of organization, the detection of unconscious meaning, i.e. the interpretative work – which is always at the center of what the psy-choanalyst does – has a different point of reference than in the clinical situation. Psychoanalytic interpretation, which in its essence aims for a transference relationship, always has a reference point outside the current relationship situation, which is supposed to be interpreted, an Archimedean point so to speak. In a clinical situation, this would usually be some kind of theory from developmental psychology, a meta-psychology etc. Inter-pretations have such a backdrop; they refer to, even if this reference

remains implicit. Thus, for the psychoanalytical work in organizations, it has to apply, that a theory of normal and dysfunctional human organizations must provide the interpretational background or the point of reference.

(Becker, 2003 [1998], p. 54)

Becker sees the function of psychoanalysts in organizations as follows: (1) they examine the unconscious working relationships within the context of the particular organization by (2) utilizing their clinical experience of detecting and diagnosing disturbances in a differentiated and qualified manner and (3) they examine these working relationships against the backdrop of the organization (Becker, 2003 [1998], p. 59). He warns against disregarding this reference to the organizational context in the interpretative work, "because, in my experience if a clinical-familialistic perspective is favored over the organizational one, the disturbance continues into the supervision. Even 'correct' interpretations have no potency of change, if they are applied in the wrong context" (Becker, 2003 [1998], p. 59).

In principle, it is more productive to think about the difference between the interpretation in therapy and supervision based on the assignment, instead of simply recommending caution or restraint at the level of behavior. Of course, it is debatable whether the distinction "familialistic" versus "organizational" is to the point. The unconscious matrix of the enterprise and the inner world of the subject are interlocked, and in both, patterns of earlier interactional experience are sedimented (at least as long as enterprises are still made up of human beings). Thus, the distinction shouldn't be made by substituting the personal unconscious with an institutional one, but should be deduced from the assignment. A patient enters into psychotherapy with the assignment to change those modes of experiencing and behaving which he experiences as pathological. Interpretations within the framework of the interpretational triangle will always implicitly be based on the assignment. The (implicit) interpretation quoted above (see Chapter 3.2.1) in the example from Sies and Löwer-Hirsch (2000) was deduced – in accordance with the triangle of insight – from the symptom (lacking sales success), with reference to genesis/personality ("have to be a dirty swine") and the countertransference (feeling pressed), which reads: "and you probably think this isn't noticeable immediately!" This sentence, uttered in the consulting context, implies that it is the found relation between an egosyntonic personality trait, business-related problems and the current interaction in regard to the assignment which should be investigated. The sentence could be continued as follows: "Perhaps this is one of several reasons why you keep receiving negative feedback from clients even though you put in a lot of effort." Had the scene unfolded at the beginning of a therapeutic first interview, it would imply that the relation conveys something about the client's personality, and the sentence could be continued: "Perhaps this helps us to understand why you feel so bad. Maybe you do not just professionally go against the grain, even though you try hard." The text interpretation can, as in this case, actually even be identical; its meaning, however, differs according to the framework agreement. In the supervisorial space, it is agreed that the insights achieved should be made professionally usable; in the therapeutic space, they should be made usable in a personal or health-related way. To clarify this, the same scene could be imagined as part of a private conversation and then the sentence "and you probably think this is not noticeable straight away!" would have a hint of friendly mockery, it would probably trigger laughter, but it wouldn't set in motion any deepening work process.

3.2.3 Relationship

The therapeutic relationship is the most effective factor for therapeutic success, no matter which therapeutic procedure is applied (Lambert & Barley, 2002). The same is true for the supervisorial field, in which the relationship, next to the interpretation based on insight, is the second most effective factor; and also for coaching, in which a positive relationship experience can become a crucial element (Migge, 2005, p. 18). For executives especially, a confidence-based relationship with an independent consultant can be a most valuable space, as they receive mainly flattering feedback in their vocational environment and have to be extremely careful about showing indecision or weakness, due to the high, often distorted, expectations which are projected onto them because of their position. In this very specific relationship, the client has to have the opportunity to allow emotions and to develop transference (Sell, Möller & Benecke, 2018). It is the supervisor's task to notice the phenomena and to interpret them with regard to the work assignment. Other than in a therapy, the work assignment is not to influence a symptom or the personality structure of the client, but to clarify the dysfunctional aspects of his task, to afford him an extended perception of his vocational field and, in consequence, further degrees of freedom for his decisions.

The same is true for the countertransferences that occur in supervision and coaching just as in therapy: They too are internally interpreted by the supervisor (usually without an explicit announcement) and referred to the primary task of the supervision. Some of the most common countertransference reactions are feelings of inferiority or superiority. The former can perhaps take the shape of envy, if the client earns much more than the supervisor/coach and can afford a much higher standard of living. On the other hand, supervisors can easily slip into grandiose feelings of superiority and surmise that they are more capable of assessing the client's decisions than he is himself. Both of these countertransferences have to be highlighted and referred to the supervisorial assignment. The envious reaction, for example, has its origins in an early level of relatedness, in which the magical fulfillment of relatively unstructured needs by an envied, almighty object is yearned for. Envious reactions with a supervisor could indicate the existence of such magical expectation within the supervisorial field, either within the client himself or when – and this happens often with entrepreneurs and charismatic leaders – such expectations are being directed at the client or fostered by him. The supervisor will have to note such unconscious figurations; as experience shows, such envious feelings dissolve as soon as the supervision can return to its work assignment. The other countertransference reaction, in which the supervisor possibly fantasizes himself to be the better executive, could represent a concordant identification with a grandiose personality trait of the client, or it could be the reaction to an unconscious appeal for advice and help from the client. With high-ranking executives, who daily have to make important decisions, this kind of transference is actually quite common. Within the protected space of the supervision, they can release rejected traits of insecurity and neediness. However, both countertransference reactions may also be the expression of unconscious business dynamics. The "magical" expectation, which becomes perceptible as envy, could be part of an institutional myth, which becomes solidified in the leadership role and therefore is noticeable in the executive supervision. Such a myth could be characterized as Bion's "basic assumption", proposing that the task of the institution could be accomplished by a charismatic leader or a Messiah. Gaining awareness of this myth could help the leader – and through him – the organization to overcome this "basic assumption" state and to once more actively fulfill the primary task. The second countertransference mentioned – the fantasy of knowing better – can likewise be reflecting an institutional dynamic. Whether it projects a sublime matching (concordant) or a helper role (complementary), both could be patterns coming from the unconscious of the enterprise (from those blindly reproduced basic assumptions within the interactive forms of the institution) and carried by the leader into the supervisorial space. In this case, the supervisor's feeling of superiority would be a symptom and could be perceived, analyzed and processed together with the client. The following interpretation could be an opening for such a processing:

> Within myself, I feel the impulse to give you advice as to how you would best decide in this situation. This, however, is not part of my work assignment. I ask myself, if this is perhaps something you also sense, in the form of an invitation to assume the role of the magician.

Such could be the wording building on the analytical hypothesis, whereby the countertransference is of the grand concordant type. If, after further data collection, the supervisor comes to the conclusion that his helper impulse is based on a complementary role-taking, corresponding to a rejected neediness of the client (and of the enterprise), then the wording could be: "I wonder if maybe a sort of decisional dilemma remains, which obviously cannot be resolved with the available methods and experience, and which now motivates me, all of a sudden, to try to advise you." Within the literature on psychodynamic coaching, the opinion is sometimes held that analytical supervisors in this situation should indeed follow their intuition and give vocational advice. Löwer-Hirsch and West-Leuer (2017), for example, argue for an active consulting style. In the form of a "selective authenticity", the consultant could very well point out straightforward alternatives for action, as, for example, in the case of a female supervisee displaying a very harsh style of leadership in dealing with an employee whom she had criticized severely. The female supervisor says to her:

> I am sorry, but in your treatment of the employee XY, I am not quite with you. Your severe criticism will have offended him. And this derogates his

work and negates your leadership style. I know you are pressed for time and maybe his way of working is a bit pedestrian; but maybe you have failed to notice, that with his thoroughness he actually only wanted to please you. This is something I would praise him for.

(Löwer-Hirsch & West-Leuer, 2017, Kindle pos. 343–352)

The authors justify their intervention as follows:

In this to-and-fro-identification (at times with the client and then again with her employee) the consultants assume the role of an auxiliary ego, to which the client can adapt herself. Mainly she embarks on confrontations, because in her private life she experiences herself as being estranged and isolated from her family. She realizes, albeit grudgingly, that she needs help.

(Löwer-Hirsch & West-Leuer, 2017, Kindle pos. 352–354)

The consultants' success justifies their intervention:

The coaching ended with her promotion to the position of a senior government official, a position corresponding with her function. She was very pleased. Beyond that, she decided to go into psychotherapy, in order to get a handle on her private situation.

(Löwer-Hirsch & West-Leuer, 2017, Kindle pos. 355–356)

From our point of view, this case example mirrors an unresolved transference, which is being exteriorized to another setting by referring the client to psychotherapy. It is likely that a comparable dynamic will unfold there and that the therapist, just like the coaches, will also blunder into the role of an advisor; however, the dynamic of transference and countertransference will be interpretable and thus can be resolved. However, this assessment should not be understood as being too critical. In supervision and coaching, just as in therapy and coaching, it is common for analysts to act out the roles they have taken, failing to display the required abstinence and instead giving a judgmental reaction. In some circumstances, this can actually benefit the process; the supervisee (or analysand) then feels that his supervisor (or analyst) is not a robot following rules, but that he or she allows him/herself to be moved and to become involved. Nevertheless, such situations must be reflected on and analyzed in retrospect; otherwise the supervision loses its analytical potency. In particular, sequences manifesting mutual role-playing can later clearly be recognized as "scenes" and, as such, be worked through.

3.3 In transition between psychoanalysis, psychodynamic counseling and classical coaching

Even the experienced business counselor or classical coach may experience his first steps into psychodynamic counseling as a fundamental vocational change, which triggers anxiety and insecurity, comparable to starting a career. Even if, by means of modular training, he has already mastered some psychodynamic elements, he will have some difficulty in assuming the calm attitude of an experienced analyst who thinks it sufficient to open up an analytic space. This insecurity will be transferred to those clients who may be doubtful as to what they will receive for their money from every hour of counseling. The threatening dilemma is: "without experience, no clients; and without clients, no experience". However, we think it is a mistake that only a training which equals the training of an analyst qualifies one for psychodynamic counseling.

It will be easier for a counselor or a client to start psychodynamic work if, to begin with, they use manuals, instruments and efficiency-optimized methods that have their origin in the transition between psychoanalytical thinking, quantitative-scientific psychology and the result-orientated striving of business. Such methods provide a training on, at least, the setting and the thinking in psychoanalytic categories; and sticking to a single method leads counselor and client quickly to the emotional experience of success. In the beginning, it might seem tempting to view this transitional stage as an end result. However, an extensive training in psychodynamic counseling work under the supervision of an experienced psychoanalyst, as well as increased experience, helps the counselor to forego his clinging to instruments and to place more trust in the analytic process. The client, so to speak, is weaned more and more from "doing" and finds out how much more he receives, if the counselor gives him less.

For the analyst who wishes to extend his range by psychodynamic counseling work, the approach of an efficiency-driven method of optimization may seem completely absurd. Through his work with his patients, he masters the methods of psychoanalysis reliably and completely. Why should he fall back on modified procedures, which are not even "real" psychoanalysis? There is nothing to be said against an analyst who mainly treats patients, and is happy if an occasional, self-reflective, open and unbiased executive seeks him out. If, however, the analyst wishes to set up a second string to his bow, offering psychodynamic counseling alongside his psychoanalytic work, he will have to brave the tempest of business life, come up with a self-promoting website, and look for clients in order to bring himself into play. In business, coaches, supervisors and counselors putting themselves forward for selection has been termed "pitching". As if auditioning for a theater part, the analyst has to present himself and allow himself to be compared to the counselor who preceded him for interview and the one following him. And he will have to answer questions such as: "Why are you the right counselor to receive our budget?" "What is your process?" and "How will our executives benefit from your work?" Quite a few analysts will then wish they had helpful instruments and manuals in their presentation case. Another analyst might demur that he does not even want such clients. But then, of course, he will only rarely have business clients. The market in which analysts and open and unbiased executives looking for self-experience meet is, at best, a niche, especially since psychoanalysis is – with the exception of some countries – not established as a method in business and it thus lacks established trust.

A market for psychodynamic counseling – which trains many counselors who then face potential clients – will not manage without compromises, allowing the partly known to happen next to the new, to establish commitments and to develop gradually from doing to being. On the other hand, of course, it can be held that such a market would not even be desirable.

For those readers who wish to be part of such a transition, we want to show what could actually happen in such a "walk-through room", using the example of free association, the main method of psychoanalysis.

3.3.1 The practice of free association in a non-clinical context

Free association is a well-established technique to disclose unconscious mental representations of objects and their relationships (Freud, 1923a, p. 237; Kubie, 1952; Macmillan, 2001). If, however, the plan is to apply free association in social structures, such as companies or industries, it is most unlikely that enough individuals will be found who are prepared to lie down on a couch and be analyzed, coming to sessions for several years. Under such circumstances, it can be helpful to have at one's command associational techniques, which are more efficient and will work more quickly to obtain insights in this non-clinical field of operation.

If we picture the mental representation of a subject as an individual map of objects, then free association is a method whereby we start at an initial object on this map and explore the environment of this starting point to find out which other objects are connected to the initial object. The association can provide conscious parts of this map. From the therapeutic point of view, it might become necessary for the patient to discover the map for himself (Bohart, 2000). These discoveries, too, have to be explored and interpreted by the patient (Ryan & Deci, 2008). This exploration happens freely, can last for several years and display unexpected twists during this process toward a healthier development. In social and business contexts, therapy and healing are not in the foreground. Above all, inexperienced counselors and clients need efficient methods to make the map, with those associative sub-areas which are relevant for their subject area visible. To satisfy the demand for efficiency, notably when working with businesses, associations clearly have to be more guided and restricted to fewer dimensions (Arbuthnott, Arbuthnott & Rossiter, 2001; Curtis, 2012; Long, 2013).

Even if free association can only be used in a restricted way in a social context, it is nevertheless worthwhile to have a look at this method's mechanisms of action. These mechanisms of action may possibly be achieved with more efficient association methods. Some first thoughts along this line can be found in early psychoanalytic literature, although the targeted direction is a different one. In his *Interpretation of Dreams*, Freud turned to the organization of thoughts in dreams. Dreams allow access to unconscious, meaningful relationships. The main aspect of this approach does not seem to be the state of sleep, but the absence of control over thoughts (Freud, 1900, pp. 592–593). After years of getting accustomed to the method of free association, the client's thoughts flow uncontrolled and thus generate unconscious material. A more efficient association method must accordingly be capable of likewise facilitating a deactivation of control, in order to bring unconscious chains of thought to light.

3.3.2 Directed association with guided imagery

Directed association as applied in katathym-imaginative psychotherapy (KIP; Leuner, 1955) is much more restricted than free association (Suler, 1989). The exchange of the instruction: "Express whatever comes to mind" for the task: "Imagine your problem as a landscape, a fairy tale being or an animal" gives a clear direction to the association. Ideally, this technique fades out all thoughts about past and future and explores the preset topic in the here and now.

Katathym-imaginative psychotherapy is the only clinically established method of directed association. It is already much more efficient than free association. Several studies have shown that KIP can significantly diminish complaints within 15 to 20 therapy sessions (Wächter & Pudel, 1980; Jung & Kulessa, 1980). The first author has treated several patients with different neurotic disorders using ultra-short-term therapies of only six sessions in the Mind Institute SE and achieved good results (Kretschmar & Tzschaschel, 2017, pp. 66–73). If a therapy can succeed with six to 20 sessions, it can be assumed that a mere analysis or diagnosis without intervention needs even less time. Based on Kretschmar's experience, after a short introduction, individuals in enterprises allow themselves to be guided into imagery, producing unconscious material even within the first hour.

3.3.3 Word association test according to C. G. Jung

A particularly efficient method of association is the word association test of C. G. Jung (Jung, 1910). In Jung's approach, the interview partner, once he hears a word the therapist says, has to call out fitting words as quickly as possible. Thus, Jung limited the association considerably. Particularly important for him was the type of response. If the patient hesitated or if his heartbeat increased, Jung took it as a sign that the word had an emotional significance. The resulting clinical diagnosis was the important part. The way in which the response was uttered was also, for Jung, indicative of possible inner conflicts within the patient.

The method seems promising for non-clinical use; it has already been utilized in criminal psychology to convict delinquents. However, the need for comprehensive training and the impracticability of heart rate measurement are not ideal preconditions for vocational deployment.

3.3.4 Limitations of clinical association methods

Jung's word association test, and even more so the directed and free association, require the user to have comprehensive training along with appropriate experience as a psychoanalyst. However, even coaches and supervisors who are not psychoanalysts need to cope with using methods of association in psychodynamic counseling work; for example, intern coaches in the organizational departments of enterprises. Thus, simpler methods are required, which could possibly even be automated by software.

Another problem of the methods discussed above is that, given the size of social systems, the amount and diversity of information gained from the individual interview partners by means of association grow to an unmanageable extent. The methods presented so far start out with a small objective (a request to associate, a symbol or a word) and end up with an unstructured multitude of results, which can neither be evaluated in studies nor manualized. To get a handle on this complexity, a much more optimized association technique is needed, which leads from fewer objectives to even fewer (and at the same time, standardized) results, which would allow their being condensed for the use of vocational clients and processed for research purposes.

3.3.5 Color-association

The method of color-association developed by the first author (Kretschmar) arises from such reflections. If we reduce associations to one single dimension – color, for example – then the results will be highly standardized and can even be merged at the level of the social system and possibly be processed in an automated way (Bachrach, Galatzer-Levy, Skolnikoff & Waldron, 1991; Cabaniss, 2008). The results received via associations of different interview partners can be compared to enable insights into the organizational thinking of sub-systems, such as enterprises or departments. It becomes clear that the usage of technical terminology and the association of these terms with colors represent a very pragmatic restriction of association, which makes it suitable for use in business (Kretschmar & Meinel, 2015).

Clients are asked to name, as quickly as possible and without thinking, a color for each of a number of words. The applied words are, for example: defeat, work council, energy, suppliers, vacation, victory, products, competitor, market, innovation, exhaustion, defense, sport, job, offense, customers, investor, employees, service, self-fulfillment. So far, studies show an associative coherence between those words to which the client affixes the same color. The coherences between words within one color group are clearly stronger and more meaningful than the coherence of words in different color groups (Kretschmar & Meinel, 2015).

The results of the described color-associations are charted (see Figure 3.2) and presented to the client in the next session to find out whether the chart accurately reflects the client's personal situation.

Figure 3.2 depicts the chart of the CEO of a very successful marketing agency. The quotations in this paragraph have been taken from the second session with this client. He sees it as his "major task" to "provide service for the market". This is where he finds his personal fulfillment. He is particularly proud of the fact that there is no work council in his enterprise – a rare occurrence in enterprises of this size. He deems it his "decisive competitive advantage, that employees develop innovations with a sportsmanlike ambition". The words defeat and

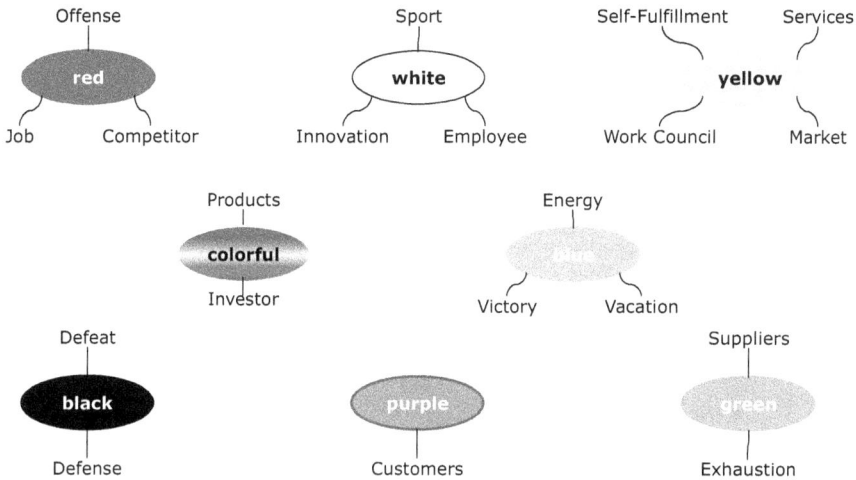

Figure 3.2 CEO of a successful marketing agency

defense were not linked with other operational terms. "The enterprise gets more requests than we can meet." Suppliers are a grueling issue because "the shopping market is difficult. It is difficult to find suppliers who render services in the demanded quality and time". The entrepreneur draws his energy from participations in tenders, which he wins against other marketing agencies, and from his vacations. The enterprise is rich enough to manage without external investors; it does not produce physical products. This is why these two terms are placed apart from the other operational words/terms.

If the method is used with several participants in a group, then it is possible to establish a context of meaning for the whole group (Kretschmar & Meinel, 2015) by applying the algorithm of seriation and cluster analysis of Hahsler, Hornik and Buchta (2008).

Without doubt, this method is far removed from psychoanalysis. Nevertheless, it does utilize an associative method, enabling it to make unconscious coherences conscious. At the same time, it represents a tool that makes it easy, even for novices, to generate working material with the client even in the first sessions. Thus, the method is positioned in the transition between psychoanalytic thinking, quantitative-scientific psychology and the result-orientated striving of business.

3.4 Discussion: Implicit estimated values and targets in coaching and organizational supervision

The different backgrounds of psychoanalytic supervision and coaching lead to different targets and implicit value propositions. Their targets could even be called contrary: While Freud saw psychoanalysis as basic research, which more or less incidentally also has healing effects, coaching entered the stage not in support of a theory, but for deliberate change (see Chapter 1.1). Different value propositions result from these different targets.

Freud had always viewed his psychoanalysis more as a scientific assignment than a therapeutic one (Freud, 1910, p. 140; 1923a, p. 234). The result of this progressive goal setting is that psychoanalysis has always been considered not just as a therapeutic practice, but also equally as psychological theory as well as a critical cultural theory (Hamburger, 2013). In the process, civilization does not emerge as the winner in every respect; psychoanalytic social criticism reproaches civilization for the price it makes us pay in the form of psychic deformation. The resulting implicit value proposal is the ideal of an autonomous and informed subject, capable of recognizing its own unconscious adjustment mechanisms and overcoming them. The consequence of these value and target propositions in respect of treatment techniques is "technical neutrality": The analyst merely has the task of helping the patient become conscious of his own unconscious motives and thereby attaining the opportunity to decide more freely. This psychoanalytic attitude (see Chapter 4.9.1), characterized by abstinence, also shapes the approach of psychodynamic supervision. Even though the task here is more clearly outlined – the supervisee expects a task-based clarification of his objectives, and a consequent improvement in terms of vocational deficits and conflicts – the clarification is supposed to happen *more psychoanalytico* and this means via the aforesaid non-suggestive, open and unbiased attitude.

Things are different in classical coaching. Here the coach is actually even challenged by the client to achieve a certain goal and to change the client in a certain desired way, with this goal in view. Coaching does not request extensive abstinence, as in psychotherapy, and as the process generally takes place much more swiftly, usually tangible targets will be defined and much shorter time frames affixed.

In psychodynamic coaching, far more psychoanalytic elements are adopted than in classical coaching. Depending on the coach's qualification level, the number of psychoanalytical elements varies considerably. The approbated psychoanalyst or depth psychologist would probably rather frame his coaching in the style of his training analysis, using psychoanalytical elements almost exclusively; while the organizational counselor or coach with a different background, who trained as a "psychoanalytically informed" coach, might utilize only a few elements. However, if the coach wants to enable the coachee to become conscious of unconscious coherences, he will give him more leeway and take a less cognitive approach than is common in classical coaching. Accordingly, a hard target agreement, as is often demanded in classical coaching, is inconceivable in psychodynamic coaching. Instead, the goal setting of the coachee is understood as the occasion for the coaching, which, via reflection and self-awareness, opens up the chance to more or less attain the target in passing.

Diverging intervention strategies ensue, also due to differing goal settings and implicit value assumptions. This is reflected in the understanding of analytic space and relationship, but also in the specific forms of intervention, such as interpretation or free association. According to the understanding of psycho-analytic executive supervision, which sees itself as applied psychoanalysis, absti-nence and neutrality are essential to reveal, within the transference field of the analytic relationship, those unconscious structures hiding in the interactive field between client and organization that is explored. This requires the supervisor to take a completely open attitude, not allowing the client to pressurize him into generating fast changes (which easily happens in a business context). The analytic attitude requires the supervisor to reflect upon such pressure. A coach might argue against this idea, saying that in business dealings, it is usually impossible to com-municate unreasonable deceleration. So the approach has to be modified in such a way that at least some focusing and efficiency are noticeable for the coachee.

On the other hand, psychodynamic coaching proceeds from a specific assignment for personal change, and accepts this. This type of coaching is psy-chodynamic in so far as it utilizes elements of psychoanalytic therapy and supervision such as transference, countertransference, interpretation and free association to fulfill its assignment. From the psychoanalytic viewpoint, the objection can be made that such an eclectic adoption of psychoanalytic elements changes them in a fashion, as some psychodynamic therapy methods also do.

This can be shown using the example of free association, which in a psycho-analytic setting should not be directed by the analyst, nor should it be suggested as a method (as was still done by C. G. Jung). Instead, an analyst considers the ana-lysand's speech as "free association", in so far as he sees exact wording, metaphors used, inconsistencies as well as patterns of rhythm, facial expression and gesticu-lation as relevant. He assumes that behind the consciously intended utterance, there is a hidden unconscious dynamic which finds expression in performance. This is why he concentrates less on what the analysand wants to say, but more on that which the analysand simultaneously reads "between the lines". This does not mean a conscious-capable sub-text, as is manifested – next to "factual informa-tion" – in the form of "self-revelation", "relationship" pointers and "appeal" in the four-sided model of Schulz von Thun (1981), but something unconscious, which makes its appearance particularly through inconsistencies and breaks (Warsitz & Küchenhoff, 2015). In order for the analyst to be able to accept these incon-sistencies and breaks, his listening cannot be selective and task-orientated, but rather must fall back on his "evenly suspended attention". In this way, through his own free associations too, he enables this fended-off level of meaning to emerge. This basic attitude can also be deployed in the supervisorial space. With enough experience and without the unfolding of a long psychoanalytical process, space can be cleared for associations even within the terms of a supervisorial assignment.

4   Indispensable background knowledge

In the previous chapters, we have repeatedly mentioned certain terms and concepts that form the backdrop for psychodynamic coaching and for psychoanalytic supervision. Now we will explain them in detail. This also provides an opportunity to outline some of the conceptual differences between the presented procedures.

4.1 The unconscious in psychoanalysis

The most important aspect of psychodynamic work is the concept of an unconscious mind. As early as 1892, Freud wrote:

> in accordance with the tendency to a dissociation of consciousness in hysteria, the distressing antithetic idea, which seems to be inhibited, is removed from association with the intention and continues to exist as a disconnected idea, often unconsciously to the patient himself.
>
> (Freud, 1892–1893, p. 122)

This detaching and making unconscious entails further repression:

> When this process occurs for the first time there comes into being a nucleus and center of crystallization for the formation of a psychical group divorced from the ego – a group around which everything which would imply an acceptance of the incompatible idea subsequently collects.
>
> (Freud, 1893b, p. 123)

Thus, the unconscious is the source of repressed content, which continues, influences thinking and acting and eludes the conscious mind. Psychoanalysis serves to make conscious what has previously been unconscious (Freud, 1896, p. 163). Such a bringing to consciousness as a principal procedure serves, not only in psychotherapy but also in coaching and supervision, to obtain new insights about one's own thinking and acting.

It would go beyond the scope of this book to attempt to even outline psychoanalysis. Rather, in this chapter, we will present a selection of techniques and principles developed by Freud and his successors, which could be useful in

DOI: 10.4324/9781003169673-4

coaching and supervision. Making conscious the previously unconscious, associative techniques, and working with transference have all proved useful. For work on the personality, an understanding of conflict and its compensation is also helpful.

From object relations psychology, which is of such importance for the economic system, working with countertransference, the understanding of inner objects and relations, as well as theory about the re-enactment of the family's origin into the present are all valuable. And last, but not least, we will also turn our attention to aspects that seem important for the intervention training of supervisors and coaches. These are the supervisor's or coach's blind spots, their ability to offer a relationship and their capability for containing.

4.1.1 The unconscious as an apparatus of the mind

The term "unconscious" was not discovered by Freud; by the turn of the 19th century, he had come upon it in numerous discourses. Philosophers – for example, Schopenhauer (cf. Buchholz & Gödde, 2005; Gödde, 1999) – as well as some of the poets of German Romanticism had tried to tour this "inner Africa", an expression coined by Jean Paul, who was born nearly a century before Freud. They were opposed by an emerging positivism and its adherents, who tried to explain all mental phenomena empirically. In this climate, Sigmund Freud re-phrased the unconscious (he did not "discover" it) as a term initially understood scientifically. One approach he witnessed lay in contemporary French psychiatry; namely, in the writings of Charcot, Bernheim and Janet. These authors had disagreed with the prevailing theory that all mental illnesses were degenerate and had presented their own contradictory approach. They had developed theories of a dissociated unconscious ("double conscience") and attempted to verify them empirically with therapeutic approaches based on hypnosis (Ellenberger, 1970). Freud first wanted to construct a physiological model of the unconscious – a "psychic apparatus" (Freud, 1950 [1895]). However, the mere neuronal model led him to a surprisingly interactive twist. He introduced "the helpful person" (Freud, 1950 [1895], p. 365), the mother who misunderstands the baby's crying, an outlet of strong emotion, as desire, as wish. What she is exactly overhearing is a call from a psychic apparatus, but she perceives instead a crying baby as she turns to it, consoles and feeds it. In this way, the attention to social relatedness stands at the very beginning of psychic development (cf. Hamburger, 1987, Chapter 3.2.1; 2013, 2016). However, the early theory of psychoanalysis did not implement this insight. For a long time, its protagonists searched solely for the mechanics of the libido and supposed that the unconscious was divested of conscious cognition by a censoring authority (thought to be neurophysiological).

4.1.2 The unconscious as homunculus

The early instinctual theory transitioned into the ego-psychological phase. The clinical experience, particularly the experience of the therapeutic relationship, which now far exceeded Freud's auto-analysis, required a more flexible theory. In

Freud's major meta-psychological revision, his "structural model" (1923b), the mind is no longer seen as a response apparatus, but as a form of discourse between authorities ("ego", "id" and "super-ego"). The structural model denotes Freud's journey from a response apparatus to the subject. The "id", the instinctual core, is an amoral entity, which does not know an external world, nor any object of pleasure, nor even space and time. It draws energy from instinctual impulses, which are not yet formed by experiences of gratification or refusal, and "wishful impulses which have never passed beyond the id, but impressions, too, which have been sunk into the id by repression" (Freud, 1933, p. 73). It is "the dark, inaccessible part of our personality" (Freud, 1933, p. 72). In the course of life's experiences, the "id" covers itself with an "outer layer", which protects it against the external world by learning to predict events and to direct behavior. This outer layer is the "ego", where consciousness, thinking, perception and the explicit memory are located. The "super-ego" is an authority which contains all collected moral values; it is partly unconscious and draws its energy from the "id", which is the reason why the imperatives of the super-ego are not always reasonably balanced. The "ego" deploys a variety of conscious, but mainly unconscious, defense mechanisms to direct the "id" (see Chapter 4.3). Of course, the "ego's" strategy is not always successful, and occasionally the "ego" is the one which is being directed. A tongue-in-cheek Freud comments:

> Often a rider, if he is not to be parted from his horse, is obliged to guide it where it wants to go; so in the same way the ego is in the habit of transforming the id's will into action as if it were its own.
>
> (Freud, 1923b, p. 24)

4.1.3 *The unconscious as relation and structure*

The third theoretical shift in psychoanalysis is the orientation toward object relations theory. It introduces a principally new concept of child development (see Chapter 4.5) and leads on to substantial consequences in terms of treatment technique. Freud himself had already used transferences as auxiliaries of analysis, as

> new editions or facsimiles of the impulses and phantasies which are aroused and made conscious during the progress of the analysis; but they have this peculiarity, which is characteristic for their species, that they replace some earlier person by the person of the physician.
>
> (Freud, 1905, p. 115)

Even if this was a key approach for the psychoanalytic method, there was still a long way to go to get to the shaping of modern treatment techniques. The fact that the analyst also experiences transferences and that both patient's and analyst's transferences have an interpretable relationship to each other was adopted much later. Even though it was clear as early as 1910 that analysts, too, react with feelings (termed countertransference), this fact was at first kept secret.

After a long debate, finally, in the 1950s, countertransference was acknowledged to be just as legitimate, significant and valuable as transference. This development triggered a psychoanalytic relationship theory, which today has become a main feature of an advanced psychoanalysis, and in which the mainly interaction-based developmental theory of psychoanalysis finds its equivalent (cf. Hamburger, 2016b).

In this way, relationship was established as a chief focus of psychoanalytic treatment technique. At the same time, the notion gained acceptance that the unconscious is not only a combination of repressed wishes, unconscious commands and regulation processes, but it is also to a great extent made up of a long-term memory, into which relational experiences are encoded, as well as their specific organization. Freud's instinctual representatives now become inner objects or "unconscious interactional organization structures" (Zelnick & Buchholz, 1991). American object relations theory, in particular, with its leading figure, Otto Kernberg (1993), frames an extensive description of the structure of this inner world formed by objects and representatives. Freud's structural model (ego – id – super-ego) is transformed into a structure theory, which describes the differentiating stages of this world of inner objects. These stages occur more or less on two axes: the axis of differentiation, setting apart the internal from the external world; and the axis of integration, blending affective positive and affective negative self- and object-concepts to receive an ambivalently perceived complete object. Kernberg (1984) describes these stages as a sequence of internalizations of object relations, and argues for the development of an early, stable "good" self-experience under the influence of a sufficiently good motherly care, which establishes the initially undifferentiated self–object-representation. Soon after, the consolidation of an early undifferentiated "bad" self–object-representation occurs. By the time the ego borders are consolidated as further development takes place, and the child finds its way around in the increasingly clear perception of its separateness from the mother, self- and object-representations are also being differentiated, but so far, neither an integrated self-concept (both good and bad ones) nor integrated conceptions of the mother and other persons exist. Only when object consistency is reached does an integration of self- and object-representation take place; partial self- and object-representations are then converted into perceptions of complete objects and a complete self (Kernberg, 1981 [1976]). The various differentiation and integration levels are linked with specific defense mechanisms and control options. On the earliest, not yet differentiated or integrated, structural levels, primitive defense mechanisms such as thought and perception disturbances, splits, chaotic character traits, impulsiveness and emotional tempests prevail; with increasing differentiation of self and object, as well as the integration of positive and negative self- and object-representations that follows, defense (repression, projection, rationalization, etc.) diminishes. The perception of self and others is gradually more subtly sketched, allows for more ambivalence and becomes more realistic. The child learns to mentalize itself and others (Fonagy, Gergely, Jurist & Target, 2018 [2002]).

Children who are healthy and cared for with sufficient empathy learn to mentalize within the first five years of their life, which means that they comprehend their own intentions and those of their caregivers. Fonagy et al. (2004 [2002]) describe the development of mentalization in four steps:

1   Teleological Mode: Around the completion of their first year, children begin to be able to predict the connection of cause and effect in the physical world without, as yet, developing a mental representation of it. They are capable of embedding such connections in targeted play situations and of optimizing their behavior to achieve their aims more effectively; also, they react with annoyance if disturbances of expected developments arise. If, at the age of one to two, the cognitive foundations of origination are being laid and an emotional order starts to develop, promoted by the biosocial feedback of affect marking, the child develops representations of the internal and external world and simultaneously begins to play with reality.

2   Psychic Equivalence Mode: At first this occurs in a mode in which representations of the internal and external world exist, but are not yet differentiated. The child experiences its thoughts as external reality. This period, which is characterized by intensive anxiety about fantasized dangers such as the crocodile under the bed, requires a balancing act between the acknowledgement of this anxiety and a staying calm by the caregivers. It can be hard for adults to accept that the child in this phase is actually incapable of differentiating between its imagination and reality. A simple test with numerous variations that can be conducted for this equating is the theory-of-mind [ToM] or false-belief test. The child is shown that the contents of a box are exchanged, for example, to sweets instead of pens. Then it is asked if another child, who is now entering the room and did not watch the exchange, will expect sweets or pens in the box. According to the psychic equivalence mode, the child will answer that the other child will expect pens in the box. Thus, it equates its own knowledge level with that of the other child and is unable to imagine that other individuals can have a false conviction in relation to reality.

3   Pretend Mode: After the equivalence mode, the child develops as an alternating state the pretend mode, in which the child can experience its thoughts as such and playfully express them. In these moments, the child enacts fantasies by playing with dolls or re-enacts real day-to-day scenes in its play, thereby making them modifiable. The self-created external representation of internal conditions is also a communication directed at the parents who accompany the child's play. If they react playfully, then the child is encouraged to further transform its as yet unmodified and unsymbolized imagination, fantasies and anxieties during its play, into interactive and narrative development, at the same time stabilizing the partition between internal and external as well as the representations of expected developments.

4   Mentalizing or Reflecting Mode: At the age of about four years, the child is able to attribute to itself and others thoughts, feelings and intentions, and it is also capable of understanding upcoming anxieties appropriately, as a mental state. Further, it is aware of the fact that others can have other notions of reality and it would pass the ToM test ("He expects sweets, as

he doesn't know that you have put pens into the box"). The reflecting mode enables the child to think about its own self and about the presumed inner life of other individuals.

(Fonagy et al., 2004 [2002], pp. 203–269)

4.2 Free association

Freud's original method of "free association" has its origin in early instinctual theory. Freud started from the premise that the unconscious parts of inner life, as the "missing links" of incomplete chains of associations, are reconstructable. At first, he tried to find the missing links by putting patients under hypnosis and then guessing the repressed content from their spontaneous utterances. Later he substituted hypnosis with the method of free association. With that, he took a step in the direction of acknowledging relatedness. Free association brought a new quality into psychoanalytic treatment: the acknowledgment of the other (Honneth, 1995 [1992]). The object of research became a subject of research (cf. Hamburger, 2016b).

4.3 Defense

Defense is not a dysfunctional process. The opposite is true: Without functioning defense, neither a psychic structure nor action adapted to reality would be thinkable. This is not only explicable in an organizational context, but also without any effort, in everyday life. Someone traveling in a car on a county road at approximately 50 mph who is approached by another vehicle going at about the same speed, and will soon pass by it with a clearance of less than 1 yard, may not be considering what would happen, at a difference in relative speed of 100 mph, if only one of the cars veered even a little. This notion must be suppressed; otherwise the resulting anxiety would enlarge the risk considerably. The concept of defense originates from the primal phase of psychoanalysis – in Freud's paper on the "Defense-Neuropsychoses" (1896), the term defense stood for all avoidance of displeasure; later, he began differentiating between the various forms of defense. In his study "Inhibitions, Symptoms and Anxiety" (1926a), defense is a fixed component of psychoanalytic terminology. During the ego-psychological phase of psychoanalytic theory, the concept became central and took on a positive connotation; the goal of an analytical treatment was now named a healthy defense. Anna Freud (1946) compiled a catalog of ten defense mechanisms (repression, regression, reaction formation, isolation, undoing, internalization [identification], projection, auto-aggression, reversal into the opposite and sublimation), which was enlarged to 26 by later authors. These ego-psychological defense concepts allowed for the inquiry into parallels to cognitive psychology (Steffens & Kächele, 1988). In addition to this descriptive differentiation targeted by ego-psychology, an object relations theoretical approach generally strives to regard the defense event in the frame of a social matrix. Already the painful affects, which the defense is meant to protect against, are connected with interactive experiences such as shame, fear of object loss, loss of love or punishment – generally, it is the social situation which paradigmatically stands for what is to be avoided. Even singular defense mechanisms are connected to certain developmental stages of object relation. The autonomous dynamic typical for ego-development is partly responsible for how an earlier trauma – for example, an object loss – can be processed (Steffens & Kächele, 1988). Whether a defense process is healthy or pathological from this viewpoint has also to do with the question of which age group is involved. Defense mechanisms like splitting, acting out and regressive fantasies, for example, are necessary and adequate for child development; however, in an adult – if they make any more than a temporary appearance – they can only represent a symptom.

Systemic and relational approaches of psychoanalysis reach further than the embedding of defense processes into object relational theory and its resulting inner object world. Mentzos (1976) understands "interpersonal defense" as a process in which the attachment figures are chosen by the subject either on condition

> that they actually adopt the according function within the defense formation or are forced to do so, or are manipulated into that direction, for example, by role assignment. The partners or "objects" enter the defense constellation as real, factually effective components and not simply as defense constellations, located in the ego of the affected person.
>
> (Mentzos, 1976, p. 23)

Such a production of the "social unconscious" (Erdheim, 1984) is relevant for the use of psychoanalytical defense concepts in organizations.

4.4 Resistance

The concept of resistance likewise has changed its meaning over time. Even in Freud's pre-analytical papers, the term could be used, on the one hand, for patients who could not be hypnotized; and on the other hand, to signify an endopsychic mechanism of defense against a thought. This endopsychic defense in therapy is apparent both as resistance to hypnosis and resistance to acknowledgment of the repressed context: "If I endeavored to direct the patient's attention to it, I became aware, in the form of resistance, of the same force as had shown itself in the form of repulsion when the symptom was generated" (Freud, 1893a, p. 268). Freud's early therapeutic attempts were often characterized by his attempt to rebut this resistance through argument:

> This resistance often conceals itself behind some remarkable excuses. "My mind is distracted to-day; the clock (or the piano in the next room) is disturbing me." I have learned to answer such remarks: "Not at all. You have at this moment come up against something that you had rather not say. It won't do any good. Go on thinking about it."
>
> (Freud, 1893a, p. 278)

Freud then advised analysts to dissolve the resistance "slowly and by degrees", whereby one

> may reckon on the intellectual interest which the patient begins to feel after working for a short time. By explaining things to him, by giving him information about the marvelous world of psychical processes into which we ourselves only gained insight by such analyses, we make him himself into a collaborator, induce him to regard himself with the objective interest of an investigator, and thus push back his resistance, resting as it does on an affective basis. ... It is an essential precondition for such psychical activity that we should have more or less divined the nature of the case and the motives of the defense operating in it.
>
> (Freud, 1893a, pp. 281–282)

This "divining" has its origin in early psychoanalysis, and later had to yield its precedence to the newly developed treatment technique of repetition in transference; however, working with resistance remained a central part of psychoanalytic technique.

The further development of psychoanalysis into a "two body psychology" (Aron, 1990) further changed the term "resistance" (Frank, 2012). Self-psychology led to a movement where the whole field prioritized empathetic relatedness toward their patients over an inquisitive analysis of resistance (Ornstein, 1996), and object relations theoretical and interpersonal psychoanalysts view resistance phenomena as necessary steps in working through resistance against the perception of feelings as well as drawing the line between self and object (Horner, 2005). In this sense, the classical concept of "resistance" is understood today as being a part of the significant scene.

Alongside such an unconscious and possibly dysfunctional dynamic of the resistance phenomenon, a resistance against entering into a psychoanalytic interpretative dialog can actually make sense; that is, if the risk of making unconscious processes conscious would be too high. This situation, called the "caterpillar-paradox", comes about if the process of making something conscious in itself blocks this very mental process. If the caterpillar had to think about how to coordinate his many legs, he (probably) wouldn't be able to walk at all. Resistance as a consequence of functional defense, as described earlier with the example of the car driver (see Chapter 4.3), protects the necessary unconsciousness against a defense that would be dysfunctional in terms of its result. The same is true for the question as to how much "laying bare" should be worked into supervision and coaching in a business context. This question is mainly relevant for psychoanalytic supervision – coaching, with its clear definition of an initial issue, already limits the space in which laying bare is allowed and tolerated, whereas the psychoanalytic attitude with its characteristic openness, the "position of not knowing", could possibly have a tendency toward overstepping the limits. A topic-orientated assignment fixation is not practicable if one plans to work with associations and evenly suspended attention. However, the fact that supervision allows developments in the enterprise to remain partially unconscious has to constantly be reflected by the supervisor, and he must decide on which interpretations he will communicate and which he will not.

In the case example previously discussed (see Chapter 2.2.2), Hirsch (2000) describes how such an uncovering process of a massive father–son conflict concerning leadership of the family business was partly successful, but how thereafter a further revealing process was prevented:

> For the first time after half a year of therapy, the son could effectively restrict the father: if he refused to stop attacking him, he would make public that the father had a criminal record (he had actually received a suspended sentence due to certain earlier financial transactions). The father then had a change of heart; he wanted to talk and wept, but nevertheless retorted that he was stuck with this – his useless – son, whom he had supported. It was essential in the therapy (which in this case really had the character of a coaching, as the patient or supervisee had naturally brought into the session the topic which now had to be treated as a focus) that the patient had to be strongly supported in his perception of his father's actions.
>
> (Hirsch, 2000, p. 42)

Beyond this practically usable aspect of the analytical reflection on the underlying psychological and family dynamic, further clarification was impossible.

> It seemed that he was satisfied with the support of his effort to dissociate himself from his father, by the confirmation and also the expansion of his view of the dynamic. He terminated the therapy because of, in his view, an absolutely indispensable appointment.
>
> (Hirsch, 2000, p. 42)

In this way, he maintained the identification with his grandiose father which he perceived as being necessary to his functioning. In this case, it cannot be decided from hindsight whether the processing of the resistance, which might have led to the dissolution of his identification (still characterized by the trauma of the father and his compensation strategy), would have been a more profound help both to the client and to the enterprise. Hirsch (2000) argues with the objective of his client, who possibly didn't want a therapy. Such a situation has previously been described by Johannes Cremerius in his study on the "psychoanalytic treatment of the rich and the powerful" (1979). He states that "patients in high political and economic positions of power only very rarely agree to a psychoanalytical treatment. Even if they turn up in the practices of psychoanalysts … they are looking for something totally different from their own psychoanalysis" (Cremerius, 1979, pp. 12–13). "They are looking for consolation and help after they have burnt their fingers" (Cremerius, 1979, p. 15). An appropriate reaction to this, however, is neither to refuse consolation and help, just because a comprehensive psychoanalytic insight is not wanted, nor to yield to fulfilling the wish for a quick repair job. The answer, if it arises from a psychoanalytic attitude, is the naming of the wishes as well as the limits.

4.5 Inner objects, relation and re-enactment

Object relations theory represents a major tendency in psychoanalysis. As has been shown in Chapter 2, its influence on the psychoanalytic business psychology of the last 70 years was essential. Accordingly, we will examine it closely here. Object relations theories "constitute the most diversified perspective in psychoanalysis, thus one can by no means only speak of one school of thought" (Boll-Klatt & Kohrs, 2014, p. 38).

The transition from an instinct-psychological to an ego-psychological conception of the mind, as Freud and his immediate associates had established and developed in Vienna, to an interactional psychoanalysis has several motives, but most importantly, one founding father: Sándor Ferenczi. Inspired by the traumatized soldiers whom he had cared for as an army doctor during World War I, Freud's creative "outpost" in Budapest had left the predetermined path of instinctual theory at an early stage to develop an intersubjective pathology and treatment technique (Hamburger, 2018). Not only did Ferenczi thus establish trauma theory, but he also exerted a lasting influence on a group of other Hungarian analysts whom he partly trained: Michael and Alice Balint, Georges Devereux, Melanie Klein, Margaret Mahler, René Spitz and others (Mészáros, 2010). These later became influential theorists and innovators of psychoanalysis. From many of these analysts, originally from Hungary, especially those who had – like the two Balints and Melanie Klein – immigrated to London came the stimuli to view the mind's functioning according to the biological model of a social organism, instead of following Freud's apparatus-model.

A further important trigger came from the very independent psychoanalyst and pediatrician Donald W. Winnicott, whose perception that a child's psyche constructs itself "a priori" only through the interaction with others had an enormous influence. His radical statement that "there is no such thing as an infant" (Winnicott, 1965, p. 39) puts the concept in a nutshell. According to the understanding of object relations theory, courses of action become important in the interaction between the real mother (and her fantasies and images) and the real child (and its fantasies and images forming in this interaction) (cf. Hamburger, 1995). The child becomes acquainted with itself by growing out of the initially undifferentiated relational matrix with the mother. Undifferentiatedness here does not mean the ability to cognitively discriminate (cf. Dornes, 1993), but the experiencing of an increasingly coherent subject reference. According to Winnicott, the child chooses a "transitional object" as a tool to get from its primary object experience – wherein it experiences, for example, the breast as an object magically dominated by its needs – to the subject–object differentiation, in which it learns to direct objects through manipulation. This process unfolds within the relationship to the "good enough mother", who adapts herself actively to the infant's needs (Winnicott, 1971, p. 12). As regards the transitional object, it is, as it were, agreed between us and the baby never to ask the question: "Have you made this up or has it been offered to you from outside?" (1975 [1953], p. 308). Admittedly, this pioneering theory wasn't empirically validated, but it was, nevertheless, based on experience.

In later empirical studies, it could be shown that from the beginning, babies really use their contact with their mother as a social biofeedback system, to playfully and in incessant repetitions try out experiences with regulation, fitting, disturbance and reparation – in this play, they become acquainted with themselves and form their basic emotional and cognitive patterns. In this interactive play, recognition itself becomes a motivational factor (Lichtenberg, 2001, 2003).

Modern psychoanalytic development psychology is dominated by paradigmatic infant research. Object relations theoretical development psychology has produced a set of metaphors which encourages empirical research; its own experimental setup, however, is no longer the analytic transition space, but the laboratory. Its opening up to academic developmental research – for instance, attachment research and its connection with the developmental concepts of object relations theory – has brought forth, for example, the concept of mentalization, which today stands at the center of psychoanalytic developmental theory.

Thus, object relations psychology is based on the concept of images, remaining from childhood, of an inner drama in which the individual plays all the parts. New experiences are undergone not in their actual forms, but through these inner images and along the lines of those old dramas. These inner images originate in subjectively perceived experiences in relation to primary objects. They are a function of the affects and wishes of the child at the time of his original experience. From the search for pleasurable experiences or the need to cope with the old dramas, there arises the notion of repeating them (Pine, 1988, pp. 571–572).

Within the context of use in psychotherapy, supervision and coaching, object relations theory seeks to find out whether a client in a certain situation behaves as the person he was or should have been, or if he behaves as the reference people (parents) were or should have been. Here are mirrored forms of belonging, closeness and security. In the more recent theory, the underlying experiences are hypothesized as being subjective and the truth-question is no longer applied (Pine, 1988, p. 581). The therapist's task is interpretation with a view to freeing the patient and thus enabling him to experience new experiences as new, and not integrate them into the old drama of his object relations (Pine, 1988, p. 585). In this, psychoanalysis represents for the patient a new, correcting object relation (Pine, 1988, p. 592).

Object relations psychology assumes as a basic principle that every human being re-enacts his inner drama in the present, regardless of whether or not a psychic disorder is present. This is what makes object relations psychology so valuable for coaching, because clients will also re-enact their inner images in business relationships (Kretschmar, 2016, p. 34). As an example, we will describe a case handled by the first author, in which a coachee grew up with his constantly fighting grandparents. This client repeatedly found himself in jobs with two bosses, who were distinctly older than he was and constantly arguing. This resulted in repeated relational patterns which were so difficult that in the end he had to fail at mediating between the two quarreling bosses. Obviously, this was a re-enactment of the drama of his inner experiences as a child, and thus showed the world in the here and now how the child stands in front of the fighting grandparents and fails to conciliate them. Another client grew up as the fourth of eight children. He was very good at cultivating his contacts during association meetings with his colleagues. However, he had difficulties with presentation in front of large groups and at accepting the role of leadership. In his family of origin, he had learned to be "right in the thick of it", but he had not learned how to lead or advance. The coach's uncovering of this re-enacting allowed the client to separate the "here and now" from the "then" and to experiment with new relational behaviors in comparable situations (Giernalczyk, Lohmer & Albrecht, 2013a, p. 21).

4.6 Transference and countertransference

Transference is a relational phenomenon between client and therapist, wherein the client shows his feelings and fantasies in relation to the therapist. These could, for example, appear in an aggressive or libidinal (i.e. erotic) form. As the therapist discloses very little about himself and effectively offers the client a projection surface, the space is there for the client to project his inner conflicts onto the therapist. The term countertransference names the corresponding emotional state of the therapist toward the client. It goes back to Ferenczi, who first mentioned it in a letter to Freud (Boll-Klatt & Kohrs, 2014, p. 44). For Freud, countertransference had little epistemic value; he saw it as the analyst's resistance and demanded "that he shall recognize this counter-transference in himself and overcome it" (Freud, 1910, pp. 143–144).

If the therapist is trained accordingly, he recognizes that these feelings that well up within him represent a type of "as if situation" and point to the client's conflict. Accordingly, he will mention this conflict to the client and will work it through with him (Rudolf, 2010, p. 213). In modern therapy, counter-transference is of outstanding importance. Some therapy forms – for example, transference-focused psychotherapy (TFP) – utilize countertransference as one of their main tools (Yeomans, Clarkin & Kernberg, 2015).

Transference processes can be utilized in businesses to identify unconscious role expectations (Mertens & Lang, 1991, pp. 66–67; Giernalczyk & Lohmer, 2012). Psychodynamic work can help us to understand and dissolve our trans-ference on superiors, clients, team members, institutions and on the coach (Lohmer & Möller, 2014, p. 47). The coach with experience in the client's vocational field analyzes his countertransference and asks himself: Would I like to do business with my client? How would I feel, if I were his colleague or superior? Do I feel motivated to outperform him as a colleague? Does the client trigger compassion in me, or would I prefer to send him away because I cannot stomach his presence? A supervisor would analyze corresponding feelings in himself which the supervisee's description of his organization has provoked. Transference in organizations simplifies dealings with other people, in so far as it helps to sort out new impressions and to "create categories of closeness" (Giernalczyk & Lohmer, 2012, p. 10). A psychoanalytic working through of transference dynamics sheds light on the contribution of autobiographical aspects to recurring relational entanglements, and should give individuals and teams in organizations the freedom to decide this way or that (Kretschmar & Senarclens de Grancy, 2016, p. 102).

The interpretation of transference phenomena can afford clients a new level of relationship with their colleagues. Intervision group work among psychodynamic counselors makes it clear how powerful this instrument actually is. In the first author's intervisional group, a business was presented, in which the counseling colleague could not make any progress with his coaching assignment. The case discussion gave rise to a strangely rough behavior by the other group members: They interrupted each other unceremoniously or stubbornly dug in their heels. At the end, one group member voiced the idea: It could well be that in this company, no one is capable of really listening. The company culture had been transferred onto the intervisional group by their colleague's story. As the next step in the process, the counselor informed the client about the intervisional group's analysis. This gave rise to the decision to offer training for active listening. In this way, it became possible to sensitize the employees to the idea that being open to others' opinion heightens their willingness to listen in turn. In this way, the general communication culture of the company was changed in a positive way (Kretschmar & Senarclens de Grancy, 2016, p. 102).

Meanwhile, there are several approaches to operationalizing countertransference for the purpose of research. The Countertransference Factors Inventory (CFI) consists of 50 items for the self-assessment of coaches and counselors and has already been applied in several studies. Meta-analyses show that countertransference reactions which are not reflected upon correlate negatively with the success of therapy; an effective management of countertransference, however, has a positive impact (Kächele & Erhardt, 2012, pp. 95–97). The Countertransference Questionnaire (CTQ) features 79 items, 58 of which can be factor analytically pooled to reduce to seven factors. A German version of the questionnaire (CTQ-D) revealed that experience-orientated therapists (art and body therapists) display a stronger positive-affectionate, protective and involved experience of countertransference; while conflict-orientated one-on-one and group therapists reacted with a more aggressive-resigned experience of countertransference. Further, it was proved that countertransference has an influence on therapy success. Indifference and aggressive-resigned feelings in countertransference right at the beginning are an important indication for unfavorable therapeutic progress (Kernhof, Obbarius, Kaufhold, Merkle & Grabhorn, 2013, p. 153). An excellent and up-to-date survey of the empirical research on countertransference can be found in Kächele, Erhardt, Seybert and Buchholz (2015).

The Operationalized Psychodynamic Diagnosis 2 (OPD-2) presents a good suggestion for the operationalization of countertransference in conjunction with conflict diagnosis. This will be explained later in this chapter and supplemented by a suggestion for further operationalization (see Chapter 4.10).

4.7 Blind spots

Freud concisely summarizes the difficulties of blind spots for the psychotherapist:

> But if the doctor is to be in a position to use his unconscious in this way as an instrument in the analysis, he must himself fulfill one psychological condition to a high degree. He may not tolerate any resistance in himself, which holds back from his consciousness what has been perceived by his unconscious; otherwise he would introduce into the analysis a new species of selection and distortion, which would be far more detrimental than that resulting from concentration of conscious attention. It is not enough for this that he himself should be an approximately normal person. It may be insisted, rather, that he should have undergone a psychoanalytic purification and have become aware of those complexes of his own which would be apt to interfere with his grasp of what the patient tells him. There can be no reasonable doubt about the disqualifying effect of such defects in the doctor; every unresolved repression in him constitutes what has been aptly described by Stekel as a "blind spot" in his analytic perception.
>
> (Freud, 1912, p. 115)

Blind spots are a challenge for supervision as well as coaching. Admittedly, some supervisors and coaches are psychoanalysts too. However, if a supervisor or coach has not gone through the self-orientation demanded here, he will possibly not be fully cognizant of his blind spot. This is why even for psychodynamic coaching and supervision, self-orientation is imperative.

4.8 Motivation, conflict and personality

Conflict is an essential element of psychoanalysis. Freud described what he had observed with his patients; namely, that conflicting affects confront one another. A conflict between affects can turn a moment into trauma (Freud, 1893b, p. 114). Later, Freud summarizes "that the outbreak of hysteria may almost invariably be traced to a psychical conflict arising through an incompatible idea setting in action a defense on the part of the ego and calling up a demand for repression" (Freud, 1896, pp. 209–210).

Nowadays, it is assumed that an unconscious, unresolved conflict resulting from an individual biography gives rise to typically conflicting self- and object-images, interpersonal behaviors, emotions and general behavior. In this situation, conflicting patterns of experience and behavior serve as the defense of typically conflicting inner aspects. Thus, what becomes visible is not the conflict as such, but the manifestation of the defense. The analyst/supervisor/coach can then extrapolate from these signs of defense to the underlying unconscious conflicting topic (Benecke & Möller, 2013, p. 189). Chapter 4.10.3 describes how such a manifestation can be operationalized within the framework of Operationalized Psychodynamic Diagnosis (OPD) through the client's tangible observable behavior as well as the analyst/supervisor/coach's countertransference (see Chapter 4.10.3). OPD also describes the conflict as "unconscious internal clashes of diametrically opposed motivational bundles" (OPD Task Force, 2008, p. 1075).

In this way, the whole concept of personality may originate from conflict and compensation. This compensation is the consequence of motivation, experience and behavior. Whether compensation is pathological or not depends on its severity. Sachse (2020, p. 3) defines the formation of personality as a psychological unit with a continuum, ranging from a "minor personality style"/"mild form" to a "major clinical disorder"/"severe form". It can be deduced from this that instruments for the clinical diagnosis of conflicts and personality disorder can also be used to diagnose personal styles in coaching. If some features of a personality disorder are present, but not all the criteria for a pathological disorder are met, then we can at least assume a corresponding *style*. The *Persönlichkeits-Stil und Störungs-Inventar* (*Personality Style and Disorder Inventory*) presents an excellent overview of styles and their corresponding disorder (Kuhl & Kazén, 2009, p. 20).

4.9 Analytic space, relationship offer and containing

4.9.1 The significance of analytic space, relationship and containing in supervision and coaching

Relationship

The debate about relationship in psychoanalysis has a long tradition. At first, relationship was rated as a source of knowledge similar to the ideas, symptoms and dreams of the patient. In 1905, Freud designated transference as the "most powerful ally" of analysis (Freud, 1905, p. 116). From the 1950s, the view became widely accepted that countertransference, which had initially been disowned and then regarded with great skepticism, is similarly enlightening (Racker, 1953). With Franz Alexander's ego-psychological concept of "corrective emotional experience", relationship turned into a therapeutic factor. Alexander referred to Freud's intuitive approach, which had been much more flexible in the field than in his theoretical writings on treatment techniques. He fell back on Ferenczi's "active technique" (Ferenczi & Rank, 1956 [1923]) and reckoned that "in all forms of etiological psychotherapy, the basic therapeutic principle is the same: to re-expose the patient, under more favorable circumstances, to emotional situations which he could not handle in the past" (Alexander & French, 1946, p. 66). The technical variations suggested by Alexander, French, Horney and other colleagues at the Chicago Institute for Psychoanalysis were controversial (Cremerius, 1979).

However, Alexander's technical innovations remained in place for the further development of the analytic relationship. They were continued by the self-psychological approaches of the Kohut School (Bergmann, 1993) and in the work at the Mount Zion Psychotherapy Research Group in San Francisco (Weiss & Sampson,

1986). Based on this institution's systematic research into effective factors of psychoanalytic processes, the Control Mastery Theory (CMT) was framed.

The group, later re-named as the San Francisco Psychotherapy Research Group (SFPRG), could prove in systematic individual case studies that patients use (1) the therapeutic relationship in itself; (2) their insights through the therapist's interpretations; and (3) testing activity to self-improve during therapy. The testing activity is differentiated in terms of (a) "transference tests" and (b) "passive-into-active tests". In a transference test, pathogenic experiences are repeated with the therapist as relationship partner. Passive-into-active tests represent a role reversal: In a re-enactment, patients treat their therapist in a way in which they themselves were treated in the pathogenic experience situation (Silberschatz, 2005). However, such healing re-enactment is only possible if the patient consciously and unconsciously feels sufficiently secure to bring forth unconscious material (Silberschatz, 2005).

Boothe & Grimmer (2005) view relationship as a major theater of analysis from its beginning. They show that in a therapeutic relationship (as in any other), the antagonism between the preservation of self and of the species, which Freud described in his theory of instincts, becomes operative: The ego instincts, which serve self-preservation, are directed toward a security-giving primary relationship; whereas the sexual drive – securing reproduction – focuses on tension relief in the form of pleasurable experiences of satisfaction. This continuous conflict between sexual exploration and attachment security leads, in the course of development, to repressions:

> The child in its various developmental sequences represses instinctual demands, [so] as not to endanger its relationship with its caregivers. However, often only these instinctual demands are banished from the child's mind, without it having to relinquish the satisfaction of its wish. The conflict between instinctual demand and self-preservation, which develops in the relationship to the outer objects, is thus internalized.
>
> (Boothe & Grimmer, 2005, p. 41)

In the further development in the self and object relations theory of psychoanalysis, this conflict – still characterized as instinctual antagonism by Freud – is described as an autonomous conflict. Relationship is no longer viewed within the frame of instinctual theory arising from the cathexis of the ego or the objects, but as an independent motivation (Lichtenberg, 2014, pp. 157–159), and it influences subsequent perception of interactions and control over them. For a long time, the dyadic relationship between mother and child was the focus of this developmental psychoanalytic relationship theory. Alongside this dyad, Abelin (1971, 1975) and Lichtenberg (2010) acknowledge in their papers the early importance of the father, who conveys essential experiences of triangular relatedness, long before the classical Oedipal phase (Mertens, 1992).

This basic pattern of dyadic and triangular relatedness is restored in the analytic and supervisorial space, if – and because – it is framed in such a way as to encourage the free relational development of the supervisee/analysand. It is the supervisor's task to frame the space in this way, and this is made possible by abstinence and a professional analytic attitude.

> A very personal relationship develops, which nevertheless is limited in respect to time, location, closeness and intimacy. It is an unequal relationship, in which only the stories and the history of the patient get attention, whereas the analyst as a private person by and large stays anonymous. This inequality allows the patient to really come into his own, but nevertheless is for many patients difficult to endure, particularly in its early stage. In the course of a psychoanalytic treatment, it is inevitable that now and again the real person of the analyst, his values and preferences beyond his professional attitude, becomes noticeable for the patient. These moments of authentic personal encounter, wherein the therapist momentarily steps out of his professional attitude, enliven the relationship and, with a hindsight view on their therapy, are usually noted by patients as [a] very distinct and essential quality.
>
> (Boothe & Grimmer, 2005, p. 45)

Authors discussing interactional psychoanalysis nevertheless assess the structure of such an asymmetrical helping relationship as a mutual process of "crediting" (Grimmer, 2005).

> The therapist ... has to be convinced that his patient has resources at his command, which allow him a solution for his problem, as well as a development and change in the future. He faces him as a potentially powerful agent and credits him with his confidence. ... A crediting attitude counteracts the self-perception and self-presentation of the patient as an unfortunate victim of a failing environment, which usually prevails at the beginning of a therapy, and encourages him to come to grips with his own role as agent.
>
> (Grimmer, 2005)

On the other hand, the analysand likewise has to credit the analyst, at the minimum, with his trust in the analyst's competence (Grimmer, 2005).

Abstinence

Bauriedl (1998) defines abstinence as an

> active and self-determined *answer* [italics in the original] of the analyst to the partly unconscious requests, wishes and feelings of the analysand. In so far as the therapist is able to develop and retain this concept of abstinence in himself, he doesn't give in or gives in less to the temptation to internally and externally join in on the scenes of his patients.
>
> (Bauriedl, 1998, p. 353)

Therapists easily give in to the temptation to cave in to their patients' manifest desires and to feel like the "better father" or the "better mother". If they do this, instead of restricting themselves to respectfully and openly (for the purpose of the ambivalence contained therein) specifying the patient's wish, they fall into the trap of reiterating the original trauma without being aware of it: Again, the patient feels recognized only and simply because this wonderful therapist is so empathetic, kind, etc. And again, the patient will conform and subject himself to this idealized therapist. The way out of this trap of reiteration is the analyst's self-analysis. He must realize his own wish to fulfill the patient's desire instead of analyzing it. If therapists only externalize these wishes to the patient, instead of feeling how the patient's desire has caused their own complementary desire (to be the idealized therapist, for example), they unconsciously re-create the original harmful situation. In the same way as the patient wishes to be healed by external recognition, the therapist himself feels a "potential or manifest threat of being seen as worthless, if one does not succeed in being the ideal, wish-fulfilling object in the eyes of the patient (and thereby in the eyes of one's own parents)" (Bauriedl, 1998, p. 353). Abstinence in the sense "of not allowing one's self to be used and not using the other" (Bauriedl, 1980, p. 52) allows the analyst to

> mentally and physically allocate the patient's space *to himself* [italics in the original] and to understand that one's own need to work effectively and gratifyingly can only be fulfilled if one tries to remain inner-psychically apart from the patient and at the same time to be connected to him.
>
> (Bauriedl, 1998, p. 353)

Due to this flexible and self-analytical abstinence, the analyst satisfies "his need as *analyst* (the need to work effectively)" and does not confuse "this role with that of a surrogate partner" (Bauriedl, 1998, p. 353; italics in the original). These detailed reflections on the psychoanalytic understanding of abstinence are particularly meaningful for the utilization of psychoanalysis in supervision.

> As [a] psychoanalyst we may be prone to accept the potential invitation to a therapeutic relationship with the client or even to invite him ourselves to a change of context, if we lose orientation in the network of social references.
>
> (Wellendorf, 1996, p. 86)

4.9.2 Containing in coaching

It was Bion who originally introduced the term "containing". What is at issue here is basically an offer of relationship. The child projects its immature emotional reaction into a container and gets a mature emotional reaction in return (Bion, 1962, p. 90). Usually, the mother provides this container in childhood. The container acts as a source of emotional assistance and supports the child in learning how to perceive feelings and how to endure them. It seems natural that the containing provided by a therapist in psychoanalysis has a rectifying effect on the patient. However, for the purpose of supervision and coaching, its utilization as a concept for business will be examined here. The concept of containing has been used in the Tavistock Institute, co-founded by Bion, for analyzing organizations and for verifying the containing ability of executives.

Even today, containing plays an important role in coaching:

> The psychodynamic concept of containment describes the major function of the coach; he is assigned to receive from the coachee his emotional tensions, unresolved conflicts and unconscious enactments, to endure them internally, to understand them and to finally return them at a suitable moment in the form of theories and suggestions.
>
> (Sell et al., 2018, p. 149)

"Initially the coach does surrogate work of experiencing emotionally what the coachee is not yet capable of" (Giernalczyk, Lohmer & Albrecht, 2013b, p. 425). However, Giernalczyk et al. do not only want to describe the containing abilities of a coach. In addition, structures need to be created in the business which allow for containing. For this, an organization needs to make room for reflecting about feelings, anxieties and needs. Unconscious rules and patterns have to be made clear. A self-reflective organizational culture has to be set up (Giernalczyk et al., 2013b, p. 432).

However, it is doubtful whether the establishment of appropriate structures is sufficient. If the ability for containment is imparted during early childhood through the relationship with the mother, as Bion says, the question has to be asked as to whether a specific executive is even suitable for containing, based on his personal early childhood development, and whether he could possibly acquire this ability, if needed, later in life. If containing is so important – and this seems to be confirmed in particular by the statements concerning primary risk (see Chapter 2.1.1) – then containing could be one of the criteria for the selection of executive personnel. This is why there is a research project that concentrates on the question as to whether and how ability for containment might be measured (see Chapter 5.2.6).

4.10 Operationalized Psychodynamic Diagnosis (OPD) in business

As psychodynamic and psychoanalytic therapists and researchers became increasingly unsatisfied with the ICD DSM-classifications of mental disorders, mainly due to their purely phenomenal approach, which undervalued unconscious phantasy and structure as relevant components of psychopathology, efforts were made to design complementary manuals.

In Germany, OPD was developed since 1992, while in the US and in the frame of the International Psychoanalytic Association, *The Psychodynamic Diagnostic Manual* (PDM) was published in 2006. Both are meanwhile available in their second version (OPD-2, PDM-2), and serve practitioners and researchers to finetune their diagnoses in addition to – not in competition with – DSM 5 and ICD 10. Both support extensive description and categorization of personality patterns, related social and emotional capacities, individual mental profiles, and personal experiences of the patient. PDM-2 is structured in three "axes" ("P-Axis – Personality Syndromes", "M-Axis – Profiles of Mental Functioning", and "S-Axis – Symptom Patterns: The Subjective Experience"). Likewise, OPD-2, which will be described in more detail below, is structured in axes. Both psychodynamic classification systems are internationally renowned; OPD, however, has a detailed formal operationalization of diagnostic criteria, which makes it more suitable for research.

4.10.1 Axes of OPD

In 1992, psychoanalysts, psychosomatically orientated therapists and psychiatrists set up a task force for OPD, to extend the symptom-based, description-orientated classification of mental disorders by adding fundamental psychodynamic dimensions. Four years later, this task force presented a manual containing a diagnostic inventory for clinical application. The OPD inventory was not a scaled instrument, but a half-standardized interview. Only later were research criteria and scaled versions of the interview questions developed. Psychodynamic diagnosis is based on five axes (OPD Task Force, 2008, p. 200):

- Axis I: Experience of Illness and Prerequisites for Treatment
- Axis II: Interpersonal Relations
- Axis III: Conflicts
- Axis IV: Structure
- Axis V: Mental and Psychosomatic Disorders.

OPD is an excellent example of the operationalization and manualization of psychodynamic work. In the following sub-sections, we will outline axes II, III and IV of OPD and evaluate them with regard to their applicability to coaching.

4.10.2 Diagnosis of interpersonal behavior

According to OPD, on axis II, a relationship-dynamic formulation can be found with the following pattern:

1   The patient experiences himself (towards or with others) time and time again as ... (response experienced as defensive)
2   Others – including the interviewer – experience the patient time and time again as ... (difficult offer of relationship)
3   Others – including the interviewer – experience themselves with respect to the patient time and time again as ... (unconsciously induced response)
4   The patient experiences others time and time again as ... (experienced attack/disappointment).

(OPD Task Force, 2008, p. 1951)

The causal loop is completed by stage 4 again influencing stage 1.

For each of the four sentences, the scaled version of OPD provides 32 items, from which some conspicuous items are to be selected and inserted into the respective sentence. From the viewpoint of the examiner, the items either apply or they do not. An ordinal scale is not provided (OPD Task Force, 2008, pp. 468–494). The items of the OPD were developed on the basis of the two levels in Benjamin's (1974) interpersonal circumplex model (cited by the OPD Task Force, 2008, pp. 1046–1055). The model conceives of four dimensions for interpersonal behavior directed at others, and four dimensions for interpersonal behavior directed to the self. Each dimension has two contradicting foci (for example, loving/attacking). Following the diagnosis, we could end up with the following formulation:

> The client experiences himself time and time again as withdrawing from others and retreating. The examiner experiences himself time and time again being dominated and controlled by the client. As a result, the examiner experiences himself time and time again as wanting to resist the client. The client experiences the examiner time and time again as wanting to damage him. Again, the client experiences himself time and time again as withdrawing from others and retreating.

The elaboration of such a relationship-dynamic formulation seems to be extraordinarily useful for supervision and coaching, especially because, as has been shown earlier, in psychodynamic counseling work, relationship topics are of particular importance (see Chapter 1.6). If the shaping of relationships between the coachee and the coach, or between the supervisee and the reference person within the organization, is seen from the OPD perspective, then essential relational schemata could be identified which possibly also exist in other relationships and could explain recurring relational problems.

The diagnosis of interpersonal behavior on the OPD model does not contain clinical terms and could be applied in supervision and coaching without modification. The application is quite easy. The coach has to go through 32 items for each relationship formulation and insert the fitting item into the sentence. The first author (Kretschmar) therefore suggests applying the diagnosis of interpersonal behavior according to OPD-2 without alteration in coaching.

For psychoanalytic supervision – at least, for the type of psychoanalytic supervision that the second author (Hamburger) practices and represents – the situation is different. Certainly, the operationalization of interpersonal behavior according to OPD-2 can be a helpful reflection tool for the supervisor, to clarify the interplay and circular reinforcements of the supervisee's relational experiencing and also its re-enactment within the supervisorial field. However, the psychoanalytic supervisor will not turn it into a specific diagnostic unit and will definitely not utilize any of the prefabricated items. A number of other inquiry instruments (Benecke & Möller, 2013) can also be useful in gathering the objectives and resources of the supervisee in an operationalized way. However, the introduction of diagnostic instruments influences from the outset the climate of encounter, nudges the supervision in a certain direction and converts it into an investigation, which reminds one of a medical or business analysis procedure. This may indeed be familiar territory for the client, but it deprives the "unusual situation of conversation" (Argelander, 1970) of its necessary unstructuredness. According to the psychoanalytic attitude, it is the supervisee's task to word his objective and the supervisor's task to accept this language of everyday life. If he hastens to translate it into professional terminology, then he removes from the supervisee's speech exactly that which should be the subject of scrutiny: the unconscious, his imagery and free associations. Frequently, business clients, in particular, look for clarity by means of operationalization and scaling – this is understandable, but has to be questioned within the supervision. However, this position does not exclude the possibility that for particular tasks – in research, for example – the utilization of reliable and valid diagnostic instruments makes sense.

4.10.3 Diagnosis of conflict and further operationalization

For the definition of ongoing and persistent conflicts, OPD falls back on traditional psychodynamic concepts of dependency, dominance, guilt and Oedipal conflict, and complements them with these new approaches. Correspondingly, OPD defines the following conflicts (OPD Task Force, 2008, p. 111):

1   Individuation versus dependency
2   Submission versus control
3   Need for care versus self-sufficiency
4   Self-worth conflict
5   Guilt conflict
6   Oedipal conflict
7   Identity conflict.

All seven types of conflict are scaled in four steps from 0 (absent) to 3 (very significant). Conflicts that cannot be assigned to types 1 to 7 (not ratable) are allocated 9 points. From this evaluation, a ranking order emerges, consisting of a main conflict and further conflicts. The conflicts are additionally assessed as mode 1 for predominantly active, 2 for mixed but active, 3 for mixed but passive, 4 for predominantly passive, and 9 for not ratable. The terms "active" and "passive" signify the according positions on the conflict axis (OPD Task Force, 2008, pp. 2066–2067). As criteria for diagnosing a conflict, OPD provides extensive textual models for the self-description of patients, including general descriptions as well as those relating to spheres of life such as family of origin (F), partnership/family (P), job/professional life (J), social context (S), wealth (W), body/sexuality (B) and illnesses (I) (OPD Task Force, 2008, p. 2076). However, these criteria are not worded as items. In the checklists for conflicts in the OPD appendix, there are further textual criteria, also differentiated according to active and passive mode (OPD Task Force, 2008, p. 2094). Furthermore, the interview tools in the OPD appendix enable the discovery of "scenic information" – how the patient and therapist interact, and how this can be interpreted (OPD Task Force, 2008, pp. 4206–4207).

The authors of OPD clearly indicate a correlation between motivation and conflict (OPD Task Force, 2008, pp. 1178–1180). If we understand conflict and motivation as two sides of one coin, conflict diagnosis using the OPD model can be employed to analyze the client's motivational structure during resource-orientated consultation work. For coaching, Benecke, Kotte and Möller (2016) suggest re-defining the OPD conflicts as basal motivational guiding themes, which are part of personality:

1 Individuation versus dependency ? attachment/autonomy
2 Submission versus control ? self-efficacy
3 Need for care versus self-sufficiency ? provision
4 Self-worth conflict ? self-worth
5 Guilt conflict ? accountability
6 Oedipal conflict ? competition
7 Identity conflict ? Identity

(Benecke et al., 2016, p. 26)

The OPD criteria for conflict diagnosis are written in an understandable vernacular and require no rewording for the consultancy setting. However, they do require a thorough structuring. The extensive descriptive texts which, in addition, are divided into a main body and appendices, would stand in the way of a broad acceptance in business. For simplification, the first author (Kretschmar) suggests arranging the self-description for each combination of the seven conflicts, two processing modes and seven spheres of life into two items each, resulting in a test composed of 196 items, which the client can fill in. Comparably, the criteria for scenic information and countertransference could be summarized for external assessment. A countertransference inventory with 42 items (seven conflicts, two modes, three items each) is suggested. For self-description and the countertransference inventory, tangible suggestions can be provided by the first author (for deployment in research projects, see Chapter 5.2.2, as well as the case examples in Chapter 6).

From the further operationalization of axis III suggested here arise the following advantages, which could possibly also lead to an improvement of clinical diagnosis:

• Tangible items allow for less interpretation than texts. This practice thus could lead to an enhancement of the interrater's reliability.
• The evaluation of the self-description by the client and of the external assessment by the coach facilitate an investigation of conflicts and modes by calculation of scale values, which is less prone to mistakes.
• Differences in the conscious self-description of the client and the external assessment of the coach, which yield unconscious contents via scenic information and countertransference, are another source of diagnostic information and can be addressed immediately during the conversation with the client.
• The evaluation of the self-description according to different spheres of life facilitates an additional statement regarding the severity of the conflict situation

per sphere of life. Although the OPD introduced the sphere of life, it has so far made no arrangements for an evaluation according to a sphere of life.

Accordingly, it is suggested that coaching should structure the OPD criteria for conflicts as described into a self-description and into an external assessment, measuring the items in a four-division scale as typical for OPD, and then utilizing the systematization with the motivational guiding themes as proposed by Benecke et al. (2016).

4.10.4 Diagnosis of structure

An essentially new approach, which has its origin both in the differentiated description of regulatory mechanisms of ego-psychology and in the interactional approach of object relations theory, is the psychoanalytic theory of structural levels (see Chapter 4.1.3 and Rudolf, Grande & Henningsen, 2010). This descriptive level of personality is mapped onto the structure axis of OPD.

OPD attempts an integration of psychodynamic concepts of structure according to Rudolf (1993, quoted in OPD Task Force, 2008, pp. 1331–1333). The structure is described in four dimensions, which accordingly establish the connection with the self and the object:

- Self-regulation and object-perception

  - Ability to self-reflect
  - Ability to perceive others realistically and as a whole

- Regulation of self and of relationships

  - Ability to regulate own impulses, affects, and self-worth
  - Ability to regulate relation to another

- Emotional internal and external communication

  - Ability to communicate internally via affects and phantasies
  - Ability to communicate with others

- Internal attachment and external relation

  - Ability to avail oneself of good internal objects for self-regulation
  - Ability to attach and detach.
    (OPD Task Force, 2008, p. 1354)

From a psychodynamic perspective, adult structure is a result of a maturational process, with the intrapsychic representation of the external world of objects being established, as well as the experiences and attitudes of the self in dealing with this object world. In the event of structural disorder, the self is neither able to be autonomous nor to regulate itself sufficiently nor to reflect. Reliable attachments cannot be established (OPD Task Force, 2008, pp. 1354–1356).

Table 4.1 Manifestation of personality styles as imbalances or disorders

Style	Imbalance	Disorder
unconventional	distrustful	paranoid
restrained	aloof	schizoid
apprehensive	mystic	schizotypal
spontaneous	inconsistent	borderline
amiable	self-promoting	histrionic
ambitious	egocentric	narcissistic
self-critical	self-doubting	avoidant
loyal	devoted	dependent
diligent	exact/perfectionistic	obsessive-compulsive
critical	stubborn/bitter	negativistic
quiet	inhibited	depressive
obliging	sacrificing	selfless
optimistic	whitewashing	rhapsodic
assertive	inconsiderate	antisocial

Structural disorders belong to psychotherapy and should not be dealt with in coaching. Consequently, we suggest that structure diagnosis, as according to OPD, should at best be utilized optionally within the frame of duty to care in order to preempt structural disorders which would require a referral to psychotherapy.

The recognition of the structural dimension of personality integration, even if not in the sense of a formalized diagnosis, is nevertheless an important aspect of psychoanalytic supervision, the more so, as the dimensions – similar to the relational formula discussed above – can not only be considered as an endopsychic structure, but also as a typical interactional form. It is indeed enlightening to ask the client, after his participation in the scrutiny of his organization's processes within supervision, to assess to what extent his self- and object-perception and his self- and object-control are differentiated; if emotional communication including affects and fantasies takes place, and how; and whether he can establish and make use of stable relationships. This has nothing to do with pathology, either the client's or (in a transferred sense) the organization's, but with a structural description of interaction.

It can, for example, be unburdening to explain the regular temper tantrums of many employees in an intensive care unit, which to date have been unspecifically ascribed to stress, as brought on by psycho-structural overload accompanied by the omnipresence of death, a combination that requires a self-distancing, a self-protection modus – an endemic splitting mechanism which prohibits the communication that relieves affects, for example, through grieving processes.

4.10.5 Means and limits of OPD

Today, OPD may be judged as an example of success for psychodynamic work. Since 2008, the OPD manual exists in its second version and has been translated into several languages. OPD is taught as standard in several international psychotherapy training institutes which are grounded in depth psychology, for the formulating of psychodynamic assessment in mandatory reports which are required for referrals for psychotherapy under health insurance cover (Arbeitskreis OPD, 2016).

However, the limits of operationalization and manualization also become apparent in OPD. The enormous effort is reflected in the sheer number authors involved – 27 (OPD Task Force, 2008, pp. 4155–4175). In spite of this effort, only a part of psychodynamic clinical work has been covered; namely, diagnosis and treatment planning. When it comes to intervention, the procedures are too diverse; thus, at best, some manuals for selected clinical scenarios exist, but because of our focus on psychodynamic counseling, we cannot expand on them here. Operationalization and manualization will not replace the pivotal elements of psychodynamic work such as self-experience, casework and supervision; they will, however, be able to augment these elements in a meaningful way.

Next to the highlighted methods of approach which are transferable to supervision and coaching, OPD conveys an important attitude of scientifically knowledgeable and quality-assured psychodynamic work (OPD Task Force, 2008, p. 18). OPD shows that psychodynamic concepts can be expressed as items and measured by scales. Comparable approaches can be found in Zimmermann, Stasch, Grande, Schauenburg and Cierpka (2014) and Ehrenthal et al. (2012). This approach will assist us in casework and research.

4.11 Discussion: On the alloying of gold – social ethics or psychoanalytic attitude?

From the psychoanalytic point of view, the idea of removing from psychoanalysis set pieces to adapt them to a business context can be viewed critically – not because of conservative inflexibility or a lack of readiness to engage in dialog, but because the elements of psychoanalytic processes that we have described (free association, relationship and transference) are closely associated with one another and with the setting.

Psychoanalysts have time and again warned about watering down the basic rules of the treatment from therapeutic ambition and a desire to yield to the wishes of the analysand, society and one's own urge to heal (Freud, 1915, p. 170). Psychoanalytic treatment gains its strength from the creation of an "unusual situation of conversation" (Argelander, 1970) and not from the grading of symptoms into a nosological grid, in the sense of a medical diagnosis. This specific approach to dialog should enable the analysand to freely structure the conversation and to thereby construct his own individual scene. Instead of using conventional conversation techniques, the analyst takes the attitude of "evenly suspended attention". This enables him to extract from the analysand's discourse that which is neither accessible in an explicit denotative sense, nor in a resonating deeper meaning (cf. Laimböck, 2011). What we hear with our "third ear" is the unconscious, which cheerfully communicates in supervision too – in the subtle nuancing of non-verbal and paraverbal communication (Buchholz, 2014; Buchholz & Reich, 2014; Buchholz, Spiekermann & Kächele, 2015). This is only possible if a frame is agreed upon, which is dedicated to the reflection of such unconscious scenic re-enactments through role ascription or assumption – this condition holds true for both supervisee and supervisor (or analyst and analysand). If the analyst is too ready to don the doctor's white coat and reacts to laments too quickly by diagnosing and clarifying, he may then damage the playfully exploring relatedness. Likewise, a supervisor introducing diagnosis instruments and behavioral recommendations may prove helpful, only not in a psychoanalytic way. The psychoanalytic supervisor is no expert with a case full of knowledge and techniques. He is an expert at enabling unusual situations of conversation in order then to decipher, together with the client, the unconscious content of the related situation – and "situation" means here according to the framework agreement, the relationship of the supervisee to the propounded vocational field or conflict. Consequently, criticism of the eclectic adoption of psychoanalytic concepts and techniques does not arise from the idea that this cannot be helpful or advantageous in some way; but that it is not compatible with major components of analysis – in particular, free association, transference and evenly suspended attention. Now, of course, supervision is not analysis and it is not based on generating an elaborate transference space. Transference phenomena matter, but they are interpreted together and in an exemplary way. Is it then not possible to apply techniques? Yes, but not without some loss: Because supervision, which specifically tries to utilize present relationship experience within the supervisorial field (Baranger & Baranger, 2008 [1961]; Vollmer & Pires, 2010) has to nurture the development of this experience and shouldn't hamper it by emphasizing techniques and specific actions.

This criticism applies also to the adoption of OPD diagnosis. OPD was developed as a structural and relational diagnosis which added to that offered by the *Diagnostic and Statistical Manual of Mental Disorders* (DSM). Since then, it has, however, developed into a convenient and verifiable diagnosis grid, utilized by many practicing international analysts (particularly in training and application contexts). In its use as an interview manual, it changes the situation of the conversation. The desire to explore particular patterns of conflict and structure renders it impossible to allow the spontaneous unfolding of the patient's communication, and at the same time, to direct one's evenly suspended attention to him, without watching out for single items. Consequently, the same objections are valid for OPD diagnosis as for psychiatric models of diagnosis; namely, that it is not process diagnosis, but classification. This stance can, as a result, possibly limit the free unfolding of the analytic space.

However, in its implementation for supervision, this could prove to be an advantage, as this setting isn't a free analytic space, but a task-based cooperation. Nevertheless, if the preservation of maximum analytic open space is appreciated, we advise that the OPD diagnosis is used, at best, as a rating procedure during the final reflection of the supervisorial conversation. In therapeutic practice, discussion of the circumplex model of interpersonal behavior (OPD axis II) has worked well in helping patients to word the circular causality of their self-experience and how they are experienced by others. However, if this is not tied to a research context, we suggest that the items are not used, but the client is allowed to express himself freely, which will feel more natural to him.

Against the criticism made above, a proponent of the idea to remove elements of psychoanalysis – we want to call them "building kit modules" – to be used in different frames might bring up two fields of application where modularization is not only useful, but also needed. The first field of application is research in psychodynamic counseling work. Research often takes place in a laboratory situation, with the researcher trying to change only one variable and to keep the others constant, if possible. From the research perspective, it seems quite legitimate to focus *only* on conflict, *only* on defense or *only* on countertransference, when working with executives and entrepreneurs, about whom, viewed through psychoanalytic eyes, we know so little in comparison to patients. In Chapter 5, we describe some research projects that use such psychoanalytic building kit modules. The results of such research will provide valuable insights into working with executives and entrepreneurs, even for fully trained psychoanalysts, who believe that they are doing the "right" thing.

But principally these insights will be of use to those coaches and supervisors who are neither psychoanalysts nor psychotherapists trained in depth psychology. As much as we want, in this book, to encourage psychoanalysts and depth psychologists to work with executives and entrepreneurs, we particularly want to convert coaches and supervisors, who so far have made their journey via other paradigms, to psychodynamic thinking and working. This second group, in particular, needs access in small steps with the help of building kit modules, instead of training that lasts five years and more (see Chapter 3.3). These are facts of the market, to which we have to adjust. An access along the lines of "sink or swim" will not occur in this target group. Every university of economics that offers a psychoanalytic specialization will have to live with the dilemma that it releases graduates with a smattering of psychoanalytic knowledge, who work with clients on the basis of this knowledge and often are very successful. Also, we should realize that they are not fiddling with patients in an irresponsible way, but working with economic subjects placed high up on the structural level, who are looking for new perspectives, but do not necessarily need an analytic space as a patient would.

Also, Freud had no training analyst and, in the beginning, no access to the complete apparatus of psychoanalysis, which he had yet to develop. He experimented with theories, perspectives and interventions. In this sense, supervisors and coaches who are interested in psychoanalysis may absolutely at first remain in their own paradigms and selectively try out more and more psychoanalytic techniques and building kit modules, experimenting with them and acquiring their own experiences. And if, after their initial enthusiasm, these consultants keep at it and adopt more and more modules and techniques, they round out their training. Maybe they will deploy a psychoanalyst as supervisor for their own cases, or will undergo their own self-orientation and thereby draw slowly closer to the training level of a psychoanalyst, without the ambition to heal patients. Instead, they might want to supervise and coach executives with the aid of their own profound business knowledge. Of course, it remains indisputable that such a consultancy service is not psychoanalysis, but psychodynamic business counseling.

The critic would partly agree with these arguments. For research, it is indispensable to determine clear and operationalized criteria, and it is OPD's great merit to have expanded the merely symptom-orientated diagnosis of the established classification systems (*International Classification of Diseases* [ICD] and DSM) by adding conflict and structure axes, and thereby entrenching a relational element in diagnosis. The critic could not, however, be able to approve the second part of the arguments above without qualification.

However, it is possible to settle on the fact, as suggested, that the term "psychodynamic" is broader than the term "psychoanalytic". It indicates at one end of the spectrum approaches which are working with psychoanalytic attitude; and at the other end, procedures which utilize analytic insights into the area of personality structure, even if these are based on other paradigms.

5 The state of research

In this chapter, we will outline the state of research on coaching and super-vision (with regard to organizational contexts and psychodynamic approaches) and give information on the most important methods. In both areas, the state of research is by no means consolidated; so far, studies can hardly build on an established stock of findings. As the numerous, and partly very diverse fields of action and paradigms of intervention would lead one to expect, very diverse research approaches materialize: Explorative and hermeneutic approaches take up a lot of space; however, there are also social science concepts such as action research – particularly originating in management and psychotherapy research – as well as first attempts at empirical impact research.

5.1 Supervision research

There is a shortfall of research both on psychodynamic coaching and psycho-analytic supervision. The craft of psychoanalytic supervision was developed in response to the practical requirements of analytical training and was only later reinforced by research. Although there were survey and single-case studies in the 1960s (cf. Hamburger & Mertens, 2016), they were often one-sided and did not include the perspective of supervisees (Cabaniss, Glick & Roose, 2001). A specialty of research approaches with a focus on psychoanalytic as well as general supervision is their multi-perspectivity: We find social-scientifically influenced studies (Rappe-Giesecke, 2013; Möller, 2001; Haubl, 2013) next to effectiveness and process studies originating in the tradition of psychotherapy research (Hechler, 2005; Buchholz, 2016; Mertens & Hamburger, 2016; Erhardt, Bergmann, Kalisch, Senf & Hamburger, 2016); qualitative-hermeneutic studies stand next to quantitative-empirical ones, which often use a triangulation of methods (i.e. Nagell, Steinmetzer, Fissabre & Spilski, 2014; cf. the literature review in Hamburger & Mertens, 2016).

5.1.1 Efficacy research

Efficacy is a hard term to define in the context of the many approaches and appli-cations of supervision. When it is employed in training, it denotes a specific

DOI: 10.4324/9781003169673-5

increase in competence in the areas of relational and reflective ability. When used in an institutional context, as in team or executive supervision, then indicators like an improvement of the institutional climate and job satisfaction, or ultimately even benchmarking figures, would be relevant, characterizing the fulfillment of the institution's primary task. However, such global indicators are influenced by too many factors to ascribe their efficacy to supervision. One of the rare attempts to directly measure the efficacy of supervision, based on the result of the supervised action, originates in behavior therapy research. Sipos (2001) analyzed 51 female patients with anorexia nervosa who were treated with a structured therapy program, with and without supervision of the therapist performing behavior therapy. The supervised group showed a significant improvement in the quality of the therapy process; however, there was no greater reduction in anorexia nervosa symptoms than in the non-supervised group (which the female author ascribes to a ceiling effect). Interestingly, supervision seems to have less influence on the direct output, but more influence on the quality of relationship between the supervisor and his patient. Research results that prove an immediate influence on the output – for example, Kilminster and Jolly (2000); Bambling, King, Raue, Schweitzer and Lambert (2006) – all relate to significantly reduced concepts of supervision, in the sense of instructions combined with a certain treatment method. Where supervision is not geared to rehearsal of techniques, but to reflecting process quality, research results tend to mirror instead an improvement in relational quality (Willutzki, Tönnies & Meyer, 2005; Schay, Dreger & Siegele, 2006). Likewise, for non-clinical utilization of supervision, Petzold, Schigl, Fischer and Höfner (2003), in their literature survey, note a research deficit regarding the impact of supervision on the client system.

However, efficacy research that is operationalized to the output is not really suitable for supervision. Haubl (2012) criticizes the use of the term "efficacy", adopted from psychotherapy research, which is based on the ideal of a control group design. He contrasts it with the model of "effectiveness", the practical testing of the supervision approach in its field of utilization, which is used in naturalistic studies. Likewise, the objective of supervision is never an a priori defined constant. It is only negotiated in the course of the process.

> The wording of the objective in supervision itself is a dynamic process. Unconscious motives are just as much an issue as an asked for conscious structure of motive. ... Efficacy research in supervision must not harm the supervisorial process by asking if its work target has been met/not met. Supervision isn't just a linear process, which can be shown in a pre-post comparison.
>
> (Möller, 2001, p. 87)

And this objective is not explicitly determined, even if this would be desirable (Moga & Cabaniss, 2014). Accordingly, supervision likewise cannot be casually defined. The self-assessment of supervisors and supervisees has proved feasible, even though it is prone to desirability bias. Studies about satisfaction with supervision regularly score high results (Steinmetzer, Nagell & Fissabre, 2016).

Orlinsky and Ronnestad (2005) examined more than 5,000 therapists and con-
cluded that supervision is more than predominantly assessed as helpful: Alto-
gether, 95 per cent of those asked, currently in supervision, assessed it as
"beneficial", and 79 per cent as "highly beneficial" for their current development. Psychotherapists valued supervision as significant, particularly at the
beginning of their training, but not only then: Most interviewees reported that
they made more use of supervision than they were required to. Fifty-three per
cent of therapists with seven to 15 years of work experience, and 39 per cent
with 15 to 25 years of work experience stated that they still made use of
supervision on a regular basis (Orlinsky & Ronnestad, 2005, pp. 3411–3419).

The quality of the working relationship is regarded as the main effect factor of
supervisorial success. From a psychotherapeutic perspective, Scobel (1991 [1989],
p. 51) suggests four factors of supervisorial effect: (1) personal relief for the psychotherapist (supervisee) through introspection; (2) the supervisor as the accepting
conscious mind of the supervisee; (3) the processing of psychological conflict; and
(4) insight and change. Horvath and Greenberg (1989) developed an instrument
called the Working Alliance Inventory (WAI), which measures the aspects of the
working relationship mentioned by Bordin (1979): the task within the framework
of the session, the mutual bond and the goal to be reached.

A study of 78 supervisor–supervisee pairs from 28 psychoanalytic training institutes (Nagell et al., 2014; Steinmetzer et al., 2016) focused on the influence of supervision on the analytical identity of the supervisee; the satisfaction of all involved; as
well as the difference between the assessment of the supervisor and the supervisee
("fit"). Furthermore, it considered differences between novice and advanced supervisees and supervisors as well as the coherence of different supervisorial styles and
the layout of the supervisorial frame in terms of identity and satisfaction. As a result,
four working styles were identified: The "experience and relationship oriented"
work style showed the highest satisfaction rate in both participant groups, followed by the "encouraging-supportive" work style. More common, however, were
the "defensive controlling" and the "pragmatic" work style (Steinmetzer et al., 2016,
p. 78). The study showed that the supervisees' expectations and the supervisors'
assumptions were far from being always congruent. A further result was that

> the supervisorial relationship … in the advanced stage was more anxiety-
> free, more open, more fruitful and more characterized by willingness to
> learn. The evaluation of the factors "identity" and "satisfaction" reinforce
> this impression, as more advanced pairs were also more satisfied with the
> supervision, saw a greater profit for the patient and the supervisee and a
> more distinct "analytical identity" of the supervisee.
>
> (Steinmetzer et al., 2016, p. 78)

5.1.2 Process research

As in newer psychotherapy research, so in supervision research too, the quantitative capture of efficacy is less relevant than the identification of effect factors

and task-specific strengths. In this case, the delaying of research on supervision has been an advantage: The emphasis on effect size had only led to the familiar result that all examined forms of psychotherapy showed comparable results, however, with differing psychotherapy procedures. As the dodo in Lewis Carroll's *Alice's Adventures in Wonderland* says: "everybody has won and all must have prizes". Subsequently, the research on efficacy refrained from generalizing comparisons and proceeded to disorder-specific studies and specifically to approaches of process research. The process research on supervision draws on isolated preliminary studies.

At an early stage, individual psychoanalysts had begun to describe supervisorial progress in detail. Fleming and Benedek (1966; cf. Hamburger & Mertens, 2016) compared the supervision of two training candidates, one with a newly begun and one with an advanced treatment. Four hundred audio transcripts were compiled and reduced to five sessions each. The sessions were rated according to therapeutic progress and supervisorial teaching; learning problems were also identified. In the results, the following primary tasks of supervision appear: (1) support of the treatment process; (2) support of the candidate regarding his development in relation to the psychoanalyst; and (3) the objectification of his learning experiences.

This as yet roughly coded study of supervisorial transcripts was refined further with the advancement of procedures for process analysis. Buchholz (2016) points out that "a detailed process analysis of the actual communication during the session ... comes closer to the specifics of supervision than research, oriented toward an outcome or abstractly defined content, skills, interventions, etc., which have first to be interpreted" (p. 84). For this, he uses the method of conversation analysis, which reacts particularly to the "how of speaking".

> In supervision, the small and fleeting particles, the "how" of speaking, is just as relevant (to access the atmosphere and reception of the spoken) as "what" is being said. This includes details of the verbal, mimic, vocal and gestural [type].
> (Buchholz, 2016, p. 84)

As a result of his conversation-analytical process study, Buchholz (2013, 2016) determines a stage model of supervision. Using a framework of interactive, cognitive and affective task orientations, the model describes the development from "non-professional" over different phases of study up to the "novice", and finally, the "experienced professional". Here we must highlight the results of this study concerning the affective task: The supervisorial process here could be described as a transition from the stage of "apathy" (differences are being denied), through the stages of "incongruence" ("someone notices that there is 'still something' but is as yet not able to face it with complete attention") and "exploration" ("curiosity to use affective experiencing to deepen understanding") up to the stage of "integration" ("even complicated or tabooed, for example, sexual feelings can be perceived in supervision and become part of the conversation") (Buchholz, 2013; 2016, p. 88).

Busse, Hansen and Lohse (2013) consider the course of a session by identifying moments of "re-centering" in the session transcripts. In the end, standardized coding processes such as the Instrument zur Kodierung von Diskussionen (IKD) (Instrument for Coding of Discussions; Schermuly & Scholl, 2011) can become the bedrock of an empirical study of relevant process variables (Kotte & Möller, 2013).

Many of the research efforts so far belong to the fields of psychotherapy and social work or are situated in associated training contexts. In these fields, supervision, as a rule, aims to impart, maintain and expand individual skills.

5.1.3 Analysis of institutions, action research and ethnographic method

Sociological research has made an ample contribution to supervision. Such research has extensively demonstrated objective hermeneutics by taking the example of a supervision session in a psychoanalytically orientated clinic for psychosomatic medicine (Oevermann 1993a, 1993b, 2010 [2001]). Sequential analysis, a method principally applicable to all interaction protocols and serving to disclose action-relevant deep structures within a society, strives to reconstruct the unfolding of a text along its chronological axis to determine, without bias and by everyday knowledge of every single speech segment, its action-directing relevance for the social system examined (for example, the supervision group). In the analysis of the session, which discusses the imminent ending of the in-patient therapy of an anorexic female patient, interesting overlaps of institutionally and psychodynamically relevant aspects become apparent. The patient had developed a strong cathexis for the clinic and the one-on-one therapist, and the latter finds himself caught in the middle, between the demands of a time-limited hospitalization and an unfolding therapeutic relationship, which he wants to shape according to the model of a free psychoanalytic practice with a flexible time frame. The author interprets this as a "relationship trap – namely, to reduce the externally determined structural problem to an internal working bond dynamic and to expect to solve it in this way" (Oevermann, 2010 [2001], pp. 249–250; see also 1993a, 1993b); a relationship trap which is reflected in the lack of differentiation between individual and team supervision and in an unresolved working bond in the supervision itself. However, Oevermann's "objectivity" has to be doubted; this is because throughout his discussion, his decided assessment becomes visible between the lines – namely, that the only "state of the art" treatment for the anorexic patient is "an analytically oriented psychotherapy … within which the working bond 'a priori' would have no time limit but would be ended in a flexible way, according to its organic self-determined development" (Oevermann, 2010 [2001], p. 253; see also 1993a, 1993b). Oevermann's analysis designates a socio-structural problem, which becomes visible as a conflict between profitability and process autonomy, with supervision taking place in the framework of psychosomatic medicine. At the same time, it misses the point, because it determines the conflict between stationary reality and an idealized psychoanalytically orientated therapy concept to be "insoluble" (Oevermann, 2010 [2001], p. 255; see also 1993a, 1993b). In this respect, Oevermann's project is significant for our issue – namely, supervision in organizations: If the "great analysis" looms in the background as an unreflected ideal, then supervisorial processes can change into a "lose–lose" situation; the analytic situation implicitly desired by both cannot be established and the desire turns into failure. By contrast, the analytical attitude in the institutional field is precisely maintained because the limitation and tight focus are clearly acknowledged.

Other groups of sociological researchers have likewise used data from supervisions as the subject of their social science papers and have radicalized Oevermann's approach. According to Buer (2012, p. 47), "good supervisors are to be seen as the primary researchers: together with their supervisees they gain experiences in a mutual process with the aim to change the experiences the supervisee brought along". According to Buer (2012), the process method is the abduction, a creative oscillating between solution patterns created either in an inductive way (by generalizing experiences) or in a deductive way (by subsuming according to rules). He views the task of the supervisor in this "research-setting" as providing space for a creative loosening up. Buer sees this as an example of action research, which is then secondarily documented and analyzed in different ways by researchers; as examples, he mentions the projects of Möller (2001), Siller (2008) and Gotthardt-Lorenz, Hausinger and Sauer (2012, 2013). The latter compare the proceeding in supervision with the process of the progressive formation of hypotheses arising from content, as in grounded theory; in this way, they likewise see the supervisorial process itself as a research process.

This emphasis on the supervisor as a researcher in her/his own field is well known in the history of psychoanalysis: In his "postscript" to the question of lay analysis, Freud (1926b) describes a program to acquire a gradual clarification within the framework of the analytical situation with ever more precise nosological and personality-focused psychological skills – these skills will then be available, on the one hand, for the clarification of psychological fundamentals; and on the other, as arguments in discourses in cultural and social theory, for example. The problem of this program is that it has often been seen as self-empowerment and a circular justification of theory and practice. Of course, this was not Freud's intention; on the contrary, he cautioned against the careless utilization of supposedly complete insights in practice and viewed the analytical process as an open research situation.

A comparable objection was raised to the conception of supervision as a research process. The

> aspiration to use supervision as an "applied science" risks counterproductive effects. Because, with this aspiration in mind it has to be demanded of supervisors to be and … to remain "state-of-the-art". Leaving aside the fact that most research results remain controversial, supervisors who accept this challenge are an exception: most of them ignore research results or notice only those approving their own practice.
>
> (Haubl, 2012, p. 349)

As in the case of research linked to psychoanalysis, if the supervisor-researcher succumbs to the temptation only to see (and to confirm) his own concepts instead of differentiating them in implementation and being open to the unknown, then her/his research results will not convince. Action research offers the opportunity to learn something new and to conceptualize, but there is no guarantee. To adequately meet the demands of qualitative research, minimum requirements such as adequate documentation of the processes and a transparent segmentation are necessary. If these are adhered to, then convincing social-scientific results can be found through supervision as a social-scientific instrument of research (Rappe-Giesecke, 2013).

Using the material from supervision groups in this way, typical communicative structures in institutions can be reconstructed. Giesecke and Rappe-Giesecke (1997) examined the processes of Balint groups as developing forms of communication, in which "normal forms of expectation" are being negotiated and changed. From the human-factors science viewpoint, the demand for supervision shows a problematization of work environments (Siller, 2008, 2016) and constitutes a mirror of institutional structures and processes. In this way, supervision processes serve as "research instruments ... to, with their help, clarify typical professional and institutional attitudes in a psychoanalytic sense" (Becker, 1995b, p. 186).

Möller (2001) uses an innovative methodology, converting the interviewed supervision experts into researchers in their own field, by inviting them to form their own hypotheses and to describe their own actions. After an initial standard format analysis of audiotaped supervision sessions based on the method of Giesecke and Rappe-Giesecke (1997), followed by a depth-hermeneutic evaluation taking into account irritations and breaks, the experts were asked to listen again, in stimulated recall-interviews to their sessions, one intervention after the other, together with the researcher, and to give an as exact account as possible of which reflections, feelings, secondary thoughts, etc., engaged them in that moment, to receive as accurate as possible an account of the group process. In this way, the dynamic between the experts and the researcher was incorporated in a self-reflecting way. In her results, the researcher found types of interventions which she again presented to the experts for validation. From the interpretational acting on the first level (of the supervised therapy), via the supervisorial interpretation, the norm model and depth-hermeneutic analysis, the self-confronting interview, typing and the renewed triangulation with the experts, through to the final appropriation by the readers, Möller unfolds a process of identification of criteria, fruitful in practice, for "good" supervision (2001, p. 95). Möller presents 18 skill areas as her result. They touch on aspects such as task orientation, field competence, triangulation competence, abstinence, transference, resistance, resource orientation and the understanding of different roles by supervisors.

Ethno-psychoanalytic approaches in social research are a neighboring field of action research, going back to the work of Georges Devereux (1967) and to the ethno-psychoanalytic research tradition (Parin, Morgenthaler & Parin-Matthèy, 1963, 1971; Adler, 1993; Nadig, 1986). Its significance for supervision within organizations is to be seen in "ethno-psychoanalysis, teaching us to allow our own culture to become foreign to us" (Möller & Pühl, 2012, p. 283). On the other hand, "the entering of a consultant into a new organizational culture equals a 'going into the foreign to discover a foreign culture'" (Nadig, 1986). Becker (1995b) similarly sees team supervision as "ethno-psychoanalysis of psychiatric institutions". The methodology focuses mainly on the term "organizational culture" as a – for the members of the organization – partially conscious, partially unconscious pattern of anthropology, norms and symbol systems. In detail, these are:

1   World view, anthropological premises on human behavior, concepts of truth as well as assumptions on contexts, environment, interhuman interaction and humanitarian questions;
2   Norms and regulations for staff, moral values, style of manners with colleagues and clients;
3   Code of conduct, dress code, interior decoration, rituals, identity-establishing narrations about founder, staff and history of organization.

(Möller & Pühl, 2012, p. 279)

Types of organizations as well as culture-defining leaders (including their style-defining personal pathology, cf. Möller & Pühl, 2012, p. 280) can be delineated, as can their opponents and also the institutional mythology. Such myths are only faintly comprehensible by means of processual diagnosis and by contextual understanding (Möller & Pühl, 2012, p. 281).

Beyond organizational diagnosis, the ethno-psychoanalytic approach is also useful for practical reference. Möller & Pühl (2012) transfer this model to organization analysis by, on the one hand, emphasizing the necessity of "introducing a dialog structure to induce, cultivate and maintain understanding and comprehending [of] processes" (p. 286), because "the only thing the participants in this process of cultural analysis have at their command is the relationship they experience with one another" (p. 286). On the other hand, they also draw a very practical conclusion from the ethno-psychoanalytical approach for supervisorial work in organizations:

The consultant, too, must have the opportunity of oscillating between two cultures, namely between the foreign, advice seeking, and his own familiar culture. His own culture is made up of his study group, where he can discuss sensitive situations of his consultancy work.

(Möller & Pühl, 2012, p. 286)

It is vital to have this meta-supervision as an assisting background in order not to become absorbed by the foreign culture (for example, no longer understanding it due to being too close) or to protect oneself against it by devaluing it.

5.1.4 Scenic-narrative microanalysis in supervision research

The method of scenic-narrative microanalysis (SNMA; Hamburger, 2017) has been developed since 2007, in the context of the re-analysis of interviews with contemporary witnesses (Laub & Hamburger, 2017). The procedure serves to identify significant moments of relatedness in interview interaction, taking into account verbal, paraverbal, mimic and gestural signals, and directing its focus onto conscious and unconscious resonance phenomena (Boston Change Process Study Group, 2002, 2008; Stern, 2004). In the psychoanalytic interview, and in supervisorial situations too, there occur unconscious scenes between analyst and supervisee or analysand (Lorenzer, 1970; Argelander, 1970), and these scenes implicitly contain exactly that which cannot be remembered consciously. Trained experts in scenic-narrative microanalysis first describe the material independently of each other, and then evaluate it with respect to the pre-dominant transference–countertransference scene in the interview situation. After every evaluation round, they discuss the results in a joint session, and the participants try to find a consensus on the processed interview. This consensus session is also recorded and transcribed. After the session, the moderators phrase a hypothesis which, in conclusion, is presented to the rater group and changed if necessary, either by consensus or by documenting the dissenting single votes. In the result, all documented phases of the evaluation process are brought together and the evaluation and consensus process is summarized in a transparent way. This narrative summary corresponds to a classical clinical-casuistic reconstruction, but with a changed goal setting, in accordance with the assignment of the studied process (interviews with contemporary witnesses, supervision session, etc.); and with enhanced validity and reliability, by means of reflection on the research process at different levels as well as a commitment to the meticulously documented material. This very sophisticated research method was developed on the basis of video testimonies from the *Yale Video Testimony Study* (Hamburger, 2015, 2017), and has subsequently been further refined using numerous videos of various types of interaction. The SNMA approach rests mainly on the assumption that paraverbal, mimic and gestural signal levels contribute and go back to the dynamic of earlier rhythmic com-munication highlighted in developmental-psychoanalytical research (Sander, 1988; Stern 1995; Beebe & Lachmann, 2002) in analogy to musical rhythm experiences (Grassi, 2014). The earliest experiences of entrainment turn into independent sources of motivation for the infant (Lichtenberg, 2014, pp. 157–159) and are more significant than the libidinal sources of instinct assumed by Freud. The process of psychotherapeutic sessions can be described in the same way (Stern & Boston Change Process Study Group, 2012 [2010]; Beebe & Lachmann, 2002) and the same is true for aesthetic processes (Hamburger & Wernz, 2015). Rhythm is being studied as a concurrence of the conversation participant's experience of presence in "now moments" or "moments of meet-ing" (Stern, 2004). This concurrence is experienced as the arrival of an expec-tation. The SNMA is a rater process, which recognizes such moments in the documented conversation protocols. In a second step, they are analyzed in her-meneutic focus groups, where multi-modal matching (i.e. in speech rhythm and in mimic-gestural rhythmizations) has to be considered.

The first results of utilizing this microanalytic method with supervision pro-tocols in the area of youth aid (Lechat, 2017) show that the method is able to capture a subliminal group dynamic, which is possibly connected to the dynamic of the case in the sense of a psychoanalytic parallel process. In the context of supervision and coaching, an ongoing study on change management in German institutions of youth aid working with SNMA is particularly important (Schmidt, in preparation).

5.2 Coaching research

5.2.1 Previous results

In 2005, Künzli published a comparative summary of 22 empirical research papers on impact and effect factors in executive coaching, published up to 2004 in the German and Anglo-Saxon language regions. At that time, retrospective cross-section studies predominated, using their own questionnaires and qualitative evaluation with usually fewer than ten participants (Künzli, 2005, pp. 233–234).

Outstanding at this time is the study by Thach (2002) with N = 281 and three measurement time points. In a large company, 281 executives took part in a coaching process, which began with a questionnaire containing 17 questions about leadership skills. Two follow-up inquiries were carried out with reduced questionnaires. The result was that leadership skills were estimated as being 55 to 60 per cent higher than before (Thach, 2002, pp. 205–214).

In 2003, a German questionnaire study with 42 coaches, 27 clients and 36 further coach–client dyads assessed influencing variables, effects and effect coherencies in coaching. The results showed that coaching is an effective intervention with a positive impact on the client's self-reflection and behavior. Willingness to change and psychological strain on the client's side, as well as the transparency of the coaching concept and the coach's use of a participatory approach are the elements that promise success (Jansen, Mäthner & Bachmann, 2003, p. 253).

Early coaching research had some deficiencies. Randomized control trials (RCTs) were non-standard, effect sizes were not determined and the quality criteria of many measuring instruments were more than obscure. However, during the last ten years, studies have clearly become more professionalized. A study by Leonard-Cross (2010, cited by Möller, 2016, p. 3) showed that after a biennial coaching, participants, in comparison to a control group, showed higher results in terms of a belief in their self-efficacy. Möller (2016, p. 3) cites further positive effects in terms of performance changes, more effective leadership, enhanced interpersonal relationships, better cooperation and communication skills, changed management of conflict, improved self-reflection, self-acceptance and personality development (Möller, 2016, p. 3).

From the most up-to-date overview of core results of existing meta-analyses of coaching studies, which are underpinned by quantitative data and sufficient information about the determination of effect sizes, it is clear that recent research literature has improved in quality (Kotte, Hinn, Oellerich & Möller, 2016, p. 6). Based on the available meta-analyses, coaching has positive effects, even if effect sizes fluctuate noticeably within and between the meta-analyses.

Accordingly, impact research and effect factor research will become less necessary. It is obvious, however, that the coachee rates the coaching success significantly higher than others do. Future studies should in consequence be based also on external assessment, alongside self-assessment, so as not to overestimate coaching success. So far, no clear link between coaching of a specific duration and coaching success could be established. In this respect, future research will also have to embrace the "seriousness" of the objective (Kotte et al., 2016, p. 6).

Face-to-face coaching and mixed forms, including e-mail contacts, Skype meetings and other forms of communication, cannot be differentiated with respect to their impact. The importance of the coach–coachee relationship for coaching success can be meta-analytically confirmed. When it comes to a coach's distinguishing features for coaching success, then internal as opposed to external coaches seem to have an advantage, due to their knowledge about the company and its line of business. With respect to qualifications, a mix of psychological and organizational know-how is more efficient than just psychological or just organizational knowledge. Finally, meta-analyses provide evidence for significant differences between samples amongst student coaches and "real" coaches (i.e. professionals) in such a way that the effect on students leads to an overestimation of the effects in the field. This result emphasizes the need for validated coaching research, using real coaches and professionals as coachees (Kotte et al., 2016, p. 7).

Focusing on psychodynamic consulting work, it is notable that currently only studies about efficiency exist, and these do not differentiate between the coaching methods used; and that the analysis of effect factors refers only to formal and not to method-specific aspects. So far, there are no studies on psychodynamic coaching. Generally, there are also no studies about coaching which compare the efficiency of different methods. Coaching research as yet is far removed from more in-depth studies about the efficiency of single psychodynamic effect principles (for example, the interpretation of countertransference). In the following sub-section, the authors present their own research projects, which deal with partial aspects of psychodynamic coaching. The line of thinking behind these projects might encourage readers to further develop these fledgling approaches or to design new research approaches of this kind.

5.2.2 *Personality tests from a psychodynamic perspective*

When it comes to test instruments, the psychoanalytic paradigm has to make up a lot of leeway in comparison to classical scientific psychology. The first author (Kretschmar) perceives the necessity of establishing diagnostics based on validated instruments. On the one hand, this is necessary for research purposes; and on the other hand, business clients are increasingly demanding valid methods similar to those for psychotherapy, for which health insurers as sponsors expect methodical criteria in application forms. In terms of personality diagnosis, psychoanalysis has nothing comparable to offer when it comes to a classical personality inventory such as the Revised NEO Personality Inventory (NEO-PI-R; Costa & McRae, 1992). However, if we conduct diagnosis in business counseling with classical scientific instruments, but use interventions based on psychodynamic methods, a methodological inconsistency arises. Why should we not, from the very beginning, diagnose in the personality the dimensions of conflict and motivation with which we will later work? In this respect, OPD's conflict axis (see Chapter 4.10.3) seems to offer a springboard.

In 2015, the first author developed a self-description inventory with 196 items (seven conflicts, seven spheres of life, two modes, each with two items). The items were derived from the OPD work material (OPD Task Force, 2008, pp. 4194–4199). For a better understanding, as shown in Table 5.1, these items are sorted according to conflicts (K), spheres (S), and modes (M) with the characteristics active (a) and passive (p). However, within the self-description inventory, they appear randomized and are listed according to numbering.

The assessment uses the usual four-level OPD scale from 0 (absent) to 3 (very significant). In the evaluation, to start with, points per conflict are added up, mode notwithstanding. Depending on the conflict, a score between 0 points (all 28 items absent) and up to 84 points (all 28 items very significant) can be obtained. This score serves as an indication of the general significance of the particular conflict. In a second evaluation, the points per conflict and mode are added up separately. Afterwards, the sum of the passive mode is subtracted from the sum of the active mode. Thus, per conflict, a score ranging from -42 (all passive items very significant and all active items absent) up to 42 points (all passive items absent and all active items very significant) can be reached. This score serves as an indication for the mode of the conflict. The same procedure is then repeated in the evaluation of each sphere of life.

The question as to whether it is reasonable to survey unconscious conflicts by using self-description questionnaires – meaning in a direct, explicit way and not through the assessment of an external expert – has been met with skepticism (cf. Dinger et al., 2014). Nevertheless, in recent years, instruments have been developed based on OPD's relationship and structural axes and have been verified in terms of their psychometric properties (Ehrenthal et al., 2012; Zimmermann et al., 2014).

A first empirical study (N = 187) of the self-description items of the conflict axis set forth in Table 5.1 yielded poor psychometric characteristics of the items, in terms of item difficulty, selectivity and internal consistency. Various exploratory and factor analytic trials provided no evidence that the items themselves could be sorted according to the conflict structure postulated by OPD (rather, it was the various spheres of life which could be described as underlying factors).

Furthermore, the comprehensibility of the items deduced from OPD and their apparently logical validity are doubtful, as they are often ambiguous or contain contradictory contents or intertwined statements, which again lead to results which are difficult to interpret.

Even if indications exist as to the convergent and discriminant validity of the conflict axis gathered by external assessment (Pieh, Frisch, Meyer, Loew & Lahmann,

Table 5.1 Excerpt self-description

Conflict	Sphere	Mode	No.	Item
C1	P	a	42	In a relationship my personal independence is very important for me.
C1	P	a	140	In a relationship I usually decide about the shared way of life.
C1	S	p	73	In my spare time I commit to groups and their cohesion.
C1	S	p	171	In my spare time I seek an association with groups over individual contacts.
C2	B	p	57	I gladly surrender to intimate sensations.
C2	B	p	155	I feel at the mercy of my bodily demands and needs.
C2	F	a	96	Parental power is a requirement of good care.
C2	F	a	194	During my childhood and youth I was quite a rebel.
C4	W	a	50	What you have is what you are.
C4	W	a	148	I take a pride in what I own and what I built up.
C6	J	a	18	I like vocational competition.
C6	J	a	116	I change my professional jobs frequently.
C6	P	p	49	Long-running relationships are more about safety than physical attraction.
C6	P	p	147	My intimate partner is my senior.
C7	W	p	33	Having gives more safety than being.
C7	W	p	131	I never quite know on what to spend my money.

2009; Schneider, Mendler, Heuft & Burgmer, 2008), a self-description instrument of the conflict axis that offers a balance between the requirements of reliability and validity is, however, missing to the best of our knowledge.

When it comes to the further development of a psychometric-psychodynamic personality test, we have now reached a crossroads: Either we wait for OPD-3 or we revise the concept which will definitely lead to new items and, possibly, to a different structuring of conflicts. In this case, the psychodynamic counseling work would depart from clinical OPD.

Despite all the methodological weaknesses, it is nevertheless possible, even today, to work with the self-description inventory, especially if coach and coachee analyze the results together. In the evaluation, the result must be very critically correlated to other observations. The self-description inventory has already produced positive results in the initial diagnosis of many coachings (see case examples 6.1 and 6.2 in Chapter 6).

5.2.3 Identification of blind spots in countertransference

In Chapter 4.10.3, we described how the OPD conflict axis could be utilized to analyze the motive structure and personality of a client. In the technique described here, the diagnostic criteria for countertransference in OPD are the main points of interest. As shown in Chapter 4.6, the utilization of countertransference in work with clients means that the coach makes use of her/his own unconscious as an instrument of analysis. The challenges posed to this method come from the coach's blind spots. If the coach has no conscious awareness of her/his own conflicts, then this can lead to a misjudgment of the client.

A further operationalization of the OPD conflict diagnosis is necessary for a scientific approach to the topic "countertransference". Alongside the self-description inventory, in 2015, the first author (Kretschmar) also developed a countertransference inventory with 42 items (seven conflicts, two modes, with three items each). These items were likewise drawn from the work material of OPD (OPD Task Force, 2008, pp. 4194–4199).

The assessment uses the usual four-level OPD scale from 0 (absent) to 3 (very significant). In the evaluation, the points per conflict are added up first, mode notwithstanding. Depending on the conflict, a score between 0 points (all six items absent) and 18 points (all six items very significant) can be obtained. This score serves to indicate the general significance of the particular conflict. In a second evaluation, the points per conflict and per mode are added up separately. Afterwards, the sum of the passive mode is subtracted from the sum of the active mode. Thus, for each conflict, a score ranging from -9 (all passive items very significant and all active items absent) up to 9 points (all passive items absent and all active items very significant) can be reached. This score serves as an indication for the mode of the conflict.

The countertransference inventory has already been tested by employees of the Mind Institute SE in Berlin, in the rating of clients as well as with characters featured in movies, and also in the mutual rating of colleagues. It soon became evident that colleagues who rated the same person came up with different results (raising the issue of interrater reliability). The greatest differences became apparent with conflicts in which the rater assumed himself to have a blind spot in the form of his own unresolved conflict. Other conflicts produced similar results. The results of the first test made it clear that the countertransference inventory in its present form cannot be utilized unless the problem of the rater-specific blind spots is first solved.

A solution for the problem of blind spots can only be found if rater-specific deviation can be systematized. These deviations could then be subtracted out by means of rater-specific corrective factors so that the inventory can become an instrument with adequate interrater reliability, which could be handled even by untrained raters. We will explain the analysis of systematic deviations by reference to Figure 5.1, using the example of care conflict.

To begin with, the raters R1 up to R7 employ the countertransference inventory on clients C1 up to C7. A sample result is shown in Figure 5.1. Then an objective rating is subtracted from the implemented rating, as shown in the

Table 5.2 Excerpt from countertransference inventory

Conflict	Mode	No.	Item
C1	p	1	To me X is very clinging and dependent.
C1	a	36	I think I rather don't want to have anything to do with X.
C2	p	2	I think X wants to accept a subordinate role to me.
C2	a	37	I feel debased or mortified by X.
C3	p	3	I feel constrained, exploited and blackmailed by X.
C3	a	38	To me X seems envious because others receive more.
C4	p	4	X makes me feel the need to support and affirm her/him.
C4	a	39	I feel the need to knock X off her/his perch.
C5	p	5	I feel the need to excuse X or to relieve her/him from her/his responsibility.
C5	a	40	I feel the need to confront X with her/his responsibility.
C6	p	6	I feel unattracted or lacking an erotic interest toward X.
C6	a	41	I fear in the end to be found inadequate and be dumped by X.
C7	p	7	To me X seems without an identity of her/his own.
C7	a	42	I feel the need to fix X to a certain identity.

middle part of the figure. As this is objective, the results for a client must always be the same. Alternatively, the mean value of the ratings of all raters here is assumed to be objective. It would be even better if an OPD-trained analyst issued the objective rating. The difference on the right-hand side of Figure 5.1 shows the systematic deviation of the rater in our model, which will

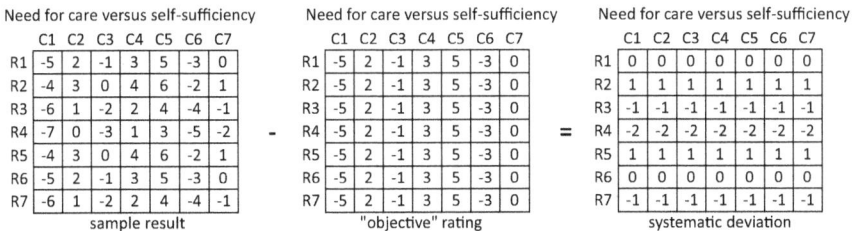

Need for care versus self-sufficiency

	C1	C2	C3	C4	C5	C6	C7
R1	-5	2	-1	3	5	-3	0
R2	-4	3	0	4	6	-2	1
R3	-6	1	-2	2	4	-4	-1
R4	-7	0	-3	1	3	-5	-2
R5	-4	3	0	4	6	-2	1
R6	-5	2	-1	3	5	-3	0
R7	-6	1	-2	2	4	-4	-1

sample result

$-$

Need for care versus self-sufficiency

	C1	C2	C3	C4	C5	C6	C7
R1	-5	2	-1	3	5	-3	0
R2	-5	2	-1	3	5	-3	0
R3	-5	2	-1	3	5	-3	0
R4	-5	2	-1	3	5	-3	0
R5	-5	2	-1	3	5	-3	0
R6	-5	2	-1	3	5	-3	0
R7	-5	2	-1	3	5	-3	0

"objective" rating

$=$

Need for care versus self-sufficiency

	C1	C2	C3	C4	C5	C6	C7
R1	0	0	0	0	0	0	0
R2	1	1	1	1	1	1	1
R3	-1	-1	-1	-1	-1	-1	-1
R4	-2	-2	-2	-2	-2	-2	-2
R5	1	1	1	1	1	1	1
R6	0	0	0	0	0	0	0
R7	-1	-1	-1	-1	-1	-1	-1

systematic deviation

Figure 5.1 Determination of rater-specific deviations

be the same with each of his clients. Even if such ideal-type deviations are not to be expected, we have had the experience that deviation within an OPD conflict is systematic, even though the figures for the actual results vary. This technique also shows coherences between the rater's own conflicts and his/her rater-specific deviation, if the raters themselves are also rated.

With such an instrument for the external assessment of business subjects, we can, for example, examine which motivation structure drawn from the OPD conflict axis and which occupational profile fit together. Fields of application for this could be career counseling and candidate selection. However, as yet, these approaches must be used with great care, as the conflict axis of OPD is not yet validated, as shown by the studies discussed in Chapter 5.2.2. Certainly, there is evidence of its validity, but there are also difficulties in showing the internal structure of conflicts in empirical studies. In this respect, both the application methods and the items themselves need a lot more work. Nevertheless, the instruments presented here have already proved to be of value in initial diagnosis in many coachings (see the case studies in Chapter 6).

5.2.4 The influence of inner objects on important life choices

In this research study, the katathym-imaginative psychotherapy described earlier is utilized in coaching for the processing of important life choices (see Chapter 3.3.2). In this sub-section, the influence of inner objects will be explained using the example of the inner mother. The decisions involved are those, made by adult persons, which influence the further structuring of life for the next years. Examples include entering into a partnership, separation, relocation to a foreign country, choice of profession or managerial decisions. As the experiences of both authors suggest, it seems to be a frequent objective of clients in terms of individuation, to sort themselves out and free themselves from the influence of their childhood person of reference when making decisions ("How do I know if it is I, or my mother within me, who wants that?"). Even if this objective cannot be completely fulfilled from an analytic perspective, as the inner mother cannot be "cut out", in this project, we will nevertheless try to clarify, to some extent at least, the influence of the inner mother by activating her in reverie.

Decision situations can be staged in reverie in many ways. If two equal alternatives for action exist, the client can imagine a path with a fork in it. He looks first in one direction and then in the other, and lets himself be drawn by the images coming up in him. In situations where a client must decide whether to hold on to certain ways of living or to change them, he can imagine a bridge over a river. He can then view and describe the landscapes on this side and on the other side of the river, and decide if he wants to cross the bridge.

If the coach doesn't touch on the topic of "mother", then the client will experience the reverie scenario described above in his present condition and state of mind. To determine the inner mother's potential influence on the situation after the client's decision (for example: "I will cross the bridge, but I am not quite sure yet"), the coach can suggest bringing in the mother: "Imagine your mother appears and you look at the bridge together." The impact of activating the mother object will then be reflected in the image, perhaps through a changed decision, whether the client crosses the bridge with his mother or leaves her on the other side. Since the mother, as an inner object, is working permanently in the client anyway and is now activated additionally, he now receives a "double mother dose". To reduce the mother's influence thereafter in his reverie, he devotes himself fully to her, empathizes with her and supplies her with all she needs. The mother will then turn her attention to these gifts; for example, a cheering, attentive crowd. After the mother's attention is diverted to herself, the client is asked to look again at the decision situation. It will then become clear whether the image has changed or if the client chooses to make a different decision (on working with inner parents, see Kretschmar & Tzschaschel, 2017, p. 112; on the transformation of objects in reverie in the case of devotion, see Kretschmar & Tzschaschel, 2017, pp. 104, 116).

This method has been tested with 11 clients so far. The following life decisions had to be made:

- accepting a job offer in a foreign country (Belgium);
- accepting a job offer in a foreign country (Africa);
- change of life partner, with two very close significant others existing (present partner and new partner);
- return to the United States after a long stay abroad;
- separation from partner (in three cases);
- taking a vocational gap-year;
- opening a new business in the United States;
- shutdown of an unprofitable but prized business branch;
- entering into a first intimate relationship.

From the conversations with these clients, the following findings emerge: Life decisions seem to be predominantly of the "bridge" type. Apparently, it all has to do with weighing attachment and habit against autonomy and advancement. If the influence of the mother is brought up, a tendency then becomes visible: In the majority of cases, clients drift away from her and decisions about crossing the bridge tend to be reinforced. This could indicate that the inner mother has an inhibiting effect on life decisions in the making. Clients experience the deactivation of the inner mother, by meeting her needs, as liberating. In two cases, the deactivation resulted in a clear reassessment and the decision not to leave the current situation as yet. In two cases, the inner mother was clearly viewed as a resource.

5.2.5 *Measuring defense*

In a further study, we initially addressed the conceptualization of psychodynamic defense mechanisms. The aim was to transfer the approach to the vocational world. The study was a first empirical attempt to identify collective psychodynamic defense mechanisms in organizations, using the Response

Evaluation Measure (REM-71), which maps 21 defense mechanisms in 71 items. The research results in three organizations (each time involving all employees) indicate that collective defense in organizations actually exists, and that the defense structures differ from one business to the next and in various work environments (Herkommer, Kretschmar, Kuchinke & Schnabel, 2017).

The study aimed to unearth initial indications that collective organizational defense mechanisms existed, in order to assess whether or not more precise research would be worthwhile.

Many further research questions follow. If business-specific defense mechanisms do exist, do the individuals choose them unconsciously or do they "infect" each other with their defense? Is the defense organizational or branch-specific? If an entrepreneur plans to make changes, which interventions would then be advisable with respect to each defense mechanism?

Finally, a psychometric test relating to defense could also be a valuable complement to diagnosis in coaching.

5.2.6 Measuring and activating containing ability

Containing is a major concept in psychoanalysis, which has already been applied in business contexts (see Chapter 4.9.2). We have shown that in the Tavistock tradition, the concept has been utilized repeatedly in connection with the function of a business as a psychic refuge, in connection with its impact in groups, and with the enduring of primary risk to avoid dysfunctional defense (see Chapter 2.1.2). Accordingly, the ability for containing seems to be a desirable skill for an executive. We do not yet venture the thesis, however, that executives can learn containing ability, because if containing was not learned in early childhood to process states of tension with the help of the mother's more mature emotional reaction, then it is doubtful whether this skill can be retroactively acquired without the support of a lengthy psychoanalysis. This task, however, would fall into the sphere of psychotherapy. It is paramount for the container to have a wide spectrum of mature emotions to be able also to provide such support.

Our aim in this project is learning how to identify containing skills in executives and how to promote their deployment. In a first step during a workshop with experienced coaches, the term coaching was fully explained in the context of the business world. It was explained that containing is at its core about orientation toward feelings and enduring them together. In this way, the executive performs the surrogate job of emotionally experiencing what the employee is not yet capable of experiencing or has not yet dared to address (cf. analogously the coaching concept according to Giernalczyk et al., 2013b, p. 425). Ideally, through this form of containing, the executive will be able to prevent the employee's defense reactions. From this, a first idea arose as to how defenses express themselves in business, and how this might be an indication of the quality of containing that the leadership offers.

A further way of measuring containing skills could be the processing of frustration or the ability to tolerate ambiguity. Clinical psychology offers numerous measuring instruments in this area; for example, the inventory for measuring the tolerance of ambiguity (IMA-40/50) and the Rosenzweig Picture-Frustration Test on latent hostility. With internal candidates, the containing achieved so far can be estimated by deducing executives' containing skills from measuring the defense mechanisms of colleagues and employees. The measurement of defense has already been outlined (see Chapter 5.2.5). Business units with low measurements of dysfunctional defense are possibly led by executives who already practice containing in their own way. However, sound judgment is needed when drawing conclusions from defense about the containing skills of executives. Not every business unit has to endure the same amount of stress, and not every executive with containing skills has made full use of them.

The concept of measuring, activating and utilizing containing skills has been applied in a medium-size services business in Berlin. In tune with the idea of training employees to be organizers and thus to awaken their "improvement fever" (Adams & Kretschmar, 1996, p. 62), we invited multipliers (influential non-managers) from the business to identify their containing skills in coaching and to learn how to utilize them. Fifteen executives, the CEOs, the employee organization head and two staff from the HR department went through a one-on-one coaching (seven to ten sessions) in three months. It was in our interest to frame a long-term and lasting process of change. In one-on-one coaching, the participants had the chance to work on a personal topic, which did not necessarily have to be part of the operational context. It was important that the participants had already experienced containing through working with the coach. Right after the coaching, these executives had team meetings with the colleagues who directly reported to them, wherein a containing space was opened. The coach assisted each executive in his first practical experience.

Results showed that through spillover of this project work, tension was reduced in all departments of the company by identifying, activating and utilizing the executives' containing skills. The staff noticed the change in interactions, which were now viewed as being kinder and more cordial. Even if neither the management's economic target nor the market had changed, the staff were better at processing tension and began every working day with anticipation. After a year, the absence rate due to sickness had reduced from 20 per cent to about nine per cent; this legitimized the project in economic terms in hindsight (Kretschmar & Senarclens de Grancy, 2017b).

5.2.7 *Influence of psychodynamic coaching on self-efficacy*

To date, there is no process research which could make any statements about the importance of the various effect factors of coaching; this has been shown at the beginning of this chapter. There is no effectiveness research regarding psychodynamic coaching. In consequence, and because of the diverse training backgrounds of coaches, it has been debated whether psychodynamic coaching should be identified not according to a job title, but on the basis of the interventions performed.

In pursuit of this identification, one can revert to the Comparative Psychotherapy Process Scale (CPPS) used in psychotherapy research. The CPPS contains items relating to the contents of the psychotherapy; for example: "My therapist interacted with me in a teacher-like (didactic) manner". Half of the items describe typical interventions of cognitive behavior therapy. The other half are concerned with typical interventions of psychodynamic-interpersonal therapy (Hilsenroth et al., 2005). In this way, the CPPS would reveal whether a behavior therapist utilizes psychodynamic interventions and vice versa. It would seem a good idea to adopt the CPPS for coaching research and adjust the items accordingly. The contents of the coaching can be determined through this procedure. For the study of other forms of interventions common in coaching, particularly systemic intervention, we still lack an additional itemization.

An instrument for measuring coaching results is needed to determine the efficiency of the various interventions. In this respect, the General Self-Efficacy Scale (GSE) has proven successful for initial and final measurement (Böning & Kegel, 2013, p. 87).

- How frequently are certain interventions applied in coaching?
- What is the coherence between single interventions and the improvement of self-efficacy?
- Which improvements are facilitated by coaching through mainly psychodynamic interventions compared to other forms of intervention?

The answers to these questions help coaching federations to obtain an overview of the actual interventions of their members, and help coaches to choose coaching methods and interventions for specific tasks (in this case, enhancement of self-efficacy). The questionnaire presented as Table 5.3 was used in one of the case examples in the next chapter (see Chapter 6.1). As the case example shows, the questionnaire can serve as important feedback for the coach even if the number of cases is small. The systematic utilization of this questionnaire in numerous coachings will result in a database, which will allow for a deeper evaluation in future years.

5.3 Discussion: Basis in science, outcome and process research

Coaching and supervision research, just like early psychotherapy research, is still situated at the stage of comparative outcome research. An explanation for this can be found in the ongoing striving for social acceptance of coaching and supervision and the accompanying distribution battles between them. If coaching research continues to develop along the lines of psychotherapy research, then in the future, a turn to process research may be expected.

We have presented several of the first author's (Kretschmar) coaching research projects, which are being conducted within the Mind Institute SE and internally termed as "atomic research". The atoms in this metaphor are psychodynamic basic terms, such as association, transference, defense, containing, conflict or introjection. First, these basic terms and their efficiency have to be understood in the business context; and then they have to be made quantifiable and manageable by

Table 5.3 Questionnaire on the form of intervention and self-efficacy

Kind/sort	No.	Item
p	1	My coach encouraged me to explore feelings that are hard for me to talk about (e.g. anger, envy, excitement, sadness, or happiness).
c	2	My coach gave me explicit advice or direct suggestions for solving my problems.
c	3	My coach actively initiated the topics of discussion and activities during the session.
p	4	My coach linked my current feelings or perceptions to experiences in my past.
p	5	My coach brought to my attention similarities between my past and present relationships.
c	6	Our discussion centered on irrational or illogical belief systems.
p	7	The relationship between the coach and myself was a focus of discussion.
p	8	My coach encouraged me to experience and express feelings in the session.
c	9	My coach suggested specific activities or tasks (homework) for me to attempt outside the session.
p	10	My coach addressed my avoidance of important topics and shifts in my mood.
c	11	My coach explained the rationale behind his/her technique or approach to treatment.
c	12	The focus of our session was primarily on future life situations.
p	13	My coach suggested alternative ways to understand experiences or events I had not previously recognized.
p	14	My coach identified recurrent patterns in my actions, feelings and experiences.
c	15	My coach provided me with information and facts about my current symptoms, disorder or treatment.
p	16	I initiated the discussion of significant issues, events and experiences.
c	17	My coach explicitly suggested that I practice behavior(s) learned in therapy between sessions.
c	18	My coach taught me specific techniques for coping with my symptoms.
p	19	My coach encouraged discussion of wishes, fantasies, dreams or early childhood memories (positive or negative).
c	20	My coach interacted with me in a teacher-like (didactic) manner.
s	21	If someone opposes me, I can find the means and ways to get what I want.
s	22	I can always manage to solve difficult problems if I try hard enough.
s	23	It is easy for me to stick to my aims and accomplish my goals.

(Continued)

Table 5.3 (Cont.)

Kind/sort	No.	Item
s	24	Thanks to my resourcefulness, I know how to handle unforeseen situations.
s	25	I am confident that I could deal efficiently with unexpected events.
s	26	I can remain calm when facing difficulties because I can rely on my coping abilities.
s	27	I can usually handle whatever comes my way.
s	28	I can solve most problems if I invest the necessary effort.
s	29	If I am in trouble, I can usually think of a solution.
s	30	When I am confronted with a problem, I can usually find several solutions.

Note: p: psychodynamic interventions, c: cognitive-behavioral interventions, s: self-efficacy The evaluation is based on four answers: 0 (hardly ever), 1 (sometimes), 2 (often), 3 (nearly always). With the introduction of such instruments in coaching, we can answer the following research questions:

operationalization and manualization. These "atoms" will be put together to form "molecules" in a second step. Examples of this development are already visible in various research approaches (In what way are containing and defense mutually dependent? Which association technique renders introjections visible?). And finally, it is necessary to test these "atoms" and "molecules" in the field and to interrelate them within the big picture. The subsequent case examples (see Chapter 6) will illustrate what this could look like.

As can be seen from the discussion sections in previous chapters, coming up with ever-new instruments is not what the second author (Hamburger) strives for. As a psychoanalyst and a supervisor, he is more inclined to personal contact than to operationalization; as a researcher, he is not concerned with the scaling of characteristics or processes, but with a process analysis orientated toward individual cases. Thus both authors could stand peacefully side by side, agreeing to differ, if it were not for the contention against the deployment of targeted intervention techniques and extensive test batteries already revealed in Chapter 4.11: both of these convey a subsumptional (classificatory) logic familiar in management. This subsumptional logic is diametrically opposed to the psychoanalytic attitude – which at best would be a problem of trademark protection – if the client has no interest in this approach, and prefers to glean something he knows from business life. This, however, does not correspond with the long-standing experience of the second author. None of his clients – entrepreneurs, managers and senior civil servants – were looking for a well-rehashed lecture from the typical consultant, but for a space offering them "unusual circumstances of conversation", characterized by evenly suspended attention and without the intention to subsume them in a diagnosis concept – above all, without the help of tests.

Then, of course, target groups might differ.

6 Case examples

The following cases originate in the counseling office of the first author (Kretsch-mar). All clients have given their consent in writing for their anonymized cases to be used for scientific purposes and publication. To protect the clients' privacy, their cases were altered in the appropriate way. Occasionally, two similar cases were condensed into one hybrid. Nonetheless, the cases were kept in such a way as to convey psychodynamic counseling work orientated toward utilization of instruments.

By way of illustration, the instruments used in counseling were explicitly placed in the foreground. The case descriptions therefore may seem provocative or give rise to the impression that the counseling work is characterized mainly by efficiency or research thinking. The case commentaries are the work of the second author (Hamburger) and reflect the view of the discerning psychoanalyst. Case examples and commentaries together yield an intended field of tension, allowing the reader to seek out his own position. The authors too have found – not least by writing this book – their positions somewhere between these poles.

6.1 Mr. L.: Fear of success

In the following section, a case from the first author's coaching practice is presented with those excerpts relevant for the topics of this book.

Mr. L., a 40-year-old entrepreneur, was booked in for coaching by his mother. She explained that her son was overworked and therefore could not manage to find a coach for himself. That is why she had intervened to look for a suitable practice. In his first interview, Mr. L. presents himself as being under high pressure and speaks very fast. He gives the impression of wanting to get as much out of the hour for himself as possible. He says he is looking for a sparring partner, who can assist him psychologically in the near future. Currently, it bothers him that he is fearful about the future and is very focused on money. Even though he has already built up a fortune, he is afraid of becoming impoverished if he has to live off his savings alone. His independence from the need to work for money, however, is his primary goal. He thinks that he would be rid of the pressure if he did not have to work anymore and was financially well provided for for the rest of his life. With the help of the coach, Mr. L. wants to overcome his fear of the future and his fixation on money. At

DOI: 10.4324/9781003169673-6

present, he must decide if he wants to sell his shares of the business he has built up, or if he wants to wait for a possible benefit from the business's increase in value. Further, he is striving to make a decision which corresponds to his personality, and that is why he wants to get to know himself better. Currently, he has the chance to sell out and to achieve financial independence, as he has always wanted. However, this idea also awakens anxiety in him as to how his life is going to continue afterwards.

Mr. L. grew up in a medium-sized town in northern Germany. His parents separated when he was two years old. His mother remarried soon afterwards. He only remembers his family with his mother and stepfather. He had hardly any contact with his biological father. After some time, his half-sister, seven years his junior, was born. His mother works as a school secretary. His stepfather works in a local municipal public order office. Mr. L. mentions his permissive upbringing. As a child, he was allowed to do anything he wanted, he says. His attachment to his mother is very strong, even today; she is his closest confidant. He respects his parents, but the poverty of the family has always disturbed him. His stepfather was not the achiever he wanted as a role model. After receiving his high school certificate as the best student of his year, he studied computer science in the nearby university.

Mr. L.'s first great love was an American girl. With her, he frequently visited her parents in the United States and began at an early stage to organize business contacts in Germany for the girl's father. He realized that he was good at bringing together investors and company founders. Today this is his main job. A couple of years ago, a distinctly older entrepreneur offered him the chance to participate in setting up a business. This business has become "extraordinarily successful" due to Mr. L.'s commitment and is now a large enterprise.

For some years now, Mr. L. has lived with a Swedish woman, eight years his junior. She has a brother who is Mr. L.'s age. As the coach remarks on the resulting restaging of both their family structures, Mr. L. agrees: "Our similar family histories unite us". Mr. L.'s partner wants to have children soon. However, he cannot imagine, he says, what he would be like as a father. His lifestyle is rather modest. He cannot bring himself to spend money and has not yet become used to the lifestyle he actually is able to afford.

The coach experiences the client as ambitious regarding his personal development, as circumspect and sober with regard to making contact, as distrusting and self-doubting. He notices the latter aspect mainly because Mr. L. worries a lot about his health and regards himself as being unsporting and physically not attractive enough – a self-assessment which is not confirmed by his appearance. As an entrepreneur, Mr. L. shows little in the way of self-aggrandizement and seems very honest. All in all, Mr. L. seems to the coach like a reliable associate whom one would gladly entrust with business. In the following diagnosis, no personality disorder can be ascertained with sufficiently appropriate criteria. Apart from his seemingly unreasonable fear of impoverishment and his worries about his health, Mr. L. shows no psychopathological symptoms.

The countertransference inventory (see Table 6.1) shows that C3 (need for care versus self-sufficiency) is clearly the main area of conflict, as it is most distinct and shows the most active mode. When confronted with these findings, Mr. L. confirms that self-reliance is his most important aim. He says that he provides others with work and his family with everything necessary. However, he cannot imagine himself having to be provided for by others. Also, he is not capable of asking for help. He would never enter into a dependent employment situation. This would make him feel imprisoned. Mr. L. confirmed the self-worth conflict (C4) which showed up in the countertransference inventory. He can only feel worthy through his achievements and without disappointing others. Later, when he completed the Business-focused Inventory of Personality (BIP), a psychometric test, he scored very low values on the "self-worth" scale in the self-description area, pointing to a disorder (compared to a reference group representing the general population, only 11 per cent scored lower, 12 per cent scored the same as him and 77 per cent had higher scores). Initially, Mr. L. denies the presence of conflict C5 (guilt/accountability), but, after working through past events, he acknowledges it. Apparently, Mr. L. developed feelings of guilt as a child because of his mother's unhappiness (marriage/divorce) and compensates for it by accusing others.

All in all, the countertransference inventory proves a suitable instrument for a first screening whereby, together with Mr. L., topics can be identified for further consolidation and analysis in the coaching process. Moreover, it brought connections to light, as he admitted, of which he had not been aware.

The color-association test was also utilized at an early stage of the coaching. When the procedure was explained to Mr. L., he doubted whether, in his current state, he would be able to think of more than one color: "All I can think of right now is blue". As Figure 6.1 shows, Mr. L. chose blue for relationship, exhaustion and hobbies. At the time of the test, he felt harnessed by his work and exhausted; the contexts in which he could imagine taking time out and refueling were his relationship and his hobbies. The other color groups were also more or less interpreted by Mr. L. himself. A vacation for him means far away (brown). At present, he needs it neither for vocational nor for private reasons. He finds fulfillment in communication (orange). What he really likes doing best is building up a network of businesspeople, making use of it and connecting it to others. Mr. L. had no idea

Table 6.1 Results of the countertransference inventory for case example

Conflict		Strength $(a + p)$	Mode $(a - p)$
C1	Autonomy	4	0
C2	Self-efficacy	4	- 4
C3	Care/Provision	8	+8
C4	Self-worth	7	+1
C5	Accountability	7	+3
C6	Competition	6	+4
C7	Identity	5	- 3

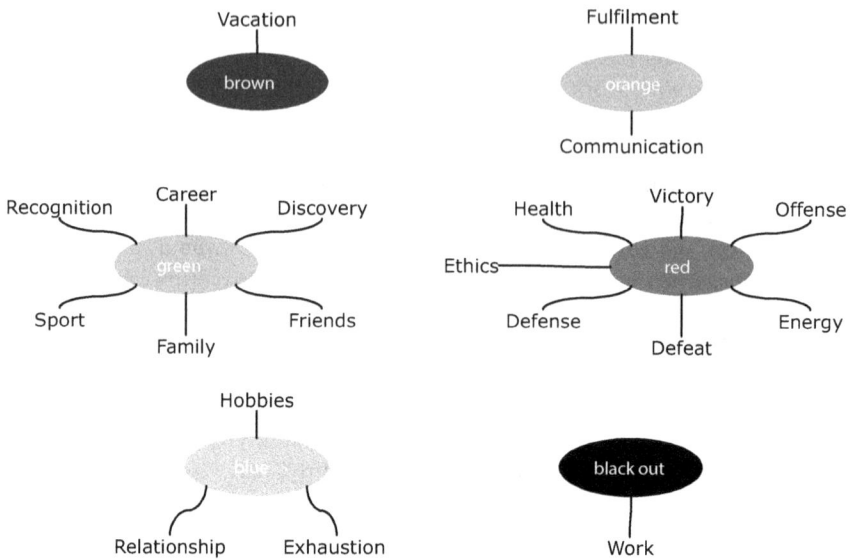

Figure 6.1 Results of color-association test for case example

whatsoever which color to pick for working. He feels as if he is "blacked out", he said. The term "work" is lost on him because he does not perceive what he is doing as work. In the center is his area of tension.

The left-hand side (Figure 6.1), according to Mr. L., shows how he could find his work–life balance in the future (green). Through a balance of career, family, friends and sport, he hopes to find recognition and to discover a new life. Today he feels the conflicts (red) of victory and defeat, offense and defense struggling within him. This costs him a lot of energy, as does the weighing of ethical aspects in his working life. He is constantly worried about his health, which adds to this area of tension.

The use of the color-association test proves helpful in revealing to the client contexts of meaning of which he had previously not been conscious. The test encourages a creative interpretation of the color patterns and supplies, alongside a social anamnesis (case history), important information about the client's experiences and actions.

We will outline the psychodynamic interpretation only to the extent that this is relevant for further utilization of the color-association test. We assume that the mother could not give up her strong attachment to the child as her own self-object in the course of the child's maturation, with the result that the client was not able to develop the self-awareness he needed independent of his mother. In consequence, he compensates for his unconscious care relationship with the mother with an unconscious striving for autonomy. Apparently, Mr. L. cannot transfer the attachment he feels to his mother to his adult relationships. Thus, his relationship to his intimate partner is more or less reduced to organizational matters, and as a business partner, he views himself rather as the "power broker in the background", a role for which he is equipped by his skill in handling large transactions and in connecting people, without involving himself with leadership responsibilities. Mr. L. has problems with business partners who in time might develop into friends. Then he could not, as he is used to, "do his own thing", but would find it difficult to hold his ground. In the area of tension between needing a friend (care) and at the same time wanting to accomplish his goals independently (autonomy), many problems arise, which are worked on during the coaching. Mr. L. seems to be trying to replace the security exuded by his mother with financial security. In the process, he avoids any caring relationship, which for him is threatening, by not letting anyone get close to him.

In the light of these reflections, there were enough indications to work on his original objective – whether or not to sell his company shares – with regard to the influence of his inner mother. In his imagination, Mr. L. develops an image of a landscape with a calm river and a bridge crossing it. He finds himself standing directly in front of the bridge. On his side of the river, there is wild grassland with wild flowers. On the other side, there is a perfectly groomed lawn without flowers. For lying down and resting, the lawn on the other side seems more suitable. At that moment, the client feels no impulse to cross the bridge. The idea unsettles him. During his imagining, the coach suggests an appearance of his mother next to him and they both look at the bridge together, which reassures the client. On this side of the bridge, the landscape no longer seems quite as wild. Now the client feels more like crossing the bridge, particularly after he realizes that he can always return.

The coach now guides Mr. L. to turn toward his mother. To the client, she seems sad. She feels worse than he does because she is older. Deep within her, she desires to be appreciated and to be strong. The thought occurs to Mr. L. that it might look like subjugation, if he appreciates his mother. The coach, therefore, asks him if he sees a possibility, in this dream world that allows for magic, of giving his mother all the appreciation and strength she desires without submitting to her. Accordingly, the client transforms his mother into superman. Using her new super powers, the mother flies away to try them out. The client now turns back to his landscape. His view is widened. In his reverie, he sees more landscape to the left and to the right. Over on the perfect lawn, a hollow has emerged, like a pond without water. The client is no longer afraid to cross the bridge, so that is what he does. On the other side, the hollow turns into a deep abyss trying to pull him down into it. The coach accompanies the client and his feelings and encourages him to surrender to them. As a consequence, Mr. L. finds himself in space, discovering a calmness he has never experienced before, and a curiosity to fly about and find new stars. With these impressions, the coach leads Mr. L. back from his reverie.

In the debriefing, coach and client interpret the reverie together. The mother keeps him on this side and limits his view. As soon as she has enough strength of her own, his view widens. To leave the mother and step into his own life causes anxiety, particularly with respect to what will happen in the future. Mr. L.

becomes intensely aware of the conflict between unconscious providing and unconscious autonomy. The coach advises him to experiment with intermediate stages between autonomy and providing, in which he tries out deeper relationships, without completely giving up his autonomy or completely giving in to providing. Part of this touches on negotiating difficult compromises with business partners whom he has grown fond of.

With the documentation of this case, the first phase of coaching comes to an end. Mr. L. has decided to sell his company shares, to reduce his contact with his mother and to consciously open himself to relationships. The coaching is to be continued in a second phase to counsel Mr. L. as he takes his new steps. Possibly, the client will have to accept a certain amount of caring by the coach, which will then be resolved with the termination of the coaching.

At the end of the first phase – lasting in total 24 hours, over the course of six months – the client filled in the research project questionnaire (see Chapter 5.2.7), requesting only items 1 to 20 because they give an indication of the type of intervention being used. The client perceived the intervention of cognitive behavior therapy as being used only "sometimes" (average = 1.0), which, of course, was intended during a coaching with a psychodynamic approach. The client "never" experienced the coach giving detailed advice or making direct recommendations to solve his problems (item 2). He also never experienced the coach as dealing with him in a didactic manner, as a teacher would with a student (item 20). However, Mr. L. often experienced the coach as explaining the basic principles behind the methods used (item 11) and explicitly suggesting that he practice between sessions the behaviors he had learned in coaching (item 17). The last two interventions do not correspond with a psychodynamic approach in its original sense. The future reduction of such interventions in supervision could perhaps be considered. In this case, however, the results of coaching research (see Chapter 5.2.1) could also be considered, showing that transparency in respect to the methods used is a factor for success.

The utilization of psychodynamic interventions, which the client experienced as encountering "often" (average = 1.9) was also intentional in a coaching with a psychodynamic approach. The client often recognized that his coach linked recurring patterns in his actions, feelings and experiences (item 14), and that he himself set off conversations about important topics, events and experiences (item 16). However, Mr. L. only occasionally observed that his coach linked his current feelings or perceptions with experiences in his past (item 4); encouraged him in experiencing and expressing his feelings during the session (item 8); or commented on the client's avoiding important topics or on mood changes (item 10). In future sessions with Mr. L., these last three interventions should be used more to allow him, in terms of the psychodynamic approach, a relational experience with the coach.

The questionnaire has proven successful in objectifying the coach's style. All in all, this case shows that all operationalized techniques used have been helpful in the coaching and have given rise to important insights for both coach and client. However, without the coach's psychodynamic background knowledge and counseling experience, as well as the client's willingness to be coached, this coaching could not have obtained such good results.

Comment of the second author

During the preliminary stages, the client already presented himself as having a strong tie to his mother, who chose the coach for him and made the appointment. Even though this initial scene is very revealing, as an analyst, I probably wouldn't have got involved and wouldn't have agreed to an appointment. I would have told the mother that the client himself had to make the call. Whether a collaboration under these circumstances could have been achieved is, of course, doubtful; because my refusal to be "used" as another "chosen one" by this mother–son dyad probably would have led mother and son to look for another consultant, who was more compliant with this interpersonal defense. However, if the collaboration had been fruitful, this prelude would have contained precious material for clarifying the work. The further course of the coaching, from my viewpoint, showed that the potential topic of a vacant post for a father ran like a common thread through the whole process. We hear that Mr. L. was left by his father when he was only two years old and apparently never again established a good contact with him. His place was taken by the mother as the closest person of reference, and "soon" by a stepfather described with conspicuous featurelessness. Here, too, no close relatedness is noticeable. The sentence, "I was allowed to do what I wanted" is more resonant of "not being looked after". The half-sister, seven years his junior, is not personified and not tangibly described; nevertheless, she comes up prominently through an interpretative idea of the coach in the initial conversation: She appears as a parallel figure of the client's partner. And here the case report takes another interesting turn: When it comes to his partner, the main thing that comes to his mind is her wish for a child. So far, a touchingly open scene has unfolded, affording coach and client ample material for a rich conversation. All these flags could provide a temptation to diagnose the client's inner world – loss of father, self-objective, in his fear of ill health, even a symbiotic mother fixation with reduced ability for enjoyment, instrumental object relations not allowed to become personal. All of this, I think, could be kept in suspension while maintaining such a promising first contact. As the coach writes, "as an entrepreneur", Mr. L. "shows little in the way of self-aggrandizement and seems very honest". However, I ask myself, whence did the decision come to fall back on the chosen number of instruments so early in the coaching process? It is clear that the coach mobilizes a whole battery of instruments to determine something diagnostically. I assume that this is part of the program and has something to do with the ongoing research project. Surely the client, as I picture him, has agreed with wholehearted interest; perhaps he wanted to be part of such a project. I would be curious to find out what kind of feelings this suggestion has set free in him. From the viewpoint of the process, however, I would not have suggested such interference, because there was a good chance that the client understood the topics that were important for him without scaling. Thus, if I reconstruct the activity from the perspective of the client's transference fantasy – without taking into account the external pressure of the research project – he seems then to fit well into the scene of transference and countertransference, which, of course, can only be assumed heuristically here. Mr. L. seeks counseling for his big decision – further capital growth of the company or ringing the cash register. With this decision, he associates pressure and impoverishment anxieties on the one (company) side; and an unknown future on the other side and the fear of having to live from his assets rather than adding to them. This seems to correlate with the topic of becoming a father. On the one hand, his wife's desire to have a child is threatening; on the other hand, the pregnancy and the birth of a child could imply completely new and binding personal relationships. Thus, he turns to the coach with the question: What is it like to become an adult man and a father, who must also endure being provided for. The coach picks up on this issue, unconsciously staging a scene by demonstrating competence through the presentation of measuring instruments, and by appearing as a leader and companion in the imaginative journey who will help him to sort out his confusing feelings regarding his mother. I assume that the aspect which was actually helpful was not the numerous operationalizations, and the coaching approach trimmed to efficiency, but the fact that someone was there for the client as a whole person on a regular, empathetic and open basis, allowing him to experience, to a certain extent, the relationship to a present and respected father, which he lacked. The objectifying approaches, as it seems to me, mainly functioned to calm the client and to signal to him that this wasn't anything close or personal, but something scientifically profound, measurable and factual. With this assurance, the client could embark on the relationship and arrive at a decision. Now he is prepared to separate from the mother-firm, which he has symbiotically served so far, and to start a new life with an open future with his own family. Here the coach addresses a part of the transference: "Possibly, the client will have to accept a certain amount of caring by the coach in this phase, which will then be resolved with the termination of the coaching". Here one can discern skepticism, and again, assurance: It could become personal occasionally, but fear not, it will not last. The future will show if the client will actually become capable of building relationships and if the wrapping up of the therapeutic relationship in a highly instrumentalized relational mode (which might be useful to induce the coaching) has been helpful in a lasting way. From my point of view, it is not so much the possible closeness, which might arise between client and coach, which has to be dissolved, but that being fended off by ratios and tools.

6.2 Ms. G.: High performance and career stress

Fighting career stress, Ms. G., 31 years old and a qualified sports scientist, booked herself in for coaching, after some research on the Internet. She explained that she works as a trainer in high-performance sport and has quite a bit of latitude as to the structuring of her job. At the same time, she is working on her habilitation, in order to teach at the sports university eventually. Her employers, she explained, overly idealize her, and see in her an efficient trainer who strives for harmony in the team. Harmony to her is very important. On one occasion, personal differences with one of her colleagues had arisen. As her circle of friends consists mainly of her colleagues, those conflicts had seeped into all of her relationships, which she had felt in every encounter. She wished to absolutely avoid that kind of situation in the future. Because she was so dedicated, numerous tasks were assigned to her. Additionally, she put herself under pressure, which had lately led her to make mistakes. Recently, she had demanded too much of an athlete who, recovering from injury, was not yet ready for top performance and had suffered a setback due to her unreasonable demands. When such things happen, she blames herself, feels inferior and goes into seclusion. Even though she gets sufficient exercise, under the circumstances described, she tends to neglect her own body. The direction of high-performance athletes, who love to occupy center stage, is not easy. Her work, she says, is rarely criticized, but if it is, then she obsesses over it for days on end. She then feels oppressed and unjustly treated, because she was already giving her best. As a trainer, she is fairly young, she says, and doesn't dare to ask colleagues for support for fear of admitting to her own inexperience. Thus, she sometimes would not feel a part of her own team. Apart from all this, she feels burdened by the recent separation from her boyfriend, who had disappointed and lied to her.

Despite the described strain, Ms. G. appears energetic and by no means exhausted or depressed. The coach soon gets the impression that Ms. G.'s stress is being transferred to him and that he is now under pressure to help her as quickly as possible.

According to her own account, Ms. G. grew up as the only child of an ideal family. When she was about ten years old, her parents' arguments seriously increased and they finally separated two years later. The father soon remarried. When Ms. G. was 18, her mother died unexpectedly in a car accident. To this day, her father and stepmother do not feel like real family to her. The coach points out here the parallel to her team of colleagues, to whom she also feels no sense of belonging. After her mother's death, Ms. G. moved into a flat she shared with older friends, who helped her work through her grief. Her remaining time in school and her sports science studies were financed with some support from her father and with several jobs on the side. In her private life, Ms. G. has had several short relationships with men, which began positively, but drifted after a year or two into a platonic ending of the male–female attraction. This also worries her. What she really wants is a long-term relationship and a family. She pictures her ideal partner as sporty, intelligent and admirable. Her only hobby is her own sport and her physical health. Personal illness or weakness is difficult for her to endure. She only calls in sick if there is absolutely no other way out.

When it comes to diligence, Ms. G. describes herself as being a bit chaotic. However, she plans a lot in advance. She functions best, she says, when she gives herself strong structures. She always has to have something planned for Saturdays. On these days, she finds it hard to be alone. She tries to treat her friends well. When she goes on vacation, she is always afraid of missing out on important private and vocational developments. Accordingly, she takes only short breaks, but she does not see this as a problem as she travels a lot with her team and always adds a day or two of private stays.

Initially, the client showed no conspicuous psychopathogenic symptoms. For further diagnosis and to clarify to her important aspects of her relational behavior and personality, the coach utilizes axis II (relationship) and axis III (conflict) of the Operationalized Psychodynamic Diagnosis (OPD-2).

From the client's account, the coach gets the impression that she mainly allows herself to be guided by the expectations of others. Thus, in their first coaching hours, he encourages her to find herself, feel her own needs and to describe her present circumstances by reference to her own feelings. It becomes apparent that Ms. G. has difficulty with this. After some exercises, her interior world is revealed as completely different from that which she presents on the surface: She is a needy girl wanting support and caring. Because of her restricted ability to perceive her inner world and to communicate it outwardly, the coach originally pictures her as being strong and resilient, a fact not corresponding to reality. This difference between the interior and the exterior also becomes apparent in her interpersonal behavior from the psychodynamic perspective (complete list of items: OPD Task Force, 2008, p. 4193):

1   Ms. G. experiences herself time and time again as harmonizing and avoiding aggression (item 6), caring very much and being worried (item 7), belittling and devaluing herself (item 27) as well as blaming herself (item 28).
2   Consequently, others – the coach, too – experience Ms. G. time and time again as shutting herself off (item 29) and not leaning on others (item 31).
3   Consequently, others – the coach, too – experience themselves with respect to the client time and time again as overlooking or ignoring Ms. G. (item 16), making themselves the center of affection (item 19) and allowing Ms. G. a lot of space (item 1).
4   Consequently, Ms. G. experiences others time and time again as neglecting and abandoning her (item 15), accusing and reproaching her (item 12).

With this established wording of interpersonal behavior, it becomes clear to Ms. G. that because she fails to communicate her needs and allows herself to be guided exclusively by other people's targets, she activates a behavioral cycle damaging to herself. During the further coaching, Ms. G. learns gradually to perceive her own needs and to communicate them. In the beginning, she finds it extremely difficult to show weaknesses and to ask for support. With increasing practice, Ms. G. realizes yet other coherences in her personal life. An emotional contact, she feels, can only occur if her life companion has an idea of how she actually feels. As it happens, that is exactly what her former boyfriends had complained about.

To determine her inner conflicts, Ms. G. completed the self-description at home between the third and fourth session. The coach filled out the counter-transference inventory and the scenic information sheet right after the fourth coaching session. The results are summarized in Figure 6.2.

In the client's self-description, top left in Figure 6.2, it becomes obvious that she behaves quite differently within her diverse spheres. In her job, she behaves passively (-7: passive mode), while she behaves in a decidedly active way (+ 10: active mode) in respect to her body. Regarding the conflicts in her self-description (bottom left in Figure 6.2), it stands out that in terms of her self-worth, the client

active	self-description	passive	sum	difference
20	family of origin (F)	17	37	3
22	partnersh./family (P)	20	42	2
19	job (J)	26	45	-7
20	social context (S)	19	39	1
22	wealth (W)	24	46	-2
26	body/sexuality (B)	16	42	10
19	illnesses (I)	14	33	5

active	countertransference	passive	sum	difference
5	autonomy (C1)	6	11	-1
1	self-efficacy (C2)	3	4	-2
7	care/provision (C3)	4	11	3
4	self-worth (C4)	4	8	0
1	accountability (C5)	7	8	-6
2	competition (C6)	5	7	-3
6	Identity (C7)	7	13	-1

active	self-description	passive	sum	difference
22	autonomy (C1)	23	45	-1
24	self-efficacy (C2)	19	43	5
22	care/provision (C3)	20	42	2
23	self-worth (C4)	15	38	8
18	accountability (C5)	20	38	-2
18	competition (C6)	21	39	-3
21	Identity (C7)	18	39	3

active	total	passive	sum	difference
27	autonomy (C1)	29	56	-2
25	self-efficacy (C2)	22	47	3
29	care/provision (C3)	24	53	5
27	self-worth (C4)	19	46	8
19	accountability (C5)	27	46	-8
20	competition (C6)	26	46	-6
27	Identity (C7)	25	52	2

Figure 6.2 Results for case example

orientates herself toward the expectation of others (+8: active mode). Thus, her self-worth doesn't derive from what she herself is, but from the role the group imposes on her. It is interesting that the coach doesn't notice the self-worth problems apparent in the countertransference (top right in Figure 6.2). Here the strong distinction that the client makes between her internal world and her external impact becomes noticeable. By contrast, the coach notices an excessive acceptance of accountability (-6: passive mode). Thus, the client, without being aware of it, takes on a particularly large quantity of guilt and responsibility.

The client developed her own interpretation of these results, under the coach's guidance. The topics of guilt and responsibility (C5: accountability) are clearly related to the mother's death. Even if the daughter cannot be to blame for the mother's accident, she feels unconscious guilt, which influences her behavior and perception. Her compensation is an excessive acceptance of responsibility, with the intention, as it were, to rectify her guilt for the mother's death. With this high level of responsibility, there is not enough space to differentiate the image of her own self and to ask the question: "Who am I without the expectation of others?" This is why the client looks for groups to orientate her in her self-worth.

During further coaching sessions, Ms. G. learns, based on everyday occurrences, to separate her guilt and responsibility in the here and now from the then and there. She begins to feel her own needs, to perceive more consciously what she is made up of and to show this self-perception more authentically to the outside world. With the help of the coach, she learns to endure tensions which arise, as she no longer strives to behave according to the expectations of the group. After 30 hours of coaching, distributed over a year, the coaching is terminated with the client's life situation greatly improved in terms of her self-perception and her interpersonal behavior.

Comment of the second author

Here, too, a process is being described that allows the client, step by step, to open up toward an empathetically approachable opposite and to process a relevant traumatic experience – the loss of the mother – in combination with her objective. She seems to have made the utilization of tools less necessary. The joint working out of the OPD circumplex formula of self-experience and how one is experienced by others seems to have helped the client to understand more of herself, and together with the coach, to transform this understanding into changed behavior. However, the question from Chapter 4.11 remains, as to whether the OPD research version with pre-formulated items, which always lead to a rather rigid wording of the cycle, is preferable to a free wording, as in the original OPD interview, which describes in its own words, in a much more empathetic and tailor-made way, the mutual conditionality in the cycle of expectations and reactions (see Chapter 4.11).

6.3 Mr. K.: Management or supervisory board?

At the recommendation of a colleague from a federation of merchants, Mr. K., the chairman of a western German enterprise for information technology, signed up for coaching. He said he was the founder of the business and had found a good solution for a particular corner of the market. His solution sells all over the world, and this is why the enterprise to date had grown to more than 500 employees.

He would soon be 50, and was thinking of changing from management of the company to the supervisory board in the next years in order perhaps to undertake other challenges in his life. However, he felt unsure about this decision and wanted, with the help of a coach, to find a more fitting solution.

Mr. K. said he had chosen the coach because he too had experience as an executive. His idea of coaching is a conversation amongst colleagues who have the same understanding of the situation. Mr. K. appears to the coach to be a reliable business partner. He seems to be neither sales-fixated nor manipulative. Mr. K. convinces with his knowledge and his professional appearance. The coach soon realizes he is glad to work with Mr. K. For his part, Mr. K. quickly comes to trust the coach and opens himself up to him accordingly.

Mr. K. grew up alone with his mother. His mother had unintentionally become pregnant during a holiday romance. At that time, the father had not been willing to move to Germany or to establish contact with the child. Mr. K. has no siblings and only a few good friends from his school days. His main interest is focused on computer sciences. He has the talent, he says, to build up good systems and to capture others' imagination with them. During the initial phase of getting to know one another, Mr. K. mentions that, a couple of years before, he had taken a course of coaching with a female psychologist who had asked him, among other questions, if he was thinking about her. He had perceived this question as unprofessional and had aborted the coaching. In the end, the fee was the only thing connecting coach and coachee. It was not his job to think about his coach. He hoped that this would not happen in the current coaching, and that the coach would refrain from continually asking him how he was feeling, because he had no answer to this question. He was a man who solved his problems rationally. Recently, he had had, occasionally, to substitute for the HR manager, who was ill.

He does not like HR work at all. Employees had come to him with personal problems, and he had been out of his depth in dealing with them. He had been very relieved when his HR manager was back on board. The limitations of his skills were another reason to think about a change. He had no interest in fundamentally changing himself, as he was happy with the way he was. Our cooperation would only have the goal of helping him further his direction in a way that was right for the resources he had.

The personality diagnosis does not supply sufficient criteria for a mental disorder, but makes visible a distrusting maverick as well as a distant restrained personality style (see Chapter 4.8). The coach develops doubts as to whether Mr. K. is open enough for a psychodynamic approach. However, Mr. K. shows himself, at an early stage, to be surprisingly enthusiastic about working with imaginative scenarios. Coach and coachee agree to begin with imaginative interventions, which will aid Mr. K. in getting to know himself better, in order to find a fitting solution for himself. As a time frame, 20 sessions in a weekly rhythm are agreed upon.

One of Mr. K.'s first imaginings is a playing room. In this playing room, he lets tin soldiers march in absolutely perfect rows and definitely has a lot of fun. An obvious preference for discipline and order also becomes visible in Mr. K.'s imagining concerning the spirit of the enterprise. The company's spirit is a small ghost, as in a children's story. The ghost watches what the employees are doing. A business culture emerges in which every single employee is under pressure to do everything to perfection. At the end of the imaginative scenario, the little ghost feels lonely and finds another ghost to fall asleep with. In the following discussion, Mr. K. interprets his reverie as a wish to fall asleep with someone. He says that he had a girlfriend in a so-called on-off relationship, from which he is presently having a break. The woman had an interest in him. But for him, a relationship came with too many obligations. During the first months of coaching, Mr. K. nevertheless succeeds in "reactivating" the relationship.

In another imagining, dealing with insoluble tasks is addressed. A bear family is playing in the woods. Mr. K. receives the task from an old man to search for a red stone in the woods. At first, Mr. K. invests ambitious effort in his search for the stone. He climbs to the peaks of mountains and searches the whole forest until he is completely exhausted and takes a break. At that point, a small fairy turns up with the question as to why he has even embarked on such an impossible task. Mr. K. decides to go back to the old man and tell him that he no longer wants the task. At that point, the old man disappears and Mr. K. can sit by the campfire with the bears. Following this imaginative scenario, Mr. K. declares that he never before had felt such feelings as during the imagining.

With the next imagining, Mr. K. returns to his original topic and addresses the question as to whether he should stay on the management board or change to the supervisory board, by visualizing a bridge. The landscape on this side is very rocky. The other side seems more inviting. The bridge looks sturdy. Mr. K. notices his impulse to cross the bridge. The coach suggests that Mr. K.'s mother appears next to him and that they look at the bridge together. As soon as the mother is there, the landscape on the other side gets darker and becomes clouded. Mr. K.

provides his mother with the attention she needs. He puts her on a stage and gives her an audience to cheer her. As a consequence, the mother disappears from the picture and a second, less sturdy, bridge appears. Mr. K. decides to cross the second bridge, which is shaky, but carries him safely over. Then Mr. K. discovers a lake and sits down to read fairy tales to a tamed crocodile.

The client interpreted the reverie as pointing to his deep need to do something for himself. Then he further mused that there was yet another variation of the path: He could drop out of the management board of his enterprise, but continue as head of the Australian subsidiary, affording him a lot of time in this country he likes so much.

At the beginning of the 20th session, Mr. K. volunteers that the budget he had allowed himself was now exhausted and that this was his last hour with the coach. He said he was very happy with the method and with the result, and that he had discovered a solution which he thought fitted his situation very well. The last hour is normally used to reflect on the progress of the coaching. After farewells had been said, the coach is left with the impression that Mr. K. would have benefited from further self-reflection, but also respects Mr. K.'s decision, precisely not to want more, but to leave it at that.

Comment of the second author

This is a very convincing example of what psychodynamic coaching could look like. As the client warns at the very beginning that he wants to have nothing to do with transference interpretations, doesn't want to be asked about his feelings and immediately defines an equal footing as a conversational basis, he drafts an initial transference scene. He doesn't want to be knocked off his stride. Obviously, the (male) coach is able to give him the security he needs and to prove to him with reasonable satisfaction, that nothing emotional beyond his control is going to happen to him here. Then comes the more than surprising turn: Precisely because his somewhat spiky presentation was accepted in deadly earnest, he could get himself involved with the imagination exercises in a surprisingly creative and playful way – in this case, there has to be complete agreement with the coach that the safety needs of the client will be supported, and thereafter his need to explore will be prompted. Whether or not the same would have been possible with accepting listening instead of guided imagination is anyone's guess – the structured framework of imagination exercises has certainly helped the client. The termination, too, is very convincing: Again, the client tries out his autonomy – and at a point where he had obtained access to feelings he had never felt before: His "budget" was exhausted. He organizes his emotionality according to management rules. The fact that the coach stands up to the test and doesn't attempt to manipulate the client into continuing on this path, on which he very obviously has not yet reached the end, gives the client a big chance. He now knows that he is capable of controlling closeness and distance. Only then, if he wants to, can he return.

7   Summary and prospects

The assignment of this book of dialog was to present models of thinking and ideal-typical utilizations as well as providing a systematic outline of the main features of psychodynamic counseling. This was no easy task, and it is by no means completed yet.

Both authors have their origins in different cultures and were interested in the area of intersection between their vocational occupations. At first, they had to come to terms with the "foreignness" of the other. This work was accompanied by feelings of indignation, the need for differentiation, and then again, convergence. It certainly has not slipped the readers' attention that alongside the strong agreement about psychoanalytic principles, a disagreement regarding the utilization remains. However, self-reflection and mutual appreciation have afforded both authors enjoyment in this work. The dialogical processing which is the foundation of this book series has proved a successful method. The analysis of challenging questions and opposite standpoints has clarified each author's own position and partly revised it. In this respect, this form of discussion has actually produced new learning.

A female colleague who very kindly read the manuscript of this book remarked afterwards: "Two men writing one book!" That a contact was not established in the form it could have been is perhaps not only due to the dialogical concept of this book series, but also to the fear of absorption, which the authors – as typical exponents of their culture – have felt. The psychoanalyst might have feared that the analytic frame is being broken, while the entrepreneur may have been apprehensive of ending up with a niche utilization of psychoanalytic work and with economic starvation. The agreement, painstakingly negotiated between the authors, is that for those who want to enjoy the benefits of psychoanalysis in business, it can be legitimate to whet the appetite of economic agents or groups with psychoanalytic concepts, as long as the work is not then termed as "psychoanalytic", but rather as "psychodynamic". Anyway, the authors agree that (possibly following) psychoanalysis in its utilization requires a psychoanalytic attitude and identity. This compromise is probably quite good, as it is equally painful for both authors. Maybe the first author will next work on a text with the title, *Psychoanalytic Bag of Tricks for Executives*, while the second author is thinking about a text called *Why Not Just Go Straight Away to the*

DOI: 10.4324/9781003169673-7

Psychoanalyst? Joking aside – there is now the need for some elaboration, which was not possible within the framework of this book. So, work on this topic has by no means come to an end with the publication of this book. At the level of principles, for example, there remains a lot to be said about regression. And we are also thinking about questions such as "Coaching sitting or lying down?" or a non-pathological issue-specific indication for a high-frequency coaching.

When working in business, it is, of course, indispensable to include systemic, social-psychological and group dynamic perspectives. On the basis of their individual vocational experience, both authors have focused their work on individual clients. But even in this instance, coach and supervisor need to keep the aforementioned perspectives in the back of their minds and to integrate them if necessary. And last, but not least, comprehensive research is needed in the areas of efficiency and process, as well as interculturally.

With these open questions and the areas of tension that we have highlighted, the reader may now find his own position. Both authors are looking forward to continuing the dialog on these topics elsewhere.

8 Index of organizations of psychodynamic coaching and psychoanalytic organizational supervision

- A.K. Rice Institute (AKRI)
- The Australian Centre for Socio-Analysis (ACSA)
- Centre for Psycho-Social Studies
- Group Relations Australia
- The Grubb Institute, London, UK
- Human Relations
- Institut für Analytische Supervision Düsseldorf (ASv; Institute for Analytic Supervision Düsseldorf)
- Institut für Psychodynamische Organisationsberatung München (IPOM; Institute for Psychodynamic Organizational Consulting Munich)
- Institut für Psychodynamische Organisationsentwicklung + Personalmanagement Düsseldorf e.V. (POP; Institute for Psychodynamic Organizational Development and Human Resource Management Düsseldorf)
- The International Society for the Psychoanalytic Study of Organizations (ISPSO)
- InterPsic, Brazil
- The Israeli Association for the Study of Group and Organizational Processes (OFEK)
- Mind Institute SE, Berlin
- Sigmund-Freud-Institut, Frankfurt am Main
- Tavistock Consulting
- The Tavistock Institute
- The Working Party for the Study of Leadership and Organisation (AGSLO)

DOI: 10.4324/9781003169673-8

References

Abelin, E. L. (1971). The role of the father in the separation-individuation process. In J. B. McDevitt & C. F. Settlage (Eds.), *Separation-Individuation. Essays in Honor of Margaret S. Mahler* (pp. 229–252). New York: International Universities Press.

Abelin, E. L. (1975). Some further observations and comments on the earliest role of the father. *The International Journal of Psychoanalysis*, 56(3), 293–302.

Adams, R. & Kretschmar, T. (1996). Machen Sie aus Ihren Mitarbeitern Organisationsprofis. *Bank Magazin*, 45(2), 62–65.

Adler, M. (1993). *Ethnopsychoanalyse: Das Unbewußte in Wissenschaft und Kultur*. Stuttgart: Schattauer.

Aichhorn, T. (Ed.) (2011). *August Aichhorn: Pionier der psychoanalytischen Sozialarbeit*. Wien: Löcker.

Alexander, F. & French, T. M. (1946). *Psychoanalytic Therapy: Principles and Applications*. New York: Ronald Press.

Arbuthnott, K. D., Arbuthnott, D. W. & Rossiter, L. (2001). Guided imagery and memory: Implications for psychotherapists. *Journal of Counseling Psychology*, 48(2), 123–132. doi:10.1037/0022-0167.48.2.123.

Argelander, H. (1970). *Das Erstinterview in der Psychotherapie*. Darmstadt: Wissenschaftliche Buchgesellschaft.

Armstrong, D. (1997). The "institution in the mind". *Free Associations*, 7(1), 1–14.

Armstrong, D. (1998). "Psychic retreats": The organizational relevance of a psychoanalytic formulation. In D. Armstrong & R. French (2005), *Organization in the Mind* (pp. 69–89). London: Karnac.

Armstrong, D. & French, R. (2005). *Organization in the Mind: Psychoanalysis, Group Relations and Organizational Consultancy*. London: Karnac.

Aron, L. (1990). One person and two person psychologies and the method of psychoanalysis. *Psychoanalytic Psychology*, 7(4), 475–485. doi:10.1037/0736-9735.7.4.475.

Bachrach, H. M., Galatzer-Levy, R., Skolnikoff, A. & Waldron, S. (1991). On the efficacy of psychoanalysis. *Journal of the American Psychoanalytic Association*, 39(4), 871–916.

Balint, M. (2002 [1954]). *The Doctor, His Patient and the Illness*. New York: International University Press.

Bambling, M., King, R., Raue, P., Schweitzer, R. & Lambert, W. (2006). Clinical supervision: Its influence on client-rated working alliance and client symptom reduction in the brief treatment of major depression. *Psychotherapy Research*, 16(3), 317–331. doi:10.1080/10503300500268524.

Baranger, M. & Baranger, W. (2008 [1961]). The analytic situation as a dynamic field. *The International Journal of Psychoanalysis*, 89(4), 795–826. doi:10.1111/j.1745-8315.2008.00074.x.

Bauriedl, T. (1980). *Beziehungsanalyse. Das dialektisch-emanzipatorische Prinzip der Psychoanalyse und seine Konsequenzen für die psychoanalytische Familientherapie.* Frankfurt am Main: Suhrkamp.

Bauriedl, T. (1994). *Auch ohne Couch.* Stuttgart: Verlag Internationale Psychoanalyse.

Bauriedl, T. (1998). Ohne Abstinenz stirbt die Psychoanalyse. *Forum der Psychoanalyse*, 14(4), 342–363. doi:10.1007/s004510050027.

Bauriedl, T. (2001). Szenische Veränderungsprozesse in der Supervision: Ursachen und Wirkmechanismen aus beziehungsanalytischer Sicht. In B. Oberhoff & U. Beumer (Eds.), *Theorie und Praxis psychoanalytischer Supervision* (pp. 27–48). Münster: Votum.

Bayerische Landesärztekammer. (2009). *Richtlinien für die Anerkennung als Lehrtherapeut/Lehranalytiker bzw. Supervisor in einem der nachfolgend aufgeführten Bausteine zum Erwerb der Zusatzbezeichnung "Psychoanalyse" bzw. "Psychotherapie".* München: Bayerische Landesärztekammer.

Becker, H. (1995a). Psychoanalyse und Teamsupervision. Einführende Bemerkungen. In H. Becker (Ed.), *Psychoanalytische Teamsupervision* (pp. 7–25). Göttingen: Vandenhoeck & Ruprecht.

Becker, H. (1995b). Angewandte Psychoanalyse in der Teamsupervision als Forschungsansatz. Zur Ethnopsychoanalyse psychiatrischer Institutionen. In H. Becker (Ed.), *Psychoanalytische Teamsupervision* (pp. 179–230). Göttingen: Vandenhoeck & Ruprecht.

Becker, H. (2003 [1998]). Psychoanalyse und Organisation. Zur Bedeutung unbewußter Sozialisation in Organisationen. *Freie Assoziation*, 1(1), 81–100. Reprinted in: B. Sievers, D. Ohlmeier, B. Oberhoff & U. Beumer (Eds.), *Das Unbewusste in Organisationen* (pp. 53–72). Gießen: Psychosozial.

Becker, H. & Becker, S. (1984). *"Höhensonne haben Sie wohl keine?": Zur Legierung des Goldes.* Frankfurt am Main: Qumran.

Beebe, B. & Lachmann, F. M. (2002). *Infant Research and Adult Treatment: Co-constructing Interactions.* Hillsdale, NJ: The Analytic Press.

Belardi, N. (1992). *Supervision. Von der Praxisberatung zur Organisationsentwicklung.* Paderborn: Junfermann.

Benecke, C., Kotte, S. & Möller, H. (2016). *Schulungsunterlagen zum Workshop OPD in Managementdiagnostik und Coaching.* 22.–23. January 2016. Unpublished manuscript, Universität Kassel.

Benecke, C. & Möller, H. (2013). OPD-basierte Diagnostik im Coaching. In H. Möller & S. Kotte (Eds.), *Diagnostik im Coaching* (pp. 183–198). Berlin: Springer.

Bergmann, G. (2016). Balintgruppen: Supervision in der Medizin. In A. Hamburger & W. Mertens (Eds.), *Supervision – Konzepte und Anwendungen. Band 1: Supervision in der Praxis – ein Überblick* (pp. 182–196). Stuttgart: Kohlhammer.

Bergmann, M. S. (1993): Reflections on the history of psychoanalysis. *Journal of the American Psychoanalytic Association*, 41(4), 929–955.

Beumer, U. (2013). "Hetzen, hetzen, hetzen." Permanente Veränderungen. In R. Haubl, G. G. Voß, N. Alsdorf & C. Handrich (Eds.), *Belastungsstörung mit System. Die zweite Studie zur psychosozialen Situation in deutschen Organisationen* (pp. 19–34). Göttingen: Vandenhoeck & Ruprecht.

Beumer, U. & Sievers, B. (2000). Einzelsupervision als Rollenberatung: Die Organisation als inneres Objekt. *Supervision. Zeitschrift für berufsbezogene Beratung*, 3, 10–17.

Bion, W. R. (1952). Group dynamics: A re-view. *The International Journal of Psychoanalysis*, 33(2), 235–247.

Bion, W. R. (1961). *Experiences in Groups and Other Papers* (1–191). London: Tavistock.

Bion, W. R. (1962). *Learning from Experience* (1–116). London: Tavistock.

Bohart, A. C. (2000). The client is the most important common factor: Clients' self-healing capacities and psychotherapy. *Journal of Psychotherapy Integration*, 10, 127–149. doi:10.1023/A:1009444132104.

Böhnisch, T. (2002). Anspruch und Wirklichkeit eines Beziehungsberufes. Eine Analyse von Verbands- und Fachzeitschriften der Supervision. *Gruppendynamik und Organisationsberatung*, 33(2), 175–195. doi:10.1007/s11612-002-0015-5.

Boll-Klatt, A. & Kohrs, M. (2014). *Praxis der psychodynamischen Psychotherapie.* Stuttgart: Schattauer.

Böning, U. & Kegel, C. (2013). Psychometrische Persönlichkeitsdiagnostik. In H. Möller & S. Kotte (Eds.), *Diagnostik im Coaching* (pp. 81–99). Berlin: Springer.

Boothe, B. & Grimmer, B. (2005). Die therapeutische Beziehung aus psychoanalytischer Sicht. In W. Rössler (Ed.), *Die therapeutische Beziehung* (pp. 37–58). Heidelberg: Springer.

Bordin, E. S. (1979). The generalizability of the psychoanalytic concept of the working alliance. *Psychotherapy: Theory, Research & Practice*, 16(3), 252–260. doi:10.1037/h0085885.

Boston Change Process Study Group (2002). Explicating the implicit: The local level and the microprocess of change in the analytic situation. *International Journal of Psychoanalysis*, 83, 1051–1062.

Boston Change Process Study Group (2008). Forms of relational meaning: Issues in the relations between the implicit and reflective-verbal domains. *Psychoanalytic Dialogues*, 18(2), 125–148. doi:10.1080/10481880801909351.

Brede, K. (2015). Steinbruch Psychoanalyse: Kritische Ausführungen zu Martin Dornes' Aufsatz "Macht der Kapitalismus depressiv?". *Psyche – Z Psychoanal*, 69(8), 745–755.

Breuninger, H. & Sellschopp, A. (Eds.). (2013). *Von der Kunst der guten Führung. Ein Projektbericht zu Female Leadership*. Stuttgart: Breuninger-Stiftung.

Brunner, M., Haubl, R., Kirchhoff, C., König, J., Lohl, J., Uhlig, T. D.et al. (2015). Editorial. *Freie Assoziation*, 18(1), 7–12.

Buchholz, M. B. (2013). Die Herausbildung psychotherapeutischer Kompetenz in der Supervision – unterwegs zur Analyse supervisorischer Konversation. Vorschlag zur Definition von Psychotherapie und für ein praktisches Modell der Supervision. In S. Busse & B. Hausinger (Eds.), *Supervisions- und Coachingprozesse erforschen. Theoretische und methodische Zugänge* (pp. 77–108). Göttingen: Vandenhoeck & Ruprecht.

Buchholz, M. B. (2014). Die Feinheiten therapeutischen Sprechens. Konversationsanalyse eines psychoanalytischen Erstgesprächs. In I. Bozetti, I. Focke & I. Hahn (Eds.), *Unerhört – Vom Hören und Verstehen: Die Wiederentdeckung der grundlegenden Methoden der Psychoanalyse* (pp. 219–240). Stuttgart: Klett-Cotta.

Buchholz, M. B. (2016). Wie Therapeuten sich bei der Arbeit beobachten: Ein prozessforschungsbasiertes Modell der Supervision. In W. Mertens & A. Hamburger (Eds.), *Supervision – Konzepte und Anwendungen. Band 2: Supervision in der Ausbildung* (pp. 83–99). Stuttgart: Kohlhammer.

Buchholz, M. B. & Gödde, G. (Eds.). (2005). *Macht und Dynamik des Unbewussten: Auseinandersetzungen in Philosophie, Medizin und Psychoanalyse*. Gießen: Psychosozial.

Buchholz, M. B. & Reich, U. (2014). Dancing insight: How psychotherapists use change of positioning in order to complement split-off areas of experience. *Chaos and Complexity Letters*, 8(2–3), 2–26.

Buchholz, M. B., Spiekermann, J. & Kächele, H. (2015). Rhythm and blues – Amalie's 152nd session: From psychoanalysis to conversation and metaphor analysis – and back again. *The International Journal of Psychoanalysis*, 96(3), 877–910. doi:10.1111/1745-8315.12329.

Buer, F. (2012). Die Supervision und ihre Nachbarformate. In H. Pühl (Ed.), *Das aktuelle Handbuch der Supervision. Grundlagen – Praxis – Perspektiven* (pp. 38–63). Gießen: Psychosozial.

Busch, H.-J. (2001). Gibt es ein gesellschaftliches Unbewußtes? *Psyche – Z Psychoanal*, 55(4), 392–421.

Busse, S. (2010). Zur Pragmatik beraterischen Handelns in Supervision und Coaching. In S. Busse & S. Ehmer (Eds.), *Wissen wir, was wir tun?* (pp. 55–103). Göttingen: Vandenhoeck & Ruprecht.

Busse, S., Hansen, S. & Lohse, M. (2013). Methodische Rekonstruktion von Wissen in Supervisionsprozessen. In S. Busse & B. Hausinger (Eds.), *Supervisions- und Coachingprozesse erforschen. Theoretische und methodische Zugänge* (pp. 14–53). Göttingen: Vandenhoeck & Ruprecht.

Cabaniss, D. L. (2008). Becoming a school: Developing learning objectives for psychoanalytic education. *Psychoanalytical Inquiry*, 28(3), 262–277.

Cabaniss, D. L., Glick, R. A. & Roose, S. P. (2001). The Columbia Supervision Project: Data from the dyad. *Journal of the American Psychoanalytic Association*, 49(1), 235–267.

Conci, M. (2005). *Sullivan neu entdecken. Leben und Werk Harry Stack Sullivans und seine Bedeutung für Psychiatrie, Psychotherapie und Psychoanalyse*. Gießen: Psychosozial.

Costa, P. T. Jr. & McCrae, R. R. (1992). *Revised NEO Personality Inventory (NEO–PI–R) and NEO Five-Factor Inventory (NEO–FFI) Professional Manual*. Odessa, FL: Psychological Assessment Resources.

Craig, J. L. (1986a). Management with feeling. *Menninger Perspectives*, 17(3), 9–13.

Craig, J. L. (1986b). Serving the business worlds. *Menninger Perspectives*, 17(3), 17–20.

Cremerius, J. (1979). Gibt es zwei psychoanalytische Techniken? *Psyche – Z Psychoanal*, 33(7), 577–599.

Curtis, R. C. (2012). New experiences and meanings: A model of change for psychoanalysis. *Psychoanalytic Psychology*, 29(1), 81–98.

Deutsche Gesellschaft für Supervision (2016). *Geschäftsbericht 2015/2016*. Accessed on 1 August 2018 at www.dgsv.de/wp-content/uploads/2017/09/geschaeftsbericht_dgsv_20161.pdf.

Deutscher Bundesverband Coaching (2011). *Coaching-Markt-Analyse 2011*. Osnabrück: DBVC Eigenverlag.

Deutscher Bundesverband Coaching (2012). *DBVC e.V. Coaching als Profession*. Osnabrück: DBVC Eigenverlag.

Deutscher Bundesverband Coaching (2016). *Internetseite des Deutschen Bundesverband Coaching*. Accessed on 15 August 2016 at www.dbvc.de.

Devereux, G. (1953). Why Oedipus killed Laius: A note on the complementary Oedipus complex in Greek drama. *The International Journal of Psychoanalysis*, 34, 132–141.

Devereux, G. (1967). *From Anxiety to Method in the Behavioral Sciences*. The Hague & Paris: Mouton.

Dietz, T., Holetz, K. & Schreyögg, A. (2012). Begriffsbestimmung. In Deutscher Bundesverband Coaching e.V. (Ed.), *Coaching als Profession* (pp. 20–21). Osnabrück: DBVC Eigenverlag.

Dinger, U., Schauenburg, H., Hörz, S., Rentrop, M., Komo-Lang, M., Klinkerfuß, M., [...] Ehrenthal, J. C. (2014). Self-report and observer ratings of personality functioning: A study of the OPD system. *Journal of Personality Assessment*, 96(2), 220–225. doi:10.1080/00223891.2013.828065.

Dornes, M. (1993). *Der kompetente Säugling. Die präverbale Entwicklung des Menschen.* Frankfurt am Main: Fischer.

Dornes, M. (2015). Macht der Kapitalismus depressiv? *Psyche – Z Psychoanal*, 69(2), 115–160.

Egloff, G. (2015). La bête noire: Kommentar zu Martin Dornes' "Macht der Kapitalismus depressiv?". *Psyche – Z Psychoanal*, 69(8), 756–765.

Ehrenberg, A. (2010 [1998]). *The Weariness of the Self. Diagnosing the History of Depression in the Contemporary Age.* Montreal: McGill–Queen's University Press.

Ehrenthal, J., Dinger, U., Horsch, L., Komo-Lang, M., Klinkerfuß, M., Grande, T. & Schauenburg, H. (2012). Der OPD-Strukturfragebogen (OPD-SF): Erste Ergebnisse zu Reliabilität und Validität. *Psychother Psych Med*, 62(01), 25–32. doi:10.1055/s-0031-1295481.

Ellenberger, H. F. (1970). *The Discovery of the Unconscious: The History and Evolution of Dynamic Psychiatry.* New York: Basic Books.

Engelmann, I. (2015). Auf dem Weg zu einer kapitalistischen Psychotherapie: Anmerkungen zu Martin Dornes' "Macht der Kapitalismus depressiv?". *Psyche – Z Psychoanal*, 69(8), 766–772.

Erdheim, M. (1984). *Die gesellschaftliche Produktion von Unbewußtheit – Eine Einführung in die ethnopsychoanalytischen Prozeß.* Frankfurt am Main: Suhrkamp.

Erhardt, I., Bergmann, J., Kalisch, C., Senf, P. & Hamburger, A. (2016). Das PQS-D-Sup: Ein Instrument zur Charakterisierung des Supervisionsstils. In W. Mertens & A. Hamburger (Eds.), *Supervision – Konzepte und Anwendungen. Band 2: Supervision in der Ausbildung* (pp. 139–156). Stuttgart: Kohlhammer.

Ferenczi, S. & Rank, O. (1956[1923]). *The Development of Psychoanalysis.* Transl. Caroline Newton (1924). New York: Dover Publications.

Fleming, J. & Benedek, T. F. (1964). Supervision: a method of teaching psychoanalysis. *The Psychoanalytic Quarterly*, 33, 71–96.

Fonagy, P., Gergely, G. & Jurist, E. L. (Eds.) (2018 [2002]). *Affect Regulation, Mentalization and the Development of the Self.* London: Routledge.

Frank, G. (2012). On the concept of resistance: Analysis and reformulation. *The Psychoanalytic Review*, 99(3), 421–435. doi:10.1521/prev.2012.99.3.421.

Freitag-Becker, E., Grohs-Schulz, M. & Neumann-Wirsig, H. (Eds.). (2016). *Lehrsupervision im Fokus.* Göttingen: Vandenhoeck & Ruprecht.

Freud, A. (1946). *The Ego and the Mechanisms of Defence.* New York: International Universities Press.

Freud, S. (1892–1893). A case of successful treatment by hypnotism. *The Standard Edition of the Complete Psychological Works of Sigmund Freud, Volume I (1886–1899): Pre-Psycho-Analytic Publications and Unpublished Drafts*, 115–128.

Freud, S. (1893a). The psychotherapy of hysteria. *The Standard Edition of the Complete Psychological Works of Sigmund Freud, Volume II (1893–1895): Studies on Hysteria*, 253–305.

Freud, S. (1893b). Miss Lucy R, case histories. *The Standard Edition of the Complete Psychological Works of Sigmund Freud, Volume II (1893–1895): Studies on Hysteria*, 106–124.

Freud, S. (1896). Further remarks on the neuro-psychoses of defence. *The Standard Edition of the Complete Psychological Works of Sigmund Freud, Volume III (1893–1899): Early Psycho-Analytic Publications*, 157–185.

Freud, S. (1896). The aetiology of hysteria. *The Standard Edition of the Complete Psychological Works of Sigmund Freud, Volume III (1893–1899): Early Psycho-Analytic Publications*, 187–221.

Freud, S. (1900). The interpretation of dreams. *The Standard Edition of the Complete Psychological Works of Sigmund Freud, Volume IV (1900): The Interpretation of Dreams (First Part)*, 9–627.

Freud, S. (1905). Fragment of an analysis of a case of hysteria. *The Standard Edition of the Complete Psychological Works of Sigmund Freud, Volume VII (1901–1905): A Case of Hysteria, Three Essays on Sexuality and Other Works*, 1–122.

Freud, S. (1910). The future prospects of psycho-analytic therapy. *The Standard Edition of the Complete Psychological Works of Sigmund Freud, Volume XI (1910): Five Lectures on Psycho-Analysis, Leonardo da Vinci and Other Works*, 139–152.

Freud, S. (1912). Recommendations to physicians practising psycho-analysis. *The Standard Edition of the Complete Psychological Works of Sigmund Freud, Volume XII (1911–1913): The Case of Schreber, Papers on Technique and Other Works*, 109–120.

Freud, S. (1913). Totem and taboo. *The Standard Edition of the Complete Psychological Works of Sigmund Freud, Volume XIII (1913–1914): Totem and Taboo and Other Works*, 7–162.

Freud, S. (1914). The Moses of Michelangelo. *The Standard Edition of the Complete Psychological Works of Sigmund Freud, Volume XIII (1913–1914): Totem and Taboo and Other Works*, 209–238.

Freud, S. (1915). Observations on transference-love (Further Recommendations on the Technique of Psycho-Analysis III). *The Standard Edition of the Complete Psychological Works of Sigmund Freud, Volume XII (1911–1913): The Case of Schreber, Papers on Technique and Other Works*, 157–171.

Freud, S. (1921). Group psychology and the analysis of the ego. *The Standard Edition of the Complete Psychological Works of Sigmund Freud, Volume XVIII (1920–1922): Beyond the Pleasure Principle, Group Psychology and Other Works*, 65–144.

Freud, S. (1923a). Two encyclopaedia articles. *The Standard Edition of the Complete Psychological Works of Sigmund Freud, Volume XVIII (1920–1922): Beyond the Pleasure Principle, Group Psychology and Other Works*, 233–260.

Freud, S. (1923b). The ego and the id. *The Standard Edition of the Complete Psychological Works of Sigmund Freud, Volume XIX (1923–1925): The Ego and the Id and Other Works*, 1–66.

Freud, S. (1926a). Inhibitions, symptoms and anxiety. *The Standard Edition of the Complete Psychological Works of Sigmund Freud, Volume XX (1925–1926): An Autobiographical Study, Inhibitions, Symptoms and Anxiety, The Question of Lay Analysis and Other Works*, 75–176.

Freud, S. (1926b). The question of lay analysis. *The Standard Edition of the Complete Psychological Works of Sigmund Freud, Volume XX (1925–1926): An Autobiographical Study, Inhibitions, Symptoms and Anxiety, The Question of Lay Analysis and Other Works*, 177–258.

Freud, S. (1927). The future of an illusion. *The Standard Edition of the Complete Psychological Works of Sigmund Freud, Volume XXI (1927–1931): The Future of an Illusion, Civilization and its Discontents, and Other Works*, 1–56.

Freud, S. (1930). Civilization and its discontents. *The Standard Edition of the Complete Psychological Works of Sigmund Freud, Volume XXI (1927–1931): The Future of an Illusion, Civilization and its Discontents, and Other Works*, 57–146.

Freud, S. (1933). New introductory lectures on psycho-analysis. *The Standard Edition of the Complete Psychological Works of Sigmund Freud, Volume XXII (1932–1936): New Introductory Lectures on Psycho-Analysis and Other Works*, 1–182.

Freud, S. (1939). Moses and monotheism. *The Standard Edition of the Complete Psychological Works of Sigmund Freud, Volume XXIII (1937–1939): Moses and Monotheism, An Outline of Psycho-Analysis and Other Works*, 1–138.

Freud, S. (1950). Project for a scientific psychology. *The Standard Edition of the Complete Psychological Works of Sigmund Freud, Volume I (1886–1899): Pre-Psycho-Analytic Publications and Unpublished Drafts*, 281–391.

Freyberger, H. J. (2016). Sollte die Supervision in der psychotherapeutischen Ausbildung zertifiziert werden? In W. Mertens & A. Hamburger (Eds.), *Supervision – Konzepte und Anwendungen. Band 2: Supervision in der Ausbildung* (pp. 170–182). Stuttgart: Kohlhammer.

Gabriel, Y. (2012). Organizations in a state of darkness: Towards a theory of organizational miasma. *Organization Studies*, 33(9), 1137–1152.

Giernalczyk, T. & Lohmer, M. (2012). *Das Unbewusste im Unternehmen. Psychodynamik von Führung, Beratung und Change Management*. Stuttgart: Schäffer-Poeschel.

Giernalczyk, T., Lohmer, M. & Albrecht, C. (2013a). Psychodynamische Zugänge zur Coachingdiagnostik. In H. Möller & S. Kotte (Eds.), *Diagnostik im Coaching* (pp. 17–31). Berlin: Springer.

Giernalczyk, T., Lohmer, M. & Albrecht, C. (2013b). Containment im Coaching. *Organisationsberatung, Supervision, Coaching*, 20(4), 425–435. doi:10.1007/s11613-013-0343-z.

Giesecke, M. & Rappe-Giesecke, K. (1997). *Supervision als Medium kommunikativer Sozialforschung*. Frankfurt am Main: Suhrkamp.

Gilmore, T. N. (2009 [2004]). Zur Psychodynamik von Führungswechseln. In B. Sievers (Ed.), *Psychodynamik von Organisationen* (pp. 221–246). Gießen: Psychosozial.

Gödde, G. (1999). *Traditionslinien des "Unbewussten": Schopenhauer, Nietzsche, Freud*. Tübingen: Edition Diskord.

Gotthardt-Lorenz, A., Hausinger, B. & Sauer, J. (2012). Die supervisorische Forschungskompetenz. In H. Pühl (Ed.), *Das aktuelle Handbuch der Supervision* (pp. 362–380). Gießen: Psychosozial.

Gotthardt-Lorenz, A., Hausinger, B. & Sauer, J. (2013). Das forschende Vorgehen in Supervisionsprozessen. In S. Busse & B. Hausinger (Eds.), *Supervisions- und Coachingprozesse erforschen. Theoretische und methodische Zugänge* (pp. 202–221). Göttingen: Vandenhoeck & Ruprecht.

Grassi, L. (2014). The dimension of sound and rhythm in psychic structuring and analytic work. *The Italian Psychoanalytic Annual*, 8, 63–82.

Greif, S. (2013). Coaching bei Stress und Burnout: Nicht ohne Diagnostik. In H. Möller & S. Kotte (Eds.), *Diagnostik im Coaching* (pp. 217–234). Berlin: Springer.

Grimmer, B. (2005). *Psychotherapeutisches Handeln zwischen Zumuten und Mut machen: Das Beziehungs- und Kommunikationskonzept der Kreditierung*. Stuttgart: Kohlhammer.

Gröning, K. (2016). Supervision – von der personenzentrierten Beziehungskunst zum sozialwissenschaftlich begründeten Format. In A. Hamburger & W. Mertens (Eds.), *Supervision – Konzepte und Anwendungen. Band 1: Supervision in der Praxis – ein Überblick* (pp. 58–70). Stuttgart: Kohlhammer.

Hahsler, M., Hornik, K. & Buchta, C. (2008). Getting Things in Order: An Introduction to the R Package seriation. *Journal of Statistical Software*, 25(3), 1–34. doi:10.18637/jss.v025.i03.

Hamburger, A. (1987). *Der Kindertraum und die Psychoanalyse. Ein Beitrag zur Metapsychologie des Traums*. Regensburg: Roderer.

Hamburger, A. (1995). *Entwicklung der Sprache*. Stuttgart: Kohlhammer.

Hamburger, A. (2013). "Arbeit in der Tiefe". Vorüberlegungen zu einer skeptischen Kulturanalyse. In H. Hierdeis (Ed.), *Psychoanalytische Skepsis – Skeptische Psychoanalyse* (pp. 123–184). Göttingen: Vandenhoeck & Ruprecht.

Hamburger, A. (2016a). Supervision in der Jugendhilfe. In A. Hamburger & W. Mertens (Eds.), *Supervision – Konzepte und Anwendungen. Band 1: Supervision in der Praxis – ein Überblick* (pp. 148–166). Stuttgart: Kohlhammer.

Hamburger, A. (2016b). Psychoanalyse und Philosophie. In H. Hierdeis (Ed.), *Austauschprozesse: Psychoanalyse und andere Humanwissenschaften* (pp. 64–88). Göttingen: Vandenhoeck & Ruprecht.

Hamburger, A. (2017). Psychoanalytische Supervision im Feld: Fallorientierte Teamsupervision in der stationären Jugendhilfe. supervision. *Mensch, Arbeit, Organisation*, 35(1), 50–56.

Hamburger, A. (2018). Ferenczi on war neuroses. In A. Dimitrijevic, G. Cassullo & J. Frankel (Eds.), *Ferenczi's Influence on Contemporary Psychoanalytic Traditions* (pp. 65–71). London & New York: Routledge.

Hamburger, A. & Mertens, W. (2016). Wirksamkeit von Supervision – ein Forschungsbericht. In W. Mertens & A. Hamburger (Eds.), *Supervision – Konzepte und Anwendungen. Band 2: Supervision in der Ausbildung* (pp. 124–138). Stuttgart: Kohlhammer.

Hamburger, A., Rauch-Strasburger, A., Bakhit, C. & Schneider-Heine, A. (2016). Die peer-to-peer Fortbildung zum psychoanalytischen Ausbildungssupervisor an der Akademie für Psychoanalyse und Psychotherapie München. In W. Mertens & A. Hamburger (Eds.), *Supervision – Konzepte und Anwendungen. Band 2: Supervision in der Ausbildung* (pp. 183–196). Stuttgart: Kohlhammer.

Hamburger, A. & Wernz, C. (2015). Aus der Zeit. Mechanik und Temporalität des Komischen in "Les Vacances de Monsieur Hulot". *Psyche – Z Psychoanal*, 69(3), 213–238.

Han, B.-C. (2015 [2010]). *The Burnout Society*. Stanford, CA: University Press.

Haubl, R. (2012). Grundsatzfragen der Supervisionsforschung. In H. Pühl (Ed.), *Das aktuelle Handbuch der Supervision* (pp. 348–361). Gießen: Psychosozial.

Haubl, R. (2013). Kollegiales Lernen in einer forschenden Interpretationsgruppe – ein erster Erfahrungsbericht. In S. Busse & B. Hausinger (Eds.), *Supervisions- und Coachingprozesse erforschen. Theoretische und methodische Zugänge* (pp. 222–236). Göttingen: Vandenhoeck & Ruprecht.

Haubl, R. & Alsdorf, N. (2012). Passen Sie gut auf sich auf. *Journal Supervision*, 2, 3–7.

Haubl, R. & Voß, G. G. (Eds.). (2011). *Riskante Arbeitswelt im Spiegel der Supervision. Eine Studie zu den psychosozialen Auswirkungen spätmoderner Erwerbsarbeit*. Göttingen: Vandenhoeck & Ruprecht.

Haubl, R., Voß, G. G., Alsdorf, N. & Handrich, C. (Eds.). (2013). *Belastungsstörung mit System: Die zweite Studie zur psychosozialen Situation in deutschen Organisationen*. Göttingen: Vandenhoeck & Ruprecht.

Hechler, O. (2005). *Psychoanalytische Supervision sozialpädagogischer Praxis: Eine empirische Untersuchung über die Arbeitsweise fallzentrierter Teamsupervision*. Frankfurt am Main: Brandes & Apsel.

Heigl-Evers, A. & Ott, J. (1996). Die psychoanalytisch-interaktionelle Methode. *Psychotherapeut*, 41(2), 77–83.

Heintel, P. & Krainz, E. E. (1994). Was bedeutet "Systemabwehr". In K. Götz (Ed.), *Theoretische Zumutungen: Vom Nutzen der systemischen Theorie für die Managementpraxis* (pp. 160–193). Heidelberg: Carl-Auer-Systeme.

Herkommer, R., Kretschmar, T., Kuchinke, L. & Schnabel, K. (2017). Kollektive Abwehrmechanismen in Organisationen. *Wirtschaftspsychologie*, 19(4), 49–59.

Hermann-Stietz, I. (2009). *Praxisberatung und Supervision in der Sozialen Arbeit.* Frankfurt am Main: Wochenschau Verlag.

Hilsenroth, M. J., Blais, M. D., Ackerman, S. J., Bonge, D. R. & Blais, M. A. (2005). Measuring psychodynamic-interpersonal and cognitive-behavioral techniques: Development of the Comparative Psychotherapy Process Scale. *Psychotherapy: Theory, Research, Practice, Training*, 42(3), 340–356. doi:10.1037/0033-3204.42.3.340.

Hirsch, M. (2000). Elemente der Supervision in der analytischen Psychotherapie. *Supervision- Mensch, Arbeit, Organisation*, 3, 36–43.

Hirschhorn, L. (2009 [1997]). The primary risk. In B. Sievers (Ed.), *Psychodynamic Studies of Organizations* (pp. 153–174). London: Karnac.

Honneth, A. (1995 [1992]). *The Struggle for Recognition: The Moral Grammar of Social Conflicts.* Cambridge: Polity Press.

Horner, A. (2005). *Dealing with Resistance in Psychotherapy.* Lanham, MD: Jason Aronson.

Horvath, A. O. & Greenberg, L. S. (1989). Development and validation of the Working Alliance Inventory. *Journal of Counseling Psychology*, 36(2), 223–233. doi:10.1037/0022-0167.36.2.223.

Hutton, J., Bazalgette, J. & Reed, B. (1997). Organisation-in-the-mind. In J. E. Neumann, K. Kellner & A. Dawson-Shepherd (Eds.), *Developing Organizational Consultancy* (pp. 113–126). London: Routledge.

International Coaching Federation (2016). Die ICF-Philosophie und -Definition von Coaching. Accessed on 3 August 2016 at www.coachfederation.de/files/icf_defintion_coaching.pdf.

International Society for the Psychoanalytic Study of Organizations (2016). Web site of the International Society for the Psychoanalytic Study of Organizations (ISPSO). Accessed on 13 September 2016 at www.ispso.org.

Jansen, A., Mäthner, E. & Bachmann, T. (2003). Evaluation von Coaching. Eine Befragung von Coachs und Klienten zur Wirksamkeit von Coaching. *Organisationsberatung, Supervision, Coaching*, 10(3), 245–254. doi:10.1007/s11613-003-0028-0.

Jaques, E. (1951). *The Changing Culture of a Factory.* London: Tavistock.

Jung, C. G. (1910). The association method. *The American Journal of Psychology*, 21(2), 219–269. doi:10.2307/1413002.

Jung, F. G. & Kulessa, C. (1980). Katamnestische Untersuchung einer 20 Stunden-Therapie mit dem Katathymen Bilderleben – Eine testpsychologische Studie. In H. Leuner (Ed.), *Katathymes Bilderleben. Ergebnisse in Theorie und Praxis* (pp. 172–185). Bern: Huber.

Kächele, H. & Erhardt, I. (2012). Is it possible to measure countertransference? *Romanian Journal of Psychoanalysis*, 5(1), 91–105.

Kächele, H., Erhardt, I., Seybert, C. & Buchholz, M. (2015). Countertransference as object of empirical research? *International Forum of Psychoanalysis*, 24(2), 96–108.

Kernberg, O. F. (1984). *Object Relations Theory and Clinical Psychoanalysis.* Lanham: Jason Aronson.

Kernberg, O. F. (1993). *Severe Personality Disorders: Psychotherapeutic Strategies.* New Haven: Yale University Press.

Kernhof, K. M., Obbarius, A., Kaufhold, J., Merkle, W. & Grabhorn, R. (2013). Gegenübertragung im stationären Therapie-Setting. *Psychotherapeut*, 58(2), 152–158. doi:10.1007/s00278-012-0942-8.

Kets de Vries Institute (2016). Website of the Kets de Vries Institute (KDVI). Accessed on 13 September 2016 at www.kdvi.com.

Kets de Vries, M., Korotov, K., Florent-Treacy. E. & Rook, C. (Eds.). (2016). *Coach and Couch: The Psychology of Making Better Leaders.* Houndmills, UK: INSEAD Business Press/Palgrave Macmillan.

Kets de Vries, M. & Miller, D. (1984). *The Neurotic Organization*. San Francisco: Jossey-Bass.

Kilminster, S. M. & Jolly, B. C. (2000). Effective supervision in clinical practice settings: A literature review. *Medical Education*, 34(10), 827–840. doi:10.1046/j.1365-2923.2000.00758.x.

Knoppers, A. (1987). Gender and the coaching profession. *Quest*, 39(1), 9–22. doi:10.1080/00336297.1987.10483853.

König, K. (1986). *Angst und Persönlichkeit. Das Konzept vom steuernden Objekt und seine Anwendungen*. Göttingen: Vandenhoeck & Ruprecht.

Korotov, K. (2013). *Peer Coaching Practice for Managers*. Scotts Valley, CA: CreateSpace Independent Publishing Platform.

Korotov, K., Florent-Treacy, E., Kets de Vries, M. & Bernhardt, A. (2012). *Tricky Coaching: Difficult Cases in Leadership Coaching*. Houndmills, UK: Palgrave Macmillan.

Kotte, S., Hinn, D., Oellerich, K. & Möller, H. (2016). Der Stand der Coachingforschung: Kernergebnisse der vorliegenden Metaanalysen. *Organisationsberatung, Supervision, Coaching*, 23(1), 5–23. doi:10.1007/s11613-016-0444-6.

Kotte, S. & Möller, H. (2013). Standardisierte Verhaltensbeobachtung als Forschungszugang zur Gruppen- und Teamsupervision mit Hilfe des IKD. In S. Busse & B. Hausinger (Eds.), *Supervisions- und Coachingprozesse erforschen. Theoretische und methodische Zugänge* (pp. 152–179). Göttingen: Vandenhoeck & Ruprecht.

Krantz, J. & Gilmore, T. N. (2009 [1986]). The splitting of leadership and management as a social defense. In B. Sievers (Ed.), *Psychodynamic Studies of Organizations* (pp. 23–50). London: Karnac.

Kretschmar, T. (2016). Psychodynamisches Coaching in Deutschland. *Coaching Magazin*, 3, 32–36.

Kretschmar, T. & Meinel, J. (2015). Using colors in a novel association technique to explore the mental representation of corporate leaders. *Socioanalysis*, 17, 12–26.

Kretschmar, T. & Senarclens de Grancy, M. (2016). Psychoanalytische Führungskräfte- und Organisationsentwicklung in Deutschland: Theoretische Fundierung und praktisches Desiderat. *Wirtschaftspsychologie*, 18(3), 99–106.

Kretschmar, T. & Senarclens de Grancy, M. (2017a). Mit dem Symptom leben lernen. Betriebliche Gesundheitsförderung und die Funktionslogik von Krankheitszeichen. *supervision. Mensch, Arbeit, Organisation*, 35(4), 29–35.

Kretschmar, T. & Senarclens de Grancy, M. (2017b). Containing als Führungsaufgabe in Zeiten der Unternehmensveränderung. *Organisationsberatung, Supervision, Coaching*, 24(1), 35–44. doi:10.1007/s11613-017-0488-2.

Kretschmar, T. & Tzschaschel, M. (2017). *The Power of Inner Pictures: How Imagination Can Maintain Physical and Mental Health*. London: Karnac.

Kubie, L. S. (1952). Problems and techniques of psychoanalytic validation and progress. In E. R. Hilgard, L. S. Kubie & E. Pumpian-Mindlin (Eds.), *Psychoanalysis as Science: The Hixon Lectures on the Scientific Status of Psychoanalysis* (pp. 46–124). Stanford, CA: Stanford University Press.

Kuhl, J. & Kazén, M. (2009). *PSSI. Persönlichkeits-Stil und Störungs-Inventar*. Göttingen: Hogrefe.

Kühl, S. (2008). *Coaching und Supervision: Zur personenorientierten Beratung in Organisationen*. Wiesbaden: VS Verlag für Sozialwissenschaften.

Künzli, H. (2005). Wirksamkeitsforschung im Führungskräfte-Coaching. *Organisationsberatung, Supervision, Coaching*, 12(3), 231–243. doi:10.1007/s11613-005-0109-3.

Laimböck, A. (2011). *Das psychoanalytische Erstgespräch*. Frankfurt am Main: Brandes & Apsel.

Lambert, M. J. & Barley, D. E. (2002). Research summary on the therapeutic relationship and psychotherapy outcome. In J. C. Norcross (Ed.), *Psychotherapy Relationships that Work: Therapist Contributions and Responsiveness to Patients* (pp. 17–32). New York: Oxford University Press.

Laub, D. & Hamburger, A. (Eds.). (2017). *Psychoanalysis and Holocaust Testimony: Unwanted Memories of Social Trauma*. London: Routledge.

Lechat, K. (2017). *Die Entfaltung des psychoanalytischen Raumes in der psychoanalytischen Supervision in der stationären Jugendhilfe im Gruppenvergleich. Eine Untersuchung mit der Szenisch-Narrativen Mikroanalyse.* Unpublished Master's thesis, International Psychoanalytic University Berlin.

Leuner, H. (1955). Experimentelles Katathymes Bilderleben als ein klinisches Verfahren der Psychotherapie. *Zeitschrift für Psychosomatik und Psychotherapie*, 6, 235–260.

Lichtenberg, J. D. (2001). Motivation: Sic transit gloria? *Psychoanalytic Inquiry*, 21(5), 589–603.

Lichtenberg, J. D. (2003). Communication in infancy. *Psychoanalytic Inquiry*, 23(3), 498–520.

Lichtenberg, J. D. (2010). Patterns of love in the four- to six-year-old period and the dispositional effect they create. *Psychoanalytic Inquiry*, 30(6), 478–484.

Lichtenberg, J. D. (2014). *Psychoanalysis and Infant Research*. London: Routledge.

Lohl, J. (2014). "Und wenn Du groß bist, dann darfst du vielleicht mal was sagen": Ein Zwischenbericht aus einem Forschungsprojekt zur Geschichte der Supervision. *Freie Assoziation*, 17(1/2), 111–129.

Lohl, J. (2016). Supervision im Blick der Sozialforschung. In A. Hamburger & W. Mertens (Eds.), *Supervision – Konzepte und Anwendungen. Band 2: Supervision in der Praxis – ein Überblick* (pp. 100–112). Stuttgart: Kohlhammer.

Lohmer, M. (Ed.). (2004). *Psychodynamische Organisationsberatung. Konflikte und Potentiale in Veränderungsprozessen.* Stuttgart: Klett-Cotta.

Lohmer, M. & Möller, H. (2014). *Psychoanalyse in Organisationen. Einführung in die psychodynamische Organisationsberatung.* Stuttgart: Kohlhammer.

Long, S. (1999). Who am I at work? An exploration of work identifications and identity. *Socioanalysis*, 1, 48–64.

Long, S. (2008). *The Perverse Organisation and its Deadly Sins*. London: Karnac.

Long, S. (2013). *Socioanalytic Methods: Discovering the Hidden in Organisations and Social Systems*. London: Karnac.

Lorenzer, A. (1970). *Sprachzerstörung und Rekonstruktion. Vorarbeiten zu einer Metatheorie der Psychoanalyse.* Frankfurt am Main: Suhrkamp.

Lorenzer, A. (1985). Der Analytiker als Detektiv, der Detektiv als Analytiker. *Psyche – Z Psychoanal*, 39(1), 1–11.

Löwer-Hirsch, M. & West-Leuer, B. (2017). *Psychodynamisches Coaching für Führungskräfte.* Wiesbaden: Springer Fachmedien.

Ludeman, K. (2009). Coaching with women. In J. Passmore (Ed.), *Diversity in Coaching: Working with Gender, Culture, Race and Age* (pp. 199–216). London: Kogan Page.

Lutzi, J. (2003). Ein Wandel der Buchhalter? – Zur Bedeutung des potentiellen Raums für Veränderungsprozesse in Organisationen. In B. Sievers, D. Ohlmeier, B. Oberhoff & U. Beumer (Eds.), *Das Unbewusste in Organisationen* (pp. 443–455). Gießen: Psychosozial.

Macmillan, M. (2001). The reliability and validity of Freud's methods of free association and interpretation. *Psychological Inquiry*, 12(3), 167–175.

Menninger, K. A. & Holzman, P. S. (1973). *Theory of Psychoanalytic Technique*. Second Edition. New York: Basic Books.

Mentzos, S. (1976). *Interpersonale und institutionalisierte Abwehr*. Frankfurt am Main: Suhrkamp.

Menzies Lyth, I. (1988). *Containing Anxiety in Institutions: Selected Essays*. London: Free Association Books.

Mertens, W. (1992). *Entwicklung der Psychosexualität und der Geschlechtsidentität. Band 1. Geburt bis 4. Lebensjahr*. Stuttgart: Kohlhammer.

Mertens, W. & Hamburger, A. (2016). Psychoanalytische Supervisionskonzepte. In A. Hamburger & W. Mertens (Eds.), *Supervision – Konzepte und Anwendungen. Band 1: Supervision in der Praxis – ein Überblick* (pp. 17–32). Stuttgart: Kohlhammer.

Mertens, W. & Lang, H.-J. (1991). Die Seele im Unternehmen: Psychoanalytische Aspekte von Führung und Organisation im Unternehmen. In G. Lenz (Ed.), *Die Seele im Unternehmen*. Berlin: Springer.

Mészáros, J. (2010). Sándor Ferenczi and the Budapest School of Psychoanalysis. *Psychoanalytic Perspectives*, 7(1), 69–89.

Migge, B. (2005). *Handbuch Coaching und Beratung*. Weinheim: Beltz.

Miller, E. J. & Rice, A. K. (1967). *Systems of Organization: The Control of Task and Sentient Boundaries*. London: Tavistock.

Moga, D. E. & Cabaniss, D. L. (2014). Learning objectives for supervision: Benefits for candidates and beyond. *Psychoanalytic Inquiry*, 34(6), 528–537.

Möller, H. (2001). *Was ist gute Supervision? Grundlagen – Merkmale – Methoden*. Stuttgart: Klett-Cotta.

Möller, H. (2016). Supervisions- und Coaching Kompetenz-Forschung. *Psychotherapie Forum*, 21(3), 74–81. doi:10.1007/s00729-015-0057-0.

Möller, H. & Hellebrandt, M. (2016). Wie wissenschaftlich fundiert sind Coaching-Weiterbildungen? *Organisationsberatung, Supervision, Coaching*, 23(1), 90–104. doi:10.1007/s11613-016-0445-5.

Möller, H. & Pühl, H. (2012). Ethnopsychoanalyse: Zum konstruktiven Umgang mit Neuem und Unbekanntem. In H. Pühl (Ed.), *Das aktuelle Handbuch der Supervision* (pp. 278–291). Gießen: Psychosozial.

Morgan-Jones, R. (2010). *The Body of the Organization and its Health*. London: Karnac.

Morgenthaler, F. (1986). *Technik. Zur Dialektik der psychoanalytischen Praxis*. Frankfurt am Main: Qumran.

Mörtl, K., Kirnoha, H. & Pos, A. (2013). Führungspositionen von Frauen. Eine qualitativ-empirische Typenbildung zu emotionalen Dilemmata. In H. Breuninger & A. Sellschopp (Eds.), *Von der Kunst der guten Führung. Ein Projektbericht zu Female Leadership* (pp. 101–126). Stuttgart: Breuninger-Stiftung.

Müller, O. (2012). *Coach-Auswahl im Personalmanagement*. Berlin: Cornelsen.

Nadig, M. (1986). *Die verborgene Kultur der Frau. Ethnopsychoanalytische Gespräche mit Bäuerinnen in Mexiko*. Frankfurt am Main: Fischer.

Nagell, W., Steinmetzer, L., Fissabre, U. & Spilski, J. (2014). Research into the relationship experience in supervision and its influence on the psychoanalytical identity formation of candidate trainees. *Psychoanalytic Inquiry*, 34(6), 554–583.

North, E. E. (1986). The psychiatrist in the executive suite. *Menninger Perspectives*, 17 (3), 5–7.

Oevermann, U. (1993a). Struktureigenschaften supervisorischer Praxis – Exemplarische Sequenzanalyse des Sitzungsprotokolls der Supervision eines psychoanalytisch orientierten Therapie-Teams im Methodenmodell der objektiven Hermeneutik. In B. Bardé & D. Mattke (Eds.), *Therapeutische Teams* (pp. 141–269). Göttingen: Vandenhoeck & Ruprecht.

Oevermann, U. (1993b). Verbatim-Transkript einer Teamsupervision. In B. Bardé & D. Mattke (Eds.), *Therapeutische Teams* (pp. 109–140). Göttingen: Vandenhoeck & Ruprecht.

Oevermann, U. (1996). Theoretische Skizze einer revidierten Theorie professionalisierten Handelns. In A. Combe & W. Helsper (Eds.), *Pädagogische Professionalität: Untersuchungen zum Typus pädagogischen Handelns* (pp. 70–182). Frankfurt am Main: Suhrkamp.

Oevermann, U. (2010 [2001]). *Strukturprobleme supervisorischer Praxis.* Frankfurt am Main: Humanities Online.

Ohlmeier, D. (2009 [2004]). Strukturen und Unbewusstes in wissenschaftlich-klinischen Organisationen und Institutionen. In B. Sievers (Ed.), *Psychodynamik von Organisationen* (pp. 97–112). Gießen: Psychosozial.

OPD Task Force (Ed.) (2008). *Operationalized Psychodynamic Diagnosis OPD-2: Manual of Diagnosis and Treatment Planning.* Boston, MA: Hogrefe Publishing.

OPD Task Force (2016). Website of the Operationalized Psychodynamic Diagnostics (OPD). Accessed on 4 October 2016 at www.opd-online.net.

Orlinsky, D. E. & Ronnestad, M. H. (2005). *How Psychotherapists Develop: A Study of Therapeutic Work and Professional Growth.* Washington, DC: American Psychological Association.

Ornstein, A. (1996). Die Angst vor der Wiederholung. Bemerkungen zum Prozeß des Durcharbeitens in der Psychoanalyse. *Psyche – Z Psychoanal*, 50(5), 444–462.

Pannewitz, A. (2012). *Das Geschlecht der Führung: Supervisorische Interaktion zwischen Tradition und Transformation.* Göttingen: Vandenhoeck & Ruprecht.

Parin, P. (1977). Das Ich und die Anpassungs-Mechanismen. *Psyche – Z Psychoanal*, 31 (6), 481–515.

Parin, P., Morgenthaler, F. & Parin-Matthèy, G. (1963). *Die Weißen denken zuviel: Psychoanalytische Untersuchungen bei den Dogon in Westafrika.* Frankfurt am Main: Suhrkamp.

Parin, P., Morgenthaler, F. & Parin-Matthèy, G. (1971). *Fürchte deinen Nächsten wie dich selbst: Psychoanalyse und Gesellschaft am Modell der Agni in Westafrika.* Frankfurt am Main: Suhrkamp.

PDM: PDM Task Force (2006). *Psychodynamic diagnostic manual (PDM).* Silver Spring: Alliance of Psychoanalytic Organizations.

PDM-2: Lingiardi, V., & McWilliams, N. (Eds.). (2017). *Psychodynamic diagnostic manual: PDM-2* (2nd ed.). New York: Guilford Press.

Petzold, H. G., Schigl, B., Fischer, M. & Höfner, C. (2003). *Supervision auf dem Prüfstand.* Opladen: Leske und Budrich.

Pieh, C., Frisch, M., Meyer, N., Loew, T. & Lahmann, C. (2009). Validierung der Achse III (Konflikt) der Operationalisierten Psychodynamischen Diagnostik (OPD). *Zeitschrift für Psychosomatische Medizin und Psychotherapie*, 55(3), 263–281. doi:10.13109/zptm.2009.55.3.263.

Pine, F. (1988). The four psychologies of psychoanalysis and their place in clinical work. *Journal of the American Psychoanalytic Association*, 36, 571–596.

Racker, H. (1953). The countertransference neurosis. In H. Racker (1988), *Transference and Countertransference* (pp. 105–126). London: The Hogarth Press and the Institute of Psycho-Analysis.

Rappe-Giesecke, K. (2013). *Supervision für Gruppen und Teams.* Berlin: Springer.

Rice, A. K. (1958). *Productivity and Social Organization: The Ahmedabad Experiment: Technical Innovation, Work Organization and Management.* London: Tavistock.

Richter, S. D. & Marchioro, M. (2013). Nun sag, wie hast du's mit der Ethik? – Menschenbilder und Ethik im Coaching. Eine Feldstudie. *Organisationsberatung, Supervision, Coaching*, 20(2), 143–161. doi:10.1007/s11613-013-0325-1.

Roundtable der Coachingverbände (2016). Profession: Coach. Ein Commitment des Roundtable der Coachingverbände. Accessed on 3 August 2016 at www.roundtable-coaching.eu.

Rudolf, G. (2010). *Psychodynamische Psychotherapie. Die Arbeit an Konflikt, Struktur und Trauma*. Stuttgart: Schattauer.

Rudolf, G., Grande, T. & Henningsen, P. (Eds.) (2010). *Die Struktur der Persönlichkeit. Theoretische Grundlagen zur psychodynamischen Therapie struktureller Störungen*. Stuttgart: Schattauer.

Ryan, R. M. & Deci, E. L. (2008). A self-determination theory approach to psychotherapy: The motivational basis for effective change. *Canadian Psychology, 49*(3), 186–193. doi:10.1037/a0012753.

Sachse, R. (2020). *Personality Disorders: A Clarification-oriented Psychotherapy Treatment Model*. Boston, MA and Göttingen: Hogrefe.

Sander, L. W. (1988). The event-structure of regulation in the neonate-caregiver system as a biological background for early organisation of psychic structure. In A. Goldberg (Ed.), *Frontiers in Self Psychology* (pp. 64–77). Hillsdale, NJ: Analytic Press.

Schay, P., Dreger, B. & Siegele, F. (2006). Die Wirksamkeit von Supervision für den Patienten – Eine Evaluationsstudie zur Wirksamkeit von Supervision für das Patientensystem in Einrichtungen der medizinischen Rehabilitation Drogenabhängiger. In P. Schay (Ed.), *Innovationen in der Drogenhilfe* (pp. 247–305). Wiesbaden: VS Verlag für Sozialwissenschaften.

Schermuly, C. C. & Scholl, W. (2011). *Instrument zur Kodierung von Diskussionen (IKD)*. Göttingen: Hogrefe.

Schmidt, S. (in preparation). *Change-Prozesse in der Jugendhilfe im Spiegel der Supervision. Eine Untersuchung mit der Szenisch-Narrativen Mikroanalyse*. Unpublished Master's thesis, International Psychoanalytic University Berlin.

Schmidt-Lellek, C. J. (2007 [2001]). Was heißt "dialogische Beziehung" in berufsbezogener Beratung (Supervision und Coaching)? Das Modell des Sokratischen Dialogs. In A. Schreyögg & C. J. Schmidt-Lellek (Eds.), *Konzepte des Coachings* (pp. 189–203). Heidelberg: VS Verlag für Sozialwissenschaften.

Schmidt-Lellek, C. J. (2012). Die Entwicklung von Coaching als Profession. In Deutscher Bundesverband Coaching e.V. (Ed.), *Coaching als Profession* (pp. 11–18). Osnabrück: DBVC Eigenverlag.

Schneider, G., Mendler, T., Heuft, G. & Burgmer, M. (2008). Validität der Konfliktachse der Operationalisierten Psychodynamischen Diagnostik (OPD-1) – empirische Ergebnisse und Folgerungen für die OPD-2. *Zeitschrift für Psychosomatische Medizin und Psychotherapie, 54*(1), 46–62. doi:10.13109/zptm.2008.54.1.46.

Schreyögg, A. (2012). Abgrenzung zu anderen Beratungsformaten. In Deutscher Bundesverband Coaching e.V. (Ed.), *Coaching als Profession* (pp. 20–21). Osnabrück: DBVC Eigenverlag.

Schreyögg, A. (2013). Coaching und/oder Supervision. Anmerkungen zur Präzisierung der beiden Beratungsformate. *Organisationsberatung, Supervision, Coaching, 20*(2), 231–237. doi:10.1007/s11613-013-0326-0.

Schulz von Thun, F. (1981). *Miteinander reden: Störungen und Klärungen*. Reinbek: Rowohlt.

Scobel, W. A. (1991 [1989]). *Was ist Supervision?* Göttingen: Vandenhoeck & Ruprecht.

Sell, C., Möller, H. & Benecke, C. (2018). Emotionsregulation und Coaching. In S. Greif, H. Möller & W. Scholl (Eds.), *Handbuch Schlüsselkonzepte im Coaching* (pp. 143–151). Berlin: Springer.

Sellschopp, A. (2013). Der Gruppenprozess. In H. Breuninger & A. Sellschopp (Eds.), *Von der Kunst der guten Führung. Ein Projektbericht zu Female Leadership* (pp. 41–82). Stuttgart: Breuninger-Stiftung.

Sies, C. & Löwer-Hirsch, M. (2000). Einzelcoaching aus psychodynamischer Sicht. *supervision. Mensch, Arbeit, Organisation*, 18(3), 31–35.

Sievers, B. (2002). "Ich lasse dich nicht, es sei denn du segnest mich!" (Genesis 32, 26): Einige Überlegungen zur Entstehung von Autorität, Erbschaft und Nachfolge. *Freie Assoziation*, 5(1), 7–37.

Sievers, B. (Ed.). (2009). *Psychodynamik von Organisationen*. Gießen: Psychosozial.

Sievers, B. (Ed.). (2015). *Sozioanalyse und psychosoziale Dynamik von Organisationen.* Gießen: Psychosozial.

Sievers, B., Ohlmeier, D., Oberhoff, B. & Beumer, U. (Eds.). (2003). *Das Unbewusste in Organisationen*. Gießen: Psychosozial.

Silberschatz, G. (Ed.). (2005). *Transformative Relationships. The Control-Mastery Theory of Psychotherapy*. London: Routledge.

Siller, G. (2008). *Professionalisierung durch Supervision*. Wiesbaden: VS Verlag für Sozialwissenschaften.

Siller, G. (2016). Zur Inanspruchnahme von Supervision – ein rekonstruktiver Forschungszugang. In W. Mertens & A. Hamburger (Eds.), *Supervision – Konzepte und Anwendungen. Band 2: Supervision in der Ausbildung* (pp. 113–123). Stuttgart: Kohlhammer.

Sipos, V. (2001). Effekte von Supervision auf Therapieprozess und Therapieergebnis bei der Behandlung von Patientinnen mit Anorexia nervosa: Ein Beitrag zur Supervisionsforschung. Accessed on 5 April 2016 at www.opus-bayern.de/uni-bamberg/volltexte/2005/17/.

Steffens, W. & Kächele, H. (1988). Abwehr und Bewältigung – Mechanismen und Strategien. Wie ist eine Integration möglich? In H. Kächele & W. Steffens (Eds.), *Bewältigung und Abwehr. Beiträge zur Psychologie und Psychotherapie schwerer körperlicher Krankheiten* (pp. 1–50). Heidelberg: Springer.

Stein, H. F. (2009). Organisatorischer Totalitarismus und Dissens. In B. Sievers (Ed.), *Psychodynamik von Organisationen* (pp. 47–78). Gießen: Psychosozial.

Steinhardt, K. (2005). *Psychoanalytisch orientierte Supervision. Auf dem Weg zu einer Profession?* Gießen: Psychosozial.

Steinmetzer, L., Nagell, W. & Fissabre, U. (2016). Forschung zur Ausbildungssupervision. In W. Mertens & A. Hamburger (Eds.), *Supervision – Konzepte und Anwendungen. Band 2: Supervision in der Ausbildung* (pp. 71–82). Stuttgart: Kohlhammer.

Stern, D. B. (1996). The social construction of therapeutic action. *Psychoanalytic Inquiry*, 16(2), 265–293.

Stern, D. N. (1985). *The Interpersonal World of the Infant: A View from Psychoanalysis and Developmental Psychology*. New York: Basic Books.

Stern, D. N. (2004). *The Present Moment in Psychotherapy and Everyday Life*. New York: Norton.

Stern, D. N. & Boston Change Process Study Group (2012 [2010]). *Veränderungsprozesse: Ein integratives Paradigma*. Frankfurt am Main: Brandes & Apsel.

Suler, J. R. (1989). Mental imagery in psychoanalytic treatment. *Psychoanalytic Psychology*, 6(3), 343–366.

Sulz, S. (2016). Supervision in der Ausbildung zum Kognitiven Verhaltenstherapeuten. In W. Mertens & A. Hamburger (Eds.), *Supervision – Konzepte und Anwendungen. Band 2: Supervision in der Ausbildung* (pp. 30–43). Stuttgart: Kohlhammer.

Szecsödy, I. (1994). Supervision: A complex tool for psychoanalytic learning. *Scandinavian Psychoanalytic Review*, 17, 119–129.

Tavistock Institute (2016). Group Relations Programme. Accessed on 13 September 2016 at www.tavinstitute.org/what-we-offer/professional-development/group-rela tions-programme..

Teising, M. (2009). Der Konflikt zwischen Laios und Ödipus. Männliche Identität im Prozess des Alterns in Übertragung und Gegenübertragung. In F. Dammasch, H.-G. Metzger & M. Teising (Eds.), *Männliche Identität: Psychoanalytische Erkundungen* (pp. 99–108). Frankfurt am Main: Brandes & Apsel.

Thach, E. C. (2002). The impact of executive coaching and 360 feedback on leadership effectiveness. *Leadership & Organization Development Journal*, 23(4), 205–214. doi:10.1108/01437730210429070.

Trist, E., Murray, H. & Trist, B. (Eds.). (1990). *The Social Engagement of Social Science, Volume 1: A Tavistock Anthology: The Socio-Psychological Perspective*. Philadelphia: University of Pennsylvania Press.

Ungar, V. R. & Busch de Ahumada, L. (2001). Supervision: A container–contained approach. *International Journal of Psychoanalysis*, 82(1), 71–81. doi:10.1516/LUM2-4C9E-PE5C-V88Y.

`Urban, C. (2011). Der Erstkontakt in der Supervision – Zur Dynamik der Anfangssituation. In E. Möller & S. Träupmann (Eds.), *Aspekte der psychodynamischen Supervision: Ein Kaleidoskop professioneller Perspektiven* (pp. 30–42). Kassel: Kassel University Press.

Vollmer Filho, G. & Pires A. C. J. (2010). Benign and disruptive disturbances of the supervisory field. *The International Journal of Psychoanalysis*, 91(4), 895–913.

von Ameln, F., Kramer, J. & Stark, H. (2009). *Organisationsberatung beobachtet. Hidden Agendas und Blinde Flecke*. Wiesbaden: VS Verlag für Sozialwissenschaften.

Wächter, H.-M. & Pudel, V. (1980). Kurzpsychotherapie von 15 Sitzungen mit dem Katathymen Bilderleben (eine kontrollierte Studie). In H. Leuner (Ed.), *Katathymes Bilderleben. Ergebnisse in Theorie und Praxis* (pp 126–147). Bern: Huber.

Warsitz, R.-P. & Küchenhoff, J. (2015). *Psychoanalyse als Erkenntnistheorie-psychoanalytische Erkenntnisverfahren*. Stuttgart: Kohlhammer.

Weigand, W. (2000). Perspektivenwechsel in der Konzeptentwicklung von Supervision – ausgelöst bei einem Gang durch die Literatur. *Supervision. Zeitschrift für berufsbezogene Beratung*, 3, 52–56.

Weigand, W. (2016). Teamsupervision. In A. Hamburger & W. Mertens (Eds.), *Supervision – Konzepte und Anwendungen. Band 1: Supervision in der Praxis – ein Überblick* (pp. 101–117). Stuttgart: Kohlhammer.

Weiss, J. & Sampson, H. (1986). *The Psychoanalytic Process: Theory, Clinical Observation, and Empirical Research*. New York: Guilford.

Wellendorf, F. (1996). Der Psychoanalytiker als Grenzgänger. Oder: Was heißt psychoanalytische Arbeit im sozialen Feld? *Journal für Psychologie*, 4(4), 79–91.

Western, S. (2012). *Coaching and Mentoring: A Critical Text*. London: Sage.

West-Leuer, B. (2000). Kontrollsupervision im Einzelsetting als kollegial-emanzipatives Beratungsverfahren. *supervision. Mensch, Arbeit, Organisation*, 18(3), 19–24.

Willutzki, U., Tönnies, B. & Meyer, F. (2005). Psychotherapiesupervision und die therapeutische Beziehung – Eine Prozessstudie. *Verhaltenstherapie und psychosoziale Praxis*, 37(3), 507–516.

Winnicott, D. W. (2014 [1953]). *Through Paediatrics to Psychoanalysis: Collected Papers*. London: Routledge.

Yeomans, F. E., Clarkin, J. F. & Kernberg, O. F. (2015). *Transference-focused Psychotherapy for Borderline Personality Disorder: A Clinical Guide*. Arlington, VA: American Psychiatric Publishing.

Zelnick, L. M. & Buchholz, E. S. (1991). Der Begriff der inneren Repräsentanz im Lichte der neueren Säuglingsforschung. *Psyche – Z Psychoanal*, 45(9), 810–846.

Zimmermann, J., Stasch, M., Grande, T., Schauenburg, H. & Cierpka, M. (2014). Der Beziehungsmuster-Q-Sort (OPD-BQS): Ein Selbsteinschätzungsinstrument zur Erfassung von dysfunktionalen Beziehungsmustern auf Grundlage der Operationalisierten Psychodynamischen Diagnostik. *Zeitschrift für Psychiatrie, Psychologie und Psychotherapie*, 62(1), 43–53. doi:10.1024/1661-4747/a000177.

Name index

Subject index

For Product Safety Concerns and Information please contact our EU
representative GPSR@taylorandfrancis.com
Taylor & Francis Verlag GmbH, Kaufingerstraße 24, 80331 München, Germany

www.ingramcontent.com/pod-product-compliance
Lightning Source LLC
Chambersburg PA
CBHW070344270326
41926CB00017B/3983

9 780367 770709